Public Choice and
Rural Development

Research Paper R-21

Public Choice and Rural Development

The proceedings of a conference sponsored by the U.S. Agency for International Development and held in Washington, D.C., in September 1979, under the auspices of Resources for the Future, Inc.

edited by
CLIFFORD S. RUSSELL and
NORMAN K. NICHOLSON

RESOURCES FOR THE FUTURE / WASHINGTON, D.C.

Resources for the Future is a nonprofit organization for research and education in the development, conservation, and use of natural resources and the improvement of the quality of the environment. It was established in 1952 with the cooperation of the Ford Foundation. Grants for research are accepted from government and private sources only if they meet the conditions of a policy established by the Board of Directors of Resources for the Future. The policy states that RFF shall be solely responsible for the conduct of the research and free to make the research results available to the public. Part of the work of Resources for the Future is carried out by its resident staff; part is supported by grants to universities and other nonprofit organizations. Unless otherwise stated, interpretations and conclusions in RFF publications are those of the authors; the organization takes responsibility for the selection of significant subjects for study, the competence of the researchers, and their freedom of inquiry.

Research Papers are studies and conference reports published by Resources for the Future from the authors' typescripts. The accuracy of the material is the responsibility of the authors and the material is not given the usual editorial review by RFF. The Research Paper series is intended to provide inexpensive and prompt distribution of research that is likely to have a shorter shelf life or to reach a smaller audience than RFF books.

Library of Congress Catalog Card Number 80-8775

ISBN 0-8018-2600-4

Copyright © 1981 by Resources for the Future, Inc.

Distributed by The Johns Hopkins University Press,
    Baltimore, Maryland 21218

Manufactured in the United States of America

Published January 1981. $12.00

v

TABLE OF CONTENTS

Preface and Acknowledgments ix

1. Introduction, Clifford S. Russell   1

2. Applications of Public Choice Theory to Rural Development --
    A Statement of the Problem, Norman K. Nicholson   . . .   17

3. Public Choice and Rural Development -- Free Riders, Lemons,
    and Institutional Design, Samuel L. Popkin   43

4. Public Choice Processes, Robert H. Bates   81

5. Public Choice Analysis of Institutional Constraints on
    Firewood Production Strategies in the West African
    Sahel, James T. Thomson   119

6. Sociological Analysis of Irrigation Water Management --
    A Perspective and Approach to Assist Decision Making,
    David M. Freeman and Max K. Lowdermilk   153
        Discussion: Kathleen O. Jackson   174

7. The Political Economy of Agricultural Extension Services
    in India, Joel M. Guttman   183

8. Peasant Behavior and Social Change -- Cooperatives and
    Individual Holdings, James Petras and Eugene Havens . .   203
        Comments: Donald N. McCloskey   226
                  T.N. Srinivasan   231

9. Three Cases of Induced Institutional Innovation, Vernon
    W. Ruttan   239

10. Does the Route to Development Pass Through Public Choice?
    Joe Oppenheimer   271

LIST OF TABLES

Page

4-1 Payoff Matrix for the Decision to Build the Dam: Costs Shared (1/2, 1/2) When Both Contribute   88

4-2 Payoff Matrix for the Decision to Build the Dam: Costs Shared (4/9, 5/9) When Both Contribute   88

4-3 The Preference Orderings of Three Farmers (1, 2, 3) Over Three Alternatives (a, b, c)   97

4-4 Another Set of Preferences Over the Three Alternatives . .   99

4-5 Preferences Employed When Person 2 Manipulates Agenda 2 . 104

4-6 Differential Dollar Values for Options 106

4-7 Total Reported Evaluation in the Absence of Bid by Farmer i for Options A through C 108

4-8 False Representations of Different Values for Options . . 110

4-9 Computations of Tax, Given False Bids: Total Reported Evaluation in the Absence 110

4-10 Change in Net Benefits from Collusion 112

6-1 Types of Irrigation Technology 163

6-2 Farmer Perception of Major Current Farm Problem by Water-course Position 170

7-1 Predictions of the Interest Group and Efficiency Theories 193

7-2 Probit Regressions of Extension Services Dummy 196

8-1 Distribution of Total Land Area, Arable Land, Permanent Cropland Natural Pastures by Size of Production Unit in 1961 205

8-2 Strikes in the Agricultural Sector from 1959 to 1968 . . . 208

8-3 Land Redistribution in Peru, 1969-79 209

8-4 Agricultural Output Per Capita for Selected Crops from 1961-1977 215

8-5 Index of Real Wages on Coastal Agro-Industrial CAPs Compared with Metropolitan Lima from 1970-1978 215

Page

8-6 Wage Differentials on Seventy-Three Production Cooperatives
     in Peru Between Permanent and Seasonal Workers, 1975 218

9-1 Factor Shares of Rice Output Per Hectare, 1976 Wet Season . . 252

9-2 Comparison Between the Imputed Value of Harvesters' Share
     and the Imputed Cost of Gama Labor 254

9-3 Average Annual Percentage Rates of Change in Various Indicators
     Thai Economic Performance, 1850 to 1950 257

LIST OF FIGURES

Page

4-1 Total costs and benefits from public good   91

4-2 A social-welfare-maximizing equilibrium   93

4-3 A representation of preferences in a single dimension   98

4-4 Preferences over two issues, with median points indicated . . 100

4-5 Regions of points which defeat (A*, B*) under majority rule . 102

4-6 Two agendas for the decision among a, b, and c, with prefer-
     ences as in Table 4-4   103

6-1 Idealized layout of main and branch watercourse system . . . 166

6-2 Sample farmer perception of major current farm problem by
     position of landholding on watercourse   169

9-1 Interrelationship between resource endowments, technical
     change, and institutional change   248

9-2 Actual demand for land-saving technical innovations 262

9-3 Dynamic adjustment path between actual and latent demands . . 262

PREFACE AND ACKNOWLEDGMENTS

This book contains the augmented proceedings of a conference held under the auspices of Resources for the Future with support from the U.S. Agency for International Development on 17 and 18 September 1979. The idea for the conference originated within AID, where people sensed the growing importance of public choice issues in rural development. It was felt that bringing development experts with rural field experience together with public choice experts having some interest in development would lead to a fruitful interchange for the participants and a valuable document for both literatures.

The initial conference plan was a tidy one, involving a review, or "state-of-the-art" paper followed by five or six papers outlining the collective choice problems encountered in the field in different substantive (as opposed to geographic) areas. Each of these papers would be discussed by two people: one from a public choice background; and one an academic or (preferably) a government official from a developing country.

The best laid conference plans are no different from those in any other part of life, and this one suffered from failures of world communications; the press of politics (public choice) in various developing countries that kept several would-be participants away; and unexplained loss of author momentum or failure of will. On the other hand, AID was flexible in the face of human and technical upset and allowed us to commission several post-conference papers that supplement those from the conference itself.

Ideally these proceedings would amount to a handbook on how to use public choice in rural development. For reasons explained in the introductory chapter and taken up at various points by the other authors, it is simply not possible to produce such a document in the current state of the art. On the other hand, we hope the contents of this book will challenge some conventional views, help practicing development experts anticipate problems, and stimulate further thinking -- even further research.

In preparing for and holding the conference we have been helped by many people. Emery Castle, then vice president, and now president of RFF, encouraged Russell to undertake this project and helped with liaison with other interested groups. Advice on potential participants was generously given by any number of people, but those we bothered most often included Robert Cameron Mitchell, Mancur Olson, Joe Oppenheimer, Samuel L. Popkin, and Vernon W. Ruttan. The organization and running of the conference itself were handled largely by Margaret Parr-Recard, with the usual valuable help of Nick Galvin of the Brookings Institution.

Clifford S. Russell
Norman K. Nicholson
July 1980

Public Choice and Rural Development

Chapter 1

INTRODUCTION

Clifford S. Russell

Why hold a conference and publish collected papers on the bizarre-
sounding topic: Public Choice and Rural Development? Everyone knows
that public choice is an abstruse subdiscipline, shared by economics and
political science, and concerned with set-theoretic proofs that democratic
government cannot work. Everyone also knows that rural development is
about rice and buffaloes and irrigation canals and the daily struggle for
existence carried on by peasant farmers and landless agricultural laborers
in the third (and fourth) world. What can these two topics possibly have
in common? Surely peasants do not make collective decisions about development. Rather development must be imposed by (rational and modernizing)
central government. Surely even if they did, public choice theory, not
having anything much to do with the real world, would not be able to help
them out.

A caricature -- of course, but not an especially extreme one -- of
the reaction one might expect (and I experienced) to the idea of the conference here reported. Like all caricatures, it contains its elements of

Editor's Note: I am grateful to Julia Allen, Emery Castle, David
Goetze, and William J. Vaughan for their criticism of an earlier draft.

truth. But it also reveals a lack of imagination and even a failure to grasp what rural development is really about. In this brief introductory essay, I hope to persuade the reader that public choice is far from irrelevant to rural development, and that while most of its lessons are negative (Don't try this; it won't work for the following reasons), the theory also has some positive things to say. Success in this modest aim will prepare the ground for the authors (and their discussants) who follow.

Background

  "Development" is a tricky concept and means different things to different people, whether because of their political beliefs, disciplinary backgrounds, feelings about technology, or their national experiences. For some it implies changes in political processes, and the balance of political power as traditionally nonelite groups are enfranchised and some form of western democracy is adopted. For others, it may mean the extension of public (government or cooperative) ownership over all, or nearly all, sectors of the economy (for example, Temu, 1979). To economists, development for a long time meant growth in per capita income; more recently, concern with redistribution of income within each nation toward its poorest citizens has begun to receive equal billing (for example, Development Dialogue, 1977; The Economist, 1979; for a cautionary note, see Srinivasan, 1977). The phrase "rural development" as used in this volume, can probably best be understood as connoting something of both the economic and political meanings above -- as referring both to efforts to increase per capita incomes in rural areas, especially the incomes of poorer peasants, and to attempts at complementary institution building.

"Public choice" has its own array of meanings, some broader, some narrower, some stressing the theoretical heritage of the field and others its empirical content.[1] The words are used here to indicate a field of analysis and experiment involving the consequences of assuming that individuals act in a rational and self-interested (or self-serving) way, not only when the context is market transactions (deciding what crops to grow or what consumer goods to buy), but also when it is a collective decision (what person to elect as village head and, indeed, whether to vote at all). In particular, each individual is assumed to be able to rank the outcomes he or she foresees resulting from his own actions, and further is assumed to act to obtain the best possible one of the outcomes.

To say, then, that the field of public choice is relevant to rural development is to say that rural development will require some collective decisions; that those decisions will often have to be made at the local, rural level; and that those participating in the decisions (the peasants with whose welfare we are concerned) can best be viewed as rational and self-interested actors. Let us work backwards through these conditions.

It is, of course, impossible to prove that peasants generally, or even peasants in region X, are rational and self-interested actors in the business of life. For that matter it is impossible to prove that the citizens of France or Japan or the United States meet this description. Indeed, probably no individual does, at all times and in all places, act in a rationally self-interested way: irrationality and selfless behavior

---

[1]The reader will find several labels, including public choice, social choice, collective choice, and political economy, used in these essays; and all standing for roughly the same approach. I have not tried to impose uniformity on the authors, even though authorities recognize subtle distinctions between the connotations of these names.

are also part of the human condition. The question, however, is not whether all the individuals in some group always behave rationally and self-interestedly. It is, rather, what kind of behavior predominates and therefore around which behavior it makes sense to design institutions. Popkin (1979), for example, makes a strong case for rational, self-interested behavior being the rule in Vietnam's rural areas. But others would point to more primitive groups and claim that they do not even have a conception of the individual; or would cite customs that appear, at least on the surface, to be irrational or selfless; or woud object on normative grounds that the public-choice assumption is pernicious and leads to all the ills of Western society. Clearly there is a deeper dispute here than can be settled in this introductory essay, and it is really only possible to assert that to begin with the assumption of predominantly selfless or irrational behavior is probably riskier than the other extreme.

What of the next condition: that at least the significant rural development decisions must be made locally? Again, a "proof" is impossible, though here a guess and assertion seem less likely to be controversial. While few developing countries may be as out of control as the Zaire pictured in recent Wall Street Journal articles (Kwitny, 1980a, 1980b), the span of control of even the most unitary government seldom extends in any complete way into the countryside. Shortcomings of transportation and communications networks and, perhaps most important, shortage of administrative skills, will make it very difficult to carry central government policies and projects into more remote rural areas. Decisions about village projects will often have to be made, and the political will to carry through these projects will have to be found, in the villages themselves.

Finally, why is it likely that collective decisions will be central to the pursuit of rural development objectives? One reason lies in the nature of the development activities and projects themselves. As The Economist (1979) has described it, the "principal problem for half of the world is how to organize rural labor for the construction of necessary local infrastructure such as fences, ditches, roads, and irrigation works." But many items of local infrastructure, for example roads and dams, produce benefits that are at least in part public or collective goods. That is, these benefits, once produced at all, cannot be denied to local residents whether or not they have contributed money or labor to the project. Thus, for example, a flood control dam supplies a public good, flood "protection," for some area downstream.[2] That is, this projection cannot in general be supplied to one farmer in the floodplain without being supplied to all others. Once the dam is built, no one in the protected area can be excluded from the protection. When the dam is being planned, there is every reason for the prospective beneficiaries to dissemble about their true prospective valuation of the protection. Depending on the link they see between their responses to planners' questions and their later shares of the costs, they will have an incentive to over or understate their desires for the dam.[3] When the dam is being constructed the prospective beneficiaries will further have reason to avoid helping out. And mobilizing

---

[2]"Protection" is itself a complicated concept, for rather than being an absolute and certain good, it is a probabilistic outcome of the interaction of rainfall and reservoir size. At some, albeit improbable, level of rainfall, protection can become disaster as dams or levees are toppled or washed out.

[3]There is some evidence that while such dissembling is rational, it is not common. Indeed, in one fascinating small study, the only person who engaged in "strategic behavior" (that is, dissembling) was a professional economist (d'Arge and coauthors, 1978).

the local underemployed labor for such projects, while sounding like a two-bird/one-stone proposition, may in fact prove extremely difficult.

Similar problems occur with other projects involving rural infra-structure, such as market roads, the establishment and protection of common woodlots as sources of wood and charcoal, and the provision of storage reservoirs and main canals for an irrigation system. Moreover, some projects with outputs that can in principle be treated as private goods, with noncontributors excluded, such as schools and clinics, will often be designed so that their outputs are de facto public goods (free public education and free medical care).

Thus, many rural development efforts face some especially difficult problems, problems that go deeper than the well-known concerns about "in-appropriate technology," peasant conservatism, and rural market imperfec-tions. (Though there are relations between, for example, large-scale technology and the extent of the public goods problem. See, for example, Chapter 6 by Freeman and Lowdermilk.) And these are exactly the problems that involve us in collective decision making.

All this will come as no surprise to many field workers who have recognized the problems and begun a search for some answers. But it may involve some changed ways of thinking for those brought up on standard development theory (with helpful "decision-makers") or related disciplines such as anthropology and sociology, which have tended to stress the peasant's cultural setting rather than his role as a more or less auto-nomous seeker after his own welfare. To show what kinds of changes these might be, I think it will be useful for me to try to describe the tone and message of the conference itself and of the resulting papers. In the

process I shall point out some of the implications for those concerned
practitioners at AID and eslewhere -- especially those whose initial reaction I may have caricatured in the first paragraph. After these introductory and background remarks, I shall set out a brief reader's guide to
the volume.

Contributions of Public Choice Theory to Planning for Rural Development

One might, on past experience, have expected to hear at the conference
the public choice academics selling "their" theory for all it was worth and
more. While our conference plan and participant selections guaranteed that
the audience would not be completely unsympathethic, no one would have been
surprised to find a strong current of skepticism among the field experts.
Instead, what I sensed throughout the conference, and what I think the
reader will find in the following pages, was a keen desire on the part of
those directly involved in rural development for more guidance, both as
positive theory and normative institutional design, than those from the
public choice background were willing to claim they could provide.

Everyone did agree that assuming rational, self-interested (or self-
ish to put it more bluntly) behavior on the part of peasant farmers and
other rural people was a good beginning. This behavior, it was further
agreed, could be expected as a general rule, not only in the private decisions such as what crops to plant and where and how to market output; but
also in the collective decision contexts, such as as those involving
infrastructure investments, the formation and operation of cooperatives,
and the influencing of agricultural extension service distribution. Setting out from this fundamental assumption of public choice theory instead
of some romantic or quasi-religious "communitarian" view of the peasantry

can, it was agreed, save a lot of headaches and avoid a lot of white
elephants, for it gives us a powerful basis for identifying schemes that
will not work. Unfortunately, as the public choice participants were
quick to point out, identifying what will not work nearly exhausts the
capability of the theory, for its strongest results are impossibility
theorems [the most famous being that of Arrow (1963) as subsequently
amended and extended by numberless others]. When it comes to positive
results, to solutions to the problems of collective choice in general or
of public goods provision in particular, the theorists have been much less
successful. Not, I hasten to add, for lack of skill or effort. The Arrow
theorem and its relatives arise from some very fundamental inconsistencies
between the behavior of rational, self-interested maximizers and the desirable properties of choice mechanisms to be used by those individuals
to make decisions collectively applicable to them all. These inconsistencies do not vanish for wishing they would. It is perhaps only a little
too strong to call them a manifestation of original sin.

One could hardly have blamed the development people had they been
considerably more impatient with this message than they in fact were.
They might have asked why public choice has done so little pushing into
positive results; so little probing of the possible? Why can it not say
more about how actual institutions are likely to behave in practice? What
about suggesting new institutional forms reflecting new knowledge? Let
us see what might be found in this conference volume with which to placate
someone asking such embarrassing questions; and, in particular, what positive results can be held out as hopeful signs for a fruitful cooperation
between the development and public choice fields. I see four such posi-

tive messages. (In the following discussion, references are to chapters
in this book unless otherwise noted.)

First, it is difficult to avoid the conclusion that, however, a
developing country's national government may be structured, however
centralized its working, and however low its tolerance for opposition,
rural development will proceed more smoothly in the long run if the puta-
tive beneficiaries participate from the beginning in planning and implementation (see chapters by Nicholson; Oppenheimer; Petras and Havens;
and, by extension, Thomson). To embark on a conscious (and sincere as
opposed to cosmetic) policy of participative or democratic decision making
is consciously to sacrifice the ability to make fast and stable decisions
for a world in which it may be difficult to reach any decision at all and
in which there is no guarantee that any decision reached has any of the
normative properties economists like to begin by insisting on. Most
important, any practical democratic system may produce a final decision to
which everyone would prefer another decision, reachable only under some
other set of rules. The payoff for this sacrifice is the rather vague
but widely agreed on prospect that the decision once taken (the investment
decided, the work or guard duty shared out, the contributions allotted)
will actually be carried out. (For a less sanguine view, see Sumra,
1979.) There is also the possibility that repeated plays of the democratic game will lead toward mutual trust, a vital ingredient in escape
from the "prisoner's dilemma" posed by collective decisions about public
goods.[4]

---

[4]The "prisoner's dilemma" is a situation in which it is optimal for
any propsective participant in a collective enterprise to opt out (to
"defect") <u>regardless</u> of the strategy followed by other would-be partici-

A second cheering note in the papers is found in the description of theoretic development of mechanisms for eliciting accurate information on consumer preferences for public goods (see Chapter 4 by Bates). These so-called incentive-compatible mechanisms still suffer from certain key infirmities of which the most important seems to be a susceptibility to manipulation by coalitions (see Chapter 10 by Oppenheimer), but they provide important clues about where to look for further refinement; and they deserve more extensive experimental work, especially in larger, real-world contexts.

The third cause for hope that I carry away from these papers is one that is mentioned only briefly by Bates: the practice of what may be called institutional engineering. In such an effort an attempt is made to analyze and design within the context of an impossibility theorem -- to explore empirically what is possible and how much of one desirable property we must give up to salvage some minimum quantity of another. (For a description of such an effort, see Ferejohn, Forsythe, and Noll, 1979.) This is hard and expensive work, for theory must be supplemented by empirical work, initially perhaps in the laboratory (for example, Smith, 1979) but inevitably requiring fullscale field trials at some point. If the first few serious efforts along these lines are any indication, the resulting choice techniques may be dependent on fairly advanced computer or communications technologies or on both. They may also require highly motivated and quite sophisticated participants. All

---

pants. If all cooperate, all, in the aggregate, will be better off than if all defect; but every individual is better off defecting. For an extensive discussion of this "game," its place in public choice theory, and the difference between single and repeated plays, see Hardin (forth-coming).

of which suggests that the public choice experts at the conference were right in being modest. (But see O'Hare, 1977, for an encouraging counter-example.)

The final positive message I find here might be read by others as a negative -- even a dangerously negative -- one. It is that an especially promising way around collective choice problems is to avoid creating such choice situations where they need not exist. We must be careful about assuming, because we currently observe problems in developing countries that the market has failed to solve, that all rural development actions must be accomplished through governments and collective organizations. If the goods and services involved can be divided, or if noncontributors can be excluded from benefits (that is, if we are, or could be, dealing with private goods), we may be well advised to take advantage of the fact and spend our efforts and money in encouraging the development of secure private titles and appropriate protective and market-clearing services (for example, see Thomson on firewood and Freeman and Lowdermilk on parts of irrigation systems. See also Ault and Rutman, 1979).

This is not to say, of course, that the market is any more a panacea than is government intervention. There will always be projects such as flood control works that may be impossible to make private. Other kinds of infrastructure will present severe practical difficulties if not impossibility (for example, roads, regional irrigation works, or agri-cultural research). In addition, markets can only operate from the exist-ing distribution of wealth, and this may be considered unacceptable even within the limited rural context. The easy answer here is to propose that redistribution be undertaken as a specific, separate policy. But it is just this separation that is almost always seen as politically impossible and hence almost never actually done.[5]

As a final comment on the utility of markets, note that in Ruttan's Chapter, changes in market situations are shown to be capable of leading to fundamental shifts in related institutional arrangements. Thus, changes in the relative scarcity of agricultural land and labor can encourage changes in the way laborers are classified and treated by the society -- without formal collective choices being made.

A Brief Reader's Guide

The book is organized into three major sections: Introduction; Areas of Substantive Interest; and a Reprise.

The first section, after this brief introduction, includes three complementary examinations of important general themes. Nicholson, in Chapter 2, provides the intellectual background from the development side, tracing earlier approaches to developing societies and describing the central problems that have exercised and continue to exercise those concerned to bring about development. Chapter 3, by Popkin, lays out the fundamental approach of public choice, shows how it applies to a number of rural development situations, and indicates some of the lessons it can teach us about organizing or collective action. He also brings in a strand from the information literature, the market for "lemons," that shows us a new dimension to the problems of monitoring and enforcing collective agreement, choosing leaders, and overcoming the prisoner's dilemma. To round out this section, Bates goes somewhat more formally into the problems of public choice under various mechanisms and shows us how the new, "incentive compatible mechanisms" are designed to work.

Against this background Chapters 5 through 8, and several accompany-
ing discussions, of the second section describe how public choice and rural
development intertwine in some areas of concern to aid donors: Thomson
discusses energy (firewood) development and protection (Chapter 5);
Freeman and Lowdermilk consider irrigation investment and maintenance
(Chapter 6); Guttman covers the provision of agricultural extension service
(Chapter 7); and Petras and Havens define land tenure (Chapter 8).

Thomson, writing on the Sahel region of Africa, describes the common
property nature of trees (hence firewood) under usual current practice.
He then discusses collective and private institutional ways around the
resulting tendency to deforestation. Irrigation is the area of concern
to Freeman and Lowdermilk, and they describe how the characteristics of
specific projects can be used to determine what decision-making units we
must look to, and whether we have to anticipate collective choice and
action problems. Guttman differs slightly in approach for he is interested
in testing the predictive power of the public choice model; an enterprise
he undertakes in the context of decisions in India about the distribution
to villages of agricultural extension services. Finally, Petras and
Havens show how a cooperative form of land tenure imposed by the national
government on Peruvian peasants failed for public-choice-related reasons
and was scrapped by informal but definite collective action.

The third section of the book may be seen as a reconsideration of
some of the themes in the first section and illustrated in the second.
Ruttan, in Chapter 9 treats induced institutional innovation, and by
using three case studies he shows how changes in market conditions can
lead to quite fundamental changes in rural society. For the most part

these changes involve the institutions defining and mediating market transactions, rather than the collective decision mechanisms of special interest in public choice. Nonetheless, the fact that the changes involve such politically volatile issues as the wage structure for agriculture _and_ are accomplished without explicit collective decisions ever being made, means this approach is a valuable complement to that of public choice proper.

In Chapter 10, Oppenheimer goes over once again the shared ground between rural development and public choice theory. His eye is skeptical and his message cautionary. He stresses the impossibility results central to public choice and the special assumptions and limitations needed to produce mechanisms that "work." If we are disappointed with Oppenheimer's negative tone, we should, I think, reflect that the enterprise of economic development, rural or otherwise, has too often in the past been hampered by enthusiastic adoption of the latest wisdom and all-purpose theoretical guide. Better to undersell than oversell a new and improved version of the truth.

There is much for rural development practitioners to learn from public choice, but there are no easy or universal answers there; only questions and universal problems. At least as yet. For now the answers will come, as they have in the past, from local wisdom, occasional flashes of brilliant insight, and lots of painful trial and error.

References

d'Arge, R., D. Brookshire, F. Blank, and R. Rowe. 1978. "Measuring Aesthetic Preferences: One Experiment on the Economic Value of Visibility." Prepared for the Western Economic Association Meetings, Hawaii, June 20-26.

Arrow, K.J. 1963. Social Choice and Individual Values (2nd ed., New York, Wiley).

Ault, David E., and Gilbert L. Rutman. 1979. "The Development of Individual Property in Tribal Africa," The Journal of Law and Economics vol. 22, no. 1 (April) pp. 163-182.

Development Dialogue. 1977. Issue on Rural Development, no. 2.

The Economist. 1979. "Business Brief," (September 15) pp. 117 and 118.

Ferejohn, John A., Robert Forsythe, and Roger A. Noll. 1979. "Practical Aspects of the Construction of Decentralized Decision-Making Systems for Public Goods," in Clifford S. Russell, ed., Collective Decisiion Making (Baltimore, Md., Johns Hopkins University Press for Resources for the Future).

Hardin, Russell. Forthcoming. "Collective Action." University of Chicago, Department of Political Science, unpublished manuscript.

Kwitny, Jonathan. 1980a. "Unrest in Zaire: Anti-Mobutu Feeling Among Masses Living in Destitution," The Wall Street Journal (June 25) pp. 1 and 16.

_____. 1980b. "African Tragedy: Zaire's Rich Soil Feeds Few Because Farming, Roads are Primitive," Policy Analysis vol. 25, no. 4, pp. 407-458.

O'Hare, Michael. 1977. "Not on My Block, You Don't," Policy Analysis vol. 25, no. 4, pp. 407-458.

Smith, V.L., ed. 1979. Research in Experimental Economics, vol. I (Greenwich, Conn., JAI Press).

Srinivasan, T.M. 1977. "Development, Poverty, and Basic Human Needs: Some Issues," Food Research Institute Studies vol. 16, no. 2, pp. 11-28.

Sumra, Suleman. 1979. "Problems of Agricultural Production in Ujamaa Villages in Handeni District," in Kwan S. Kim, Robert B. Mabele, and Michael J. Schultheis, eds., Papers on the Political Economy of Tanzania (Nairobi, Heinemann Educational Books).

Temu, P. 1979. "The Ujamaa Experiment," in Kwan S. Kim, Robert B. Mabele, and Michael J. Schultheis, eds., Papers on the Political Economy of Tanzania (Nairobi, Heinemann Educational Books).

Chapter 2

APPLICATIONS OF PUBLIC CHOICE THEORY TO RURAL DEVELOPMENT --

A STATEMENT OF THE PROBLEM

Norman K. Nicholson

Rural Development: The Need for a Paradigm

There was a time when the key knowledge that was required to direct development programs was considered to be a broad systemic understanding of the character of "traditional" society and of "modern" society (see, for example, Levy, 1966; Parsons, 1966; and Lerner, 1958). With such an understanding of traditional social structure, economy, and culture, one could anticipate the changes needed to bring about a shift to modern forms and chart a course. This model was particularly effective in anticipating the conflicts and disruptions inherent in dramatic social change. It was always less clear, however, what the dynamic or causal source of this change was to be, hence it was never really clear what policy inter-ventions might be required to bring about modernization. The conceptual model stimulated some broad-based community development interventions in developing countries but these produced no demonstrable impact on economic growth or social modernization.

The traditional/modern model failed also as an empirical description of reality in the developing world and collapsed against the background of new field studies. Attempts were made to salvage it by suggesting a typology of "traditional" systems, a variety of paths to modernity, and a variety of "modern" societies (see, Atter, 1965; Horowitz, 1966; Adelman and Morris, 1973; Binder and coauthors, 1971; and Almond and Powell, 1966). Heroic though this salvage attempt was, it still appeared inadequate to explain the diversity of conditions encountered, the continuation of traditional forms in modern guise, the difficulty of bringing about change in rural areas in general, and the remarkable speed of change in Green Revolution areas such as the Indian Punjab. Contrary to Kuhn's (1970) argument, however, the model collapsed before an alternative appeared, and studies and analyses of development fragmented into sector-specific and problem-specific approaches in which incremental and microtheoreies, usually heavily grounded in empirical data, sprang up in various disciplines. The attempt at macrosystems models that crossed disciplinary lines had, in consequence, atrophied by the early 1970s.

Only in economics have general growth and development models persisted. Attention to capital formation and savings has abated somewhat and has been replaced with a focus on technological change in altering the productivity of land and labor, but economic growth continues to be the vehicle of "modernization" in the economic models. It should be pointed out, however, that these models have not been without their critics who have argued that they misrepresent the complex social reality of rural areas by extracting economic behavior and institutions from the surrounding social context with which leaders and administrators must deal on a day-to-day basis. At the village level, it is argued, these models continue to produce unanticipated pernicious results unless they are integrated into a more holistic "rural development" perspective.

The concern with broad social change of the early modernization models
did have one beneficial effect which has assisted this integration. A good
many studies were initiated which provided elaborate information on social
structure and process at the local level -- whether in sociology or anthropology. The supply of scholars who went to the field to demonstrate the
validity of the macromodels was substantial. It is to their credit that
they honestly reported data which did not fit the assumptions. They also
produced great amounts of social analysis of microenvironments and demonstrated how the forces of modernization differentially affected different
environments and communities, producing bewildering complexity and unanticipated results. We developed, therefore, a generation of scholars
well acquainted with the microlevel conditions in less developed
countries, aware of the uniqueness of those responses to the forces of
change and dissatisfied with general models. These same scholars were
quick to identify the frequent failures of development efforts, and were
in a unique position to point out that failures were often attributable
to the lack of understanding, or monitoring, of the unique social environment into which initiatives and investments were made. The international
aid donors did not always appreciate this universally critical perspective
but in the face of obvious failure, the lack of alternative explanations,
and the credibility of many of the instances these microscholars cited,
the trend quickly came to be one of coopting them into the process.
Hardly any AID project is done today which does not incorporate micro-
analysis of a variety of disciplines to assure the project's "social
soundness."

Our understanding of the communities with which we deal and the
sensitivity of decision makers to the microprocesses at work have probably
never been higher. At the operational level, implementation teams have
become increasingly interdisciplinary with the participation of specialists in economics, public administration, anthropology, and the biological
sciences. But, in fact, this has become the only guiding principle of
rural development projects -- that they must be micro-oriented, sensitive
to local conditions and adaptive to local peculiarities, and oriented to
incremental changes in local conditions that can be brought about at the
project level. This is a satisfactory orientation for project design
but it is unrelated to any theory of change, development, or the broader
interrelationships of local to national level processes. In consequence,
the gap between the economic planners and rural development practitioners
has seldom been broader than at present. The best rural development
projects are conceptually weak and built on accumulated field experience
-- not theory. On the other hand, the economic growth models provide
little operational guidance and frequently fail to guide practice.

Thus, although the "rural development" profession has earned increasing credibility at the operational level, it still has little theoretical status as a macromodel. AID's agricultural policy statement of
1978 (USAID, 1978) for example, was a remarkable tribute to how far
this integrated rural development perspective has come, but was unable
to explain how the very real contribution of the social scientists at
the operational level might be expressed as a component of a satisfactory
growth model. Rather, it was argued that these social issues were
implementation and operational considerations and did not have any status

in a theory or model of rural growth per se -- they were questions of
technique. The social scientists felt a considerable loss of status at
thus being addressed as mere practitioners but, in fact, were unable to
convincingly articulate a response.

The result is, then, the continuation of (1) a paradigm crisis, (2) a
gap between theory and practice, (3) an extremely haphazard rural development process in which there is really no basis for reviewing rural development projects except on the processual grounds that they are not "participatory," not "disaggregate enough," that they ignore local realities, or
that they are not implementable. The character of the criticism of rural
development projects is typically quite different from the rigorous
analysis that surrounds macroeconomic policy analysis regarding price
levels, interest rates, important-export policy, capital:labor ratios.
Similarly the rural development professionals do not seem to have much to
contribute to a dialog with macroeconomic analysts because the nature of
their experience and paradigms simply does not translate into the dimensions of macromodeling.

Public Choice and Rural Development

The search for a theoretical perspective that will cross disciplinary
lines and integrate the perspectives of the economic planners with the
community-level concerns of the anthropologist has some priority and
considerable potential utility. The current interest in public choice
theory, or political economy, as an approach to development problems
arises in part because it appears to offer such a bridge between economic
analysis and analysis based on social structure and social power. In
addition to this general orientation, however, public choice theory

appears to provide a valuable insight into a specific set of development problems which practitioners have come to agree are critical to the rural development process. These problems include (1) planning and management of rural investment -- including infrastructure, agricultural research, social services, and human resource development; (2) the development of local governance systems -- such as local governments, cooperatives, water users associations; and (3) access to and management of productive resources -- that is, water, land, and trees. These problems share several characteristics: a substantial need for local participation in order to create an adequate "demand schedule" for the service or investment; the presence of externalities (positive or negative) and a degree of "publicness" in the goods supplied that suggests the need for collective action; an inadequacy of existing institutions for decision making and management to deal with the problems of equity, demand, and free riders that are rampant in these areas; and a strong bias within governments of developing countries in the direction of regulatory or administrative solutions. It is hardly surprising, therefore, that scholars and practitioners have turned to public choice theory for a perspective that will assist in dealing with these issues.

Political Economy and Public Investment in Rural Areas

Political economy has long been concerned with the difficult conceptual and practical problems of estimating demand schedules for public goods. This is doubly difficult in rural investment decisions in developing countries because of the cultural and institutional gaps which commonly prevail between the government on the one hand and the village community on the other. The cultural divisions mean that there is no particular reason to assume that either bureaucratic or political decision makers have any real understanding of the investment priorities of the villagers. The weakness of rural institutions means that there are few institutional lines of communication between the villages and the bureaucratic hierarchy. When one takes as one's target population the rural poor, the general phenomenon is made more difficult by the voicelessness and high access costs of the poor in dealing with decision makers. The problem that development practitioners call "top down planning" is very much a public choice problem.

One aspect of rural development that has given practitioners increasing difficulty and concern is the area of rural infrastructure. We are well aware of the importance of public investment in such areas as irrigation, electrification, roads, and conservation. Yet, on the other hand, such large-scale projects have increasingly come under attack as being capital rather than labor-intensive, and as being unresponsive to real local needs and capacities. There is ample reason for concern when you add to this the fact that such investments as often as not have detrimental long term effects on the welfare of the poorest in the region. Thus, the "price" signals bear little relationship to user demand, and the negative externalities are large.

Public investment in agricultural research, crucial to dynamic rural development, presents comparable problems. How much should governments invest in agricultural research and what forms should such research take? To whose demands are existing research systems responsive? How might small farm needs be more accurately and effectively reflected in the research agenda and what institutional forms would produce equitable

access to researchers by the poor and provide incentives to researchers
to respond?

Current analysis argues strongly that most agricultural research must
be in the public sector because of the "public goods" character of biological technology. Most private seed companies are in the marketing
business, not in the research business. There are also strong implications
that the relative success of the U.S. research system is largely due to
the successful politicization of the agricultural university system combined with substantial decentralization regionally. This combination
overcomes the classic public choice difficulties by permitting farm
interests fairly easy and effective access to decision making in the research system. Even in the United States, however, it is recognized
that this research system has been biased against the small farmer. The
opportunities for interaction between the research establishment and the
small farmer are even fewer in the highly centralized systems characteristic of developing countries. Replications of the U.S. system appear to
be producing comparable social effects in the third world. The question
then becomes one of finding some institutional solution to the mobilization and organization of demand.

A number of common questions seem to emerge from rural investment
decisions:

- Are the opportunities created by such projects really commensurate
  with the aspirations, capacities, and resources of the majority of
  the local population? That is, is demand highly distorted by
  institutional processes?

- Can the community sustain these investments and finance them after
  a reasonable period of adjustment? Will they do so? We typically
  find that many public goods are being overproduced by this criteria?

- How can we be sure that the distribution of costs of such investments is consistent with the distribution of benefits, and what
  constitutes a valid principle of cost allocation?

What we are seeking in the above discussion is information about the
nature of the local demand function for rural public investments. What
package of public investments does the rural community want or need and
how much are they willing to pay for? An even more important question may
be the social distribution of "effective demand" for such investments;
that is, whose needs/demands are reflected in the pattern of investment?
And how is the system of financing such investment related to the distribution of benefits? It is not enough to argue that "everyone benefits"
from public goods. We are asking how the demand of the voiceless and
powerless might be made effective in the planning and implementation
process. In other words, how can the system be made more participatory?

We have discovered that nationally conceived plans prepared by
experts are seldom really responsive to local needs and capacities. As
such, they are undoubtedly wasteful and inefficient guides to public investment. Yet it is surprising how often it is argued that this dilemma
can be resolved by more rigorous economic analysis and planning. The
weakness of this argument is clear. In an economic analysis the "goals"
or "demand" for public investment are either derived from the growth model
which is being utilized or are treated as an exogenous political "given"
which it is up to the planner to make consistent with other aspects of

the plan. The creation or articulation of the demand function for such public investment is seldom treated as part of the planning problem and process. Where planners do recognize the problem and "bottom-up" planning is attempted, it is usually not done very effectively. Our institutional ingenuity in devising participatory program development and planning processes has not been very impressive.

A concern for the institutional context for collective choice -- public decisions on the allocation of investment -- has been an important focus for analysis in the field of political economy for some time. It is the area where the economists' concern for the allocation of scarce resources, the political scientists' concern for the institutions of public choice, and the anthropologists' interest in social exchange meet, and, where the tools of each discipline can be used to improve investment decisions.

There are a number of theoretical problems which must be resolved if the integration is to succeed:

1. Political economy has yet to deal effectively with the question of power. Generally the dynamics of collective choice in the political economy models depend on mutual gains to trade. So far it has ignored the capacity to impose penalties. This is a serious weakness in real-world applications. Harsanyi (1969a and 1969b) and Parsons (1969) offer a start, but only that.

2. To a considerable extent the question of cultural diversity has been finessed by political economy. Yet different perceptions of reality, different valuation of media of exchange, and questions of "trust," are too often assumed away. What are the social requisites of an effective

exchange system and have we dealt adequately with the circumstances described by Banfield (1958) or by Siegel and Beals (1960a and 1960b)?

3. This author has yet to see any convincing treatment of the process
of institutional change in the literature of political economy. Changing
patterns of social organization and institutional development, unstable
utility schedules, great uncertainty regarding the parameters of choice
-- both individual and collective -- are all characteristic of developing
countries, but the public choice models are static. Ruttan (1978; see also
Chapter 9) has made the only convincing effort to date to deal systematically with this problem.

This is not intended to be an exhaustive list of items for a research
agenda, but merely to illustrate that some important theoretical work is
required to adapt the political economy literature to the requirements
of development practitioners.

Political Economy and Institutional Design

The theoretical and practical question we must answer is how to
structure the policy development and implementation processes so as to
relate them to effective popular input. Some of the key questions here
relate to scale of social organization, decision-making rules, the functional specificity of projects and institutions, and characteristic types
of policy which institutions must implement. We have some insights
developed in the work of Bailey (1969), Oslon (1965) or Buchanan and
Tullock (1969), but much more systematic treatment of these issues in
the context of the third world is essential.

A good example is the whole question of public decisions to leave
various functions in the private, cooperative, or public sector. Much
of our analysis is based on total systems rather than on the suitability

of certain institutional patterns for particular functions in particular
settings. A discussion such as that by Buchanan and Tullock (1969, Chapter
5), which provides a proposed analytical framework for analyzing such
choices, is very helpful but needs elaboration to LDC contexts. What
are the key components of such an analysis?

Scale of social organization can be an important consideration in
planning institutional development. The absorption capacity of rural
institutions is clearly influenced by the scale of organization through
which resources are directed. The debate between advocates of a village-
based, "bottom up" strategy, and those supporting a decentralized planning
strategy focused at intermediate levels, is one of the more active conflicts in rural development today. Resource mobilization appears to be
superior in the smaller unit, but the ability to manage externally provided
investments clearly improves at the intermediate level. For the Parsoni-
ans, the development of large-scale organization has been virtually
synonymous with modernization. Given the resources which such structures
can mobilize this is not an unreasonable proposition. Political economists
such as Olson and Tullock are more likely to stress the changes in decision-
making patterns as scale increases and how these changes effect outcomes.
But these perspectives seldom illuminate the debates of the practitioners.

We have now considerable literature on how various decision-making
rules (for example, majority rule, unanimity, and so forth) influence the
outcome of public decision-making. Yet it is seldom that this knowledge
has deliberately been applied to specific problems of the design of participatory institutions. It is surprising how often the time and energy
required for the individual to participate in local institutions is not

worth the benefit derived either by the community or the individual.
Planners tend to view participation as an _educational_ process. Villagers
either view it as a business proposition or else place much lower value
on the potential benefit of such "education" than they do on more conventional forms of learning (for example, literacy).

Functional specificity has a major impact on institutional performance.
It is common observation that single-purpose and commercially oriented cooperatives are much easier to organize and sustain than multipurpose,
communitywide structures. The reasons for this are clear. Multipurpose
organizations become politicized because of the diversity of interests
represented and, in consequence, commercial functions become confused with
public policy questions. Nevertheless, there are examples of successful
multipurpose organizations and there are gains to trade when multiple
interests are involved. How is one to evaluate the advantages of different approaches?

Policies and programs differ in the relationship which they establish
between citizen and public authority, and this, in turn, influences institutional structure and behavior. "Extractive" policies such as taxation
engender quite different relationships than "distributive" policies regarding fertilizer or institutional credit in order to raise prices to
real costs and ration scarce resources clearly disrupt established institutional practice and institutional interests in the third world as they
would in the United States. In publicly owned canal irrigation systems,
the government bureaucracy typically rations water to its clientele
because each farmer has established water _rights_. The tubewell, however,
introduces quite a different set of allocation criteria and permits water-

use decisions centered on the technical requirements of the crop. The
relative abundance of water on-farm in tubewell conditions, in comparison
with canal conditions, encourages misuse of the resource -- for example,
causing salinization. Government cannot exercise the regulatory authority
over the individual tubewells that it did over canal water, however, and
must turn to extension techniques to rationalize water use. The institutional adjustments required are substantial. The work of Theodore Lowi
is quite suggestive in relating policy types (that is, extractive, regulatory, distributive, and so forth) to the structuring of economic interests,
bureaucratic style, and characteristic institutional problems and policy
failures (Lowi, 1972). This work has yet to be systematically applied to
third world settings, however.

Institutional development depends in part on an adequate structuring
of roles within the institution. Generally, role theory has been the
preserve of the social anthropologists and has stressed functional compatibility and socialization in understanding role relationships. The
insight of Downs (1957) or Blau (1967), based on exchange models of inter-
personal relationships, has not found much application in LDC settings,
however. There is obvious scope for such analysis in models of bureaucratic behavior (especially in heavily bureaucratized economies), in
analyzing the behavior cooperative institutions, and in understanding the
key problems of leadership and various maladies of leadership (such as
functionalism).

Implementation analysis touches a number of important issues, (see,
for example, Bardach, 1977; and Wolf, 1979) and is an attempt to relate
the characteristics of policy making to the institutional problems of

implementation. This approach is almost atheoretic at this point but the perception that there may be systematic reasons for policy failure is the unifying thread in this literature. If these could be treated theoretically as inefficiencies in nonmarket exchange mechanisms, they would become tractable to much more rigorous analysis.

The problem of institutional design is increasingly recognized as a key problem of development. Many researchers and practitioners accept the value of the political economy insights and we find unmistakable evidence of the application of the approach both in their footnotes and their formal reasoning processes. Nevertheless, with the single exception of Ilchman and Uphoff (1971), we lack a systematic attempt to relate political economy theory to institution-building problems in the third world. Part of the problem has been the lack of empirical data on intermediate level institutions in LDCs. Field research has tended to be dominated by anthropologists, and their focus was the village and not policy oriented. That information gap is now being filled, but current research lacks a clear conceptual framework and theoretical base.

The problem of developing that theoretical base is made difficult, however, by excessively abstract theoretical models on the one hand and the general lack of rigor of most of the empirical field studies on the other. The gap can best be overcome, I would argue, by an attempt to come to a theoretical understanding of the design problems of specific local institutions -- credit cooperatives, water users associations, extension systems, regional planning, and so forth.

Access to Productive Assets

A concern for the interdependence (functional or otherwise) of political and economic systems is one that clearly predates more formal collective choice models. Marx or Weber provide the intellectual origins of much of this analysis, and the starting point is the manner in which mechanisms of social control are used to maintain economic systems which systematically work to the differential advantage of certain groups in society.

At the simplest level, an analysis of how control of basic productive assets (for example, land, capital or technology) can be maintained in the hands of a restricted group is fundamental to our understanding of the distribution of costs and benefits of growth.

At a somewhat more complex level, some authors have investigated how seemingly neutral economic processes, for example, the market or new technical knowledge, will have highly inequitable and unanticipated consequences for different groups or regions if no capacity for social control exists to regulate and shape these processes. Thus, the absence of the power or will to take collective (social) action may be as serious as the undue biasing of such control toward the interests of a small elite.

The patron-client literature represents yet another approach to this problem. These studies tend to stress the reciprocity (not equality of course) and the multidimensionality of exchange relationships between the powerful and the powerless. Such studies warn us against the over simplification of an "exploitation" model of rural power relationships while at the same time indicating the difficulties involved in breaking dependency ties when they are reinforced by such complex and reinforcing motivations. They further reflect the inadequacy of "market" models of villages' economic behavior (for example, Scott, 1976; Breman, 1974; and Kern, 1973).

Finally, we have a rather extensive literature on fragmented, multi-ethnic communities in which cleavages among groups inhibit mutual trust and, in consequence, both exchange and cooperation. Much analysis has centered on the rather primitive and convoluted mechanisms of political exchange characteristic of such systems. In many ways the "brokerage politics" of such communities resembles a "barter" political economy. The insights derived from this literature (for example, on the role of leadership, corruption, factionalism, and symbolic demands) seems to invite application of work by Blau (1967) and Parsons (1969) on values as media of exchange but much of the work so far is descriptive.

This literature is clearly in need of an integrating perspective, if not a theory, if we are to avoid immersion in ad hoc descriptions on the one hand or vulgar Marxism on the other. Unlike the early sixties where we had a major theory-building effort with almost no data at all, the time is now ripe for a productive interaction of the deductive model builders in political economy and the inductive, middle-range theory building of the field researchers. What is needed at this point is a strategy for proceeding with this effort and a systematic commitment of funds to the enterprise.

New Directions in Political Economy

One answer to the conceptual problems raised above would appear to be a focus on political economy models, paying particular attention to the functioning of economic institutions of various kinds. Several current approaches deserve attention.

Induced innovation model. The leading spokesman of this approach is Ruttan (1978), and his argument can be capsulized as follows: "a theory of institutional changes in which shifts in the demand for institutional change are induced by changes both in the relative prices of factors and products and in the technology associated with economic growth, and in which shifts in the supply of institutional change are induced by advances in knowledge in the social sciences."

Ruttan tends to view institutional change, then, as responsive to demands originating in changing factor prices and the disruptions they engender. But, he argues, there are inefficiencies in the adjustment of institutions to new conditions because the dynamic of power relations is not identical to market processes. As a result, the "supply" of institutional change frequently lags behind "demand" and is frequently biased by "political forces."

Institutional experimentation and innovation can, however, offer new and lower-cost ways of pursuing collective economic goals -- reconciling collective and individual goals, providing "justice" when claims on economic rights are in competition, providing collective goods such as agricultural research, or permitting very small farms to externalize certain economic functions. Ruttan argues that the pessimism of the public choice theorists concerning the effects (irrational) of institutional interventions in the market is largely a function of these lags and rigidities on the supply side and is not inherent in collective action per se. These lags and rigidities could presumably be corrected by further investment in social research or experimentation.

Institutional change and performance is brought directly into an economic analysis by this model, therefore, by making it dependent on changing technology and prices. The analysis appears to be stronger when it deals with social institutions such as land contracts between landlord and tenant than when it is applied to formal organizations such as civil bureaucracies. Recent work on agricultural research systems suggests that application to formal organization is not impossible, however. The analytical problem appears to be one of researching the motivational or behavioral aspects of nonmarket choice in formal institutions and of identifying the constraints on institutional change and adaptation that account for the lags and biases uncovered by the economic research. Current applications of public choice theory to development, outlined below, may help to correct these weaknesses.

Governance and technology. A second approach to the problem of integrating economic and political analysis can be found in the growing number of studies centering on the community governance of the production process at the local level. The argument is made that certain modes of production, irrigated agriculture for example, require certain types of supporting institutional structures. In irrigation the key is the allocative process -- who gets access to water, how much water each gets, and the timeliness of the shares. Canal irrigation inevitably requires some sort of collective allocation process. In a penetrating analysis, Maass and Anderson (1978) argue that local control, a reasonable degree of equity, and the ability to exclude nonmembers, are the keys to such irrigation management. In fact, they argue, the exclusion principle appears to take precedence over efficiency in that it can be demonstrated

that a market system of allocation would probably be more economically
optimal for farmers but is seldom used because the community might then
lose control over the resource to outsiders.

Freeman and Lowdermilk, also dealing with water management institutions, attempts (in Chapter 6) to provide somewhat more structure to the
relationship between technology and governance. They suggest a sixfold
typology of goods provided by local institutions along the dimensions of
high-medium, and low-divisibility of the goods along one axis and private
and public goods along the other. Once a certain production problem is
diagnosed to lie in a particular cell of the matrix, the characteristics
of the most suitable institutional structure for producing that goods or
service can be deduced. The line of causation still lies from the production system to the institutional structure but this approach complements
the "induced innovation" model by focusing on how the type of institution
structures farmer incentives and behavior. Field tests in Pakistan indicate that the Freeman-Lowdermilk approach provides a reasonable degree
of predictability of farmer behavior in different institutional contexts.

These approaches are certainly not deterministic and they currently
may have better explanatory than predictive power, but they do demonstrate
an intimate connection between the economic functions performed by an
institution highly influenced by the technology and demography of production, and the decision rules, scale, and organizational structure of
local institutions. The game theorists are generally unhappy with these
applications of public choice theory to development problems because they
do not yield determinate solutions, but rather a range of possible outcomes, and because the solutions do not appear to be stable in a game

theoretic sense. From an operational point of view, however, this would not appear to have much consequence and reflects the empirical reality that there are several alternative institutional paths to solving a given economic problem. These approaches also have considerable diagnostic power in ascertaining the unsuitability or irrelevance of particular institutional forms that typically "fail" because they have been imposed by national bureaucracies and display insufficient regard for the local production system, farmer incentives, and the institutional problems of collective goods development at the community level.

Collective Choice Theory. A recent study by Popkin (1979) offers another approach to the problems of integrating political and economic analysis. The analysis builds on a growing body of literature on peasant behavior that argues that peasants' collective behavior can be modeled by microeconomic models because the assumptions about rational behavior built into such models are fundamentally valid. The weakness of the models to date, however, lies in assumptions made about the goals peasants pursue in collective economic activities. In particular, Popkin argues, peasants seek to achieve maximum security, not maximum profit, in their economic behavior. The social institutions which emerge, therefore, may be subject not only to changing factor prices, but also to changing survival strategies mandated by such changing factor prices.

Popkin's work also provides a number of insights into the problems of collective action at the community level in "traditional" societies. First, collective action was extremely difficult and, in consequence, investment in public goods minimal. Second, because of the difficulty of investment in public goods, community security in time of famine was

minimal, with the result that peasants sought dyadic patron-client ties
or individualized solutions whenever possible. Community institutions
have never been, he argues, a reliable hedge against disaster. His conclusion is that rural institutions need not be slow to change in the face
of new economic opportunities if (1) those opportunities operate at the
individual and not the group level, and (2) if the new activities increase
family income security. Under these conditions, there are likely to be
powerful village-level pressures for altering "traditional" institutional
structures (independently of power structures). Whether local elites
will promote or encourage such changes or even whether they can effectively
control these pressures if they choose to become empirical questions.

A recent survey of firewood problems in Africa by Thomson (1979;
and in Chapter 5) focuses on problems of village governance of available
firewood supplies and seems to add credence to the Popkin approach.
Thomson concludes that much of the explanation for deteriorating firewood
supplies lies in the character of village-level decision rules, the lack
of decision authority at the village level, and the high personal costs
of participation combined with the potential high deprivations of coopera-
ting in group action if decisions went against one's interests (that is,
due to the character of the decision rules). The complexities of ownership in Africa, both individual and collective, make the character of
these decision rules a key constraint on firewood development. These
problems of the interaction of rights and incentive and decision rules
offer an interesting practical application of classic collective choice
theory to development problems.

In Thomson's study the growing scarcity of firewood interacts with
both formal and informal tenure rules on the one hand and the cost of

enforcement on the other to produce patterns of individual behavior which are "irrational" at both the microeconomic and macroeconomic levels. Thus, the individual underinvests in tree production because in spite of his need for wood and for windbreaks he cannot economically protect his investment against encroachment by others. Conversely, the government, recognizing the need to protect the stock of trees, attempts to protect the existing supply by regulating access rather than by altering the process by which individuals protect their investment. The result has been that neither the community nor the individual have been able to prevent free riders from poaching wood supplies.

These applications of public choice theory provide an analytical model which focuses on institutional decision rules rather than on market processes. They also shed light on such features of institutional processes as (1) the determinants of access to institutional rights and benefits, (2) the cost-benefit ratios of pursuing individual interests through various institutional processes, (3) the <u>probabilities</u> of outcome distributions, and (4) the manner in which the decision rules and institutional structure encourage short-term versus long-term or individual versus communitywide perspectives. If these approaches are less aesthetically pleasing than classic public choice models, they have the advantage of also being less static and deterministic. There would appear to be utility in employing approaches more similar to those of Harsanyi (1969a), which provide a more probabilistic and interactive model incorporating a wider range of variables. Institutional analysis, however, must permit frequent changes in the rules of the game.

References

Adelman, Irma, and Cynthia Taft Morris. 1973. Economic Growth and Social Equity in Developing Countries (Stanford, Calif., Stanford University Press).

Almond, G. and G. Powell. 1966. Comparative Politics (Boston, Mass., Little, Brown).

Atter, David. 1965. The Politics of Modernization (Chicago, Ill., University of Chicago Press).

Bailey, F.G. 1969. Strategems and Spoils (New York, Schocken).

Banfield, E. 1958. The Moral Basis of a Backward Society (New York, Free Press).

Bardach, Eugene. 1977. The Implementation Game (Cambridge, Mass., MIT Press).

Binder, Leonard and Joseph Lapalombara, eds. 1971. Crises and Sequences in Political Development (Princeton, N.J., Princeton University Press).

Blau, Peter M. 1967. Exchange and Power in Social Life (New York, Wiley).

Breman, Jan. 1974. Patronage and Exploitation (Berkeley, University of California Press).

Buchanan, James and Gordon Tullock. 1969. The Calculus of Consent (Ann Abror, University of Michigan Press).

Downs, Anthony. 1957. An Economic Theory of Democracy (New York, Harper & Row).

Harsanyi, John. 1969a. "Measurement of Social Power, Opportunity Costs, and the Theory of Two-person Bargaining Games," in Roderick Bell and others, eds., Political Power (New York, Free Press) ch. 19.

_____. 1969b. "Measurement of Social Power in n-Person Reciprocal Power Situations," in Roderick Bell, Political Power (New York, Free Press) ch. 20.

Horowitz, Irving L. 1966. Three Worlds of Development (New York, Oxford University Press).

Ilchman, Warren and Normal Uphoff. 1971. The Political Economy of Change (Berkeley, University of California Press).

Kern, Robert, ed. 1973. The Caciques (Albuquerque, University of New Mexico Press).

Kuhn, Thomas. 1970. The Structure of Scientific Revolutions (2nd ed., Chicago, Ill., University of Chicago Press).

Lerner, Daniel. 1958. The Passing of Traditional Society (Glencoe, N.Y., Free Press).

Levy, Marion J., Jr. 1966. Structure of Societies (Princeton, N.J., Princeton University Press).

Lowi, Theodore. 1972. "Population Policies and the Political System," in A.E. Kier Nash, ed., Governance and Population: The Governmental Implications of Population Change Commission on Population Growth and the American Future, Research Reports, vol. iv, pp. 283-300 (Washington, D.C., GPO).

Maass, Aruthur and Raymond Anderson. 1978. And the Desert Shall Rejoice (Cambridge, Mass., MIT Press). ch. 9.

Olson, Mancur. 1965. The Logic of Collective Action (Cambridge, Mass., Harvard University Press).

Parsons, Talcot. 1966. Societies: Evolutionary and Comparative Perspectives (Englewood Cliffs, N.J., Prentice-Hall).

_____. 1969. Politics and Social Structure (New York, Free Press) ch. 14.

Popkin, Samuel L. 1979. The Rational Peasant (Berkeley, University of California Press).

Ruttan, Vernon W. 1978. "Induced Institutional Change," in H.P. Binswanger and Vernon W. Ruttan, Induced Innovation (Baltimore, Md., Johns Hopkins University Press) ch. 12.

Scott, James C. 1976. The Moral Economy of the Peasant (New Haven, Conn., Yale University Press).

Siegel, J. and A. Beals. 1960a. "Conflict and Factionalist Dispute," Journal of Royal Anthropological Institute vol. 90, pp. 107-117.

_____. 1960b. "Pervasive Factionalism," American Anthropologist vol. 62, pp. 394-417.

Thomson, James T. 1979. "Firewood Survey: Theory and Methodology," submitted in accordance with terms of U.S. AID Purchase Order No. 147-88 under Project No. 698-0135, Program Development and Support (Firewood Survey Methodology, September 18).

U.S. Agency for International Development. 1978. Agricultural Development Policy Paper (Washington, D.C., U.S. AID).

Wolf, Charles. 1979. "A Theory of Nonmarket Failure: Framework for Implementation Analysis, Journal of Law and Economics vol. 22 (April, pp. 107-139.

Chapter 3

PUBLIC CHOICE AND RURAL DEVELOPMENT --
FREE RIDERS, LEMONS, AND INSTITUTIONAL DESIGN

Samuel L. Popkin

There is a natural affinity between public choice and the study of
rural development. Public choice can be defined as the study of nonmarket
economics, and the extension of the methodology of microeconomics to nonmarket settings. Since so much of rural development is concerned with
the analysis and design of institutions other than markets, public choice
can bridge the chasm between market economists applying rational models
of individual decision making to markets and the social scientists who
have assumed that the assumptions of economics about individual decision
making and the allocation of scarce resources were not applicable to their
study of rural institutions.

The division in the past between economists and the other social
scientists was caused in great measure by the disdain economists displayed
toward nonmarket institutions and nonmarket arrangements. Market economics
gave economists a set of elegant tools with which to discuss economic
policy, but there was no corresponding awareness by economists of the
economic role of nonmarket institutions. Although one field worker after
another wrote treatises on one or another "traditional institution" and

its role in the rural economy, economists were proudly uninterested in rural institutions other than markets. To even the best development economists, institutions other than the market were of little concern because it was assumed that market forces would dominate them. "The love of money is a powerful institutional solvent," trumpeted Sir Arthur Lewis (1962, p. iii), "many countries have indeed attitudes and institutions which inhibit growth, but they will rid themselves of these attitudes and institutions once their people discover that they stand in the way of economic opportunities." As F.G. Bailey (1971, p. 295) so aptly commented, "this is not really a statement about the nature of human motivation: rather it is a statement about the investigator himself -- about the seriousness with which he proposes to inform himself about people's values and their perceptions of the possibilities of a situation."

Ignoring institutions, however, led a generation of economists astray. A milestone in laissez-faire economic theory, Schultz's Transforming Traditional Agriculture (1964) is an excellent reference point for a brief discussion of the strengths and weaknesses of the assumptions and foci with which the free-market economists approached peasant agriculture. Examining evidence for peasant response to new opportunities and for allocation of resources at the farm level, Schultz emphasized the responsiveness of peasants to market forces. From the evidence for economic responsiveness at the household level, Schultz argued that there are two major ways to improve the position of the peasantry -- education and improved and cheaper technology. As Schultz (1964, p. 5) commented, "Once there are investment opportunities and efficient incentives, farmers will turn sand into gold."

Today it is all too easy to disparage Schultz and belittle his contributions. He wrote at a time when most non-economists had little or
no understanding of the role which market forces could play in stimulating
agricultural production, when there was little or no appreciation of the
responsiveness of the so-called traditional farmer to price incentives,
when a large number of development scholars even believed in backward-
bending labor curves -- that, that as wages or profits increased peasants
would work less.

Important as Schultz's work is, it is severely limited because of
its focus on market forces and a fixed institutional framework. By ignoring the interplay between market forces and national and local institutions,
Schultz makes prescriptions which are far too narrow and predictions which
are far too optimistic about the beneficial aspects of increased market
activity. Peasant households are indeed marginally efficient allocators
of their resources, and peasants are indeed resonsive to market forces.
To stress education and technology, however, is to ignore too many crucial
factors.

From the evidence that peasants are efficient resource allocators,
Schultz argues that traditional agricultural communities are generally
also "efficient but poor" (1964, p. 38). If that were so, then it would
be appropriate to stress education and technology as means for raising
peasant output and living standards; and institutional analysis would be
irrelevant. For if peasants were "efficient but poor," then, "no appreciable increase in agricultural production is to be had by reallocating
the factors at the disposal of farmers who are bound by traditional agriculture. Another implication is that an outside expert, however skilled

he may be in farm management, will not discover any major inefficiency in the allocation of factors (Schultz, p. 39). If, that is, villages were production maximizing for the known state of the art, then the most important measures are to give peasants schooling -- so that they can understand new methods -- and to develop new and cheaper technology (Schultz, pp. 21, 33 and 155).

As Lipton (1968) has shown, however, the conclusion that peasants are production maximizing does not pay sufficient attention to problems of risk and uncertainty facing the household. The leap from peasant efficiency to village efficiency (or production maximization for a given level of technology), moreover, assumes perfect markets in land, labor, and capital. It also fails to take sufficient account of the problem of nonmarket goods and insurance.

Individual peasant families, although they are highly efficient at the margin in allocating their labor, land, and capital, pay far more attention to risk and uncertainty that Schultz's work implies. The concern with risk means that improved insurance or welfare schemes may do as much to increase production as education or technology. Farmers concerned about survival will diverge from production maximization; the extent of the divergence will be affected by the quality of their insurance. Both risk and insurance, therefore, require more attention than Schultz gave them.

Peasants' worries about risk and insurance and the economic benefits of institutional remedies to these problems were ignored by most economists, not just Schultz. For example, the widespread practice of scattering plots was viewed by many economists as irrational. In fact, the scattering of plots substantially reduces the maximum damage that small local disasters or climatic variations can cause in a given season: mildew or rot in one area of the village, an errant herd, exceptionally light or heavy rains, and similar mini-disasters will be less likely to wipe out a peasant's entire crop when fields are scattered. Scattered plots reduce the variance of yield from year to year and thus reduce the probability of losing the entire crop, but scattering also cuts the maximum yield per farmer and for the village as a whole (McCloskey, 1976).

Scattered plots are often more desirable than a single plot per family when there is no reliable widespread insurance system. However, centuries of division sometimes lead to scattering in the extreme. In Greece, for example, Thompson found that the number and disperson of plots belonging to the typical family was far greater than that needed for in-surance value and that a majority of villagers in the eighteen villages favored a program of plot consolidation to increase production, decrease family friction over inheritances, reduce violence over access to inside plots, and put land consumed by paths and boundaries back into production. But this majority of villagers believed that a voluntary program of con-solidation would not work because the differences in fertility and soil type, as well as the problems of accurately evaluating the yield (and variance) of plots, made weighting systems for establishing equivalences difficult to establish, and there was little willingness to trust any committee of villagers to arrive at an equitable consolidation. For that reason, the general feeling was that compulsory consolidation was the only way to proceed (Thomson, 1963).

The complex problem of trading and consolidating parcels arises whenever an inheritance is shared among more than one offspring. Lipton

(1968) describes an Indian village where the farmland runs down the side
of a long slope. Soil quality varies from top to bottom of the sloped, but
varies little along a contour of the slope. If plots were divided hor-
izontally along the contours of the hill, plowing would be easier and
cheaper, and average output would be higher. Lipton (1968, p. 339) reports
that each father, however, avoids the problem of equating contours with
different averages and variances by dividing the patrimony into vertical
strips: "This saddles each generation of sons with longer, thinner sloping
strips, increasingly costy and inconvient to plough properly, i.e., re-
peatedly and across the slope." The very lack of insurance and the difficulties of comparing plots mean that for every generation the share of
land occupied by partions increases, as does the gap between actual and
potential production.

But designing workable systems of crop insurance has been an almost
insurmountable problem. The first approach, following from welfare economics followed Kenneth Arrow's dictum that "The welfare case for insurance
of all sorts is overwhelming. It follows that the government should
undertake insurance where the market, for whatever reason, has failed
to emerge (cited in Pauly, 1968, p. 531). Crop insurance has been proposed in several countries to increase production by protecting peasants
against risk. But such direct applications of the principles of welfare
economics still did not show an appreciation of peasant society (Roumasset,
1976). The very existence of insurance can effect the way farmers work
and thus can decrease productivity because it is not always possible to
separate the effects of sloth and nature. Farmers, then, can take advantage of crop insurance to decrease their own efforts and total productivity can suffer, as when the accounting units in the People's Republic

of China were enlarged to commune or county level. (Disaster insurance, however, is less likely to have a negative impact on personal effort and so is likely to increase production.)

Here is an example of the potential contribution of public choice to the analysis of nonmarket supralocal organizations for insuring peasants against crop failure. This theory focuses our attention on the disjunction between collective and individual rationality; it reminds us that although village productivity can be raised by plot consolidation or insurance schemes, it is in any individual peasant's interest to maximize his benefits hile minimizing his contributions to these public goods -- in other words, to be a free rider.[1]

Although the peasant may be highly efficient -- even individually maximizing -- when allocating his resources among various production acti-vities, it does not generally follow that villages are production maximizing for the known given technology. Given the price of water, for example, a peasant may make maximizing decisions about the allocation of resources between water, fertilizer, ploughing, and seed. But irrigation facilities, dams, or canals may be in short supply because of problems of leadership or cooperation. Peasants may use the existing water in the most efficient possible way, but new or different leadership -- with no change in tech-nology -- might improve cooperation and hence increase the supply of water. The Schultzian technology cum education approach, is inadequate for ex-plaining when and why villages will or will not cooperate to provide such public goods as more water.

---

[1] Editor's Note: "Free riding" is the phrase public choice theorists have coined to denote the act of enjoying a public good without paying for it.

The narrow market-economics approach assumes that all goods possess excludability -- if you do not pay you do not get to consume the good. However, it is not always possible to restrict benefits directly to purchasers. In the case of flood control, forest fire prevention, or the construction of irrigation channels, it is difficult to deny benefits to persons who do not contribute to the project. Whenever there is the possibility of enjoying benefits whether or not you contribute, there is the possibility of free riders.

There are also collective aspects to many divisible goods. The existence of a school or hospital or theater, even though you may be required to pay to use it, has aspects of a collective good. This is particularly true in peasant society where the limitations on savings and capital accumulation, and costly and unreliable mechanisms for enforcing contracts mean that many goods are provided on a quasi-collective rather than a market basis.

But the varieties of institutional arrangements for providing these quasi-collective goods -- despite their effects on productivity -- were rarely studied by development economists. Economists usually limited the domain of economics to explicit markets. This equation of economics and market was accepted by most other social scientists studying rural development. Rural anthropologists, sociologists, and political scientists identified the many nonmarket organizations and personalities within rural society as instances of nonmarket economic behavior, outside the domain of the rational individualist actor posited by the economists. They talked of the persistence of traditional institutions and community orientations as evidence that much of peasant society was outside the realm of eocnomics.

Much of the realm of peasant society is nonmarket but not noneconomic. It may be outside the domain of conventional market eocnomics, but public choice, as nonmarket economics, can be the bridge between economics and the study of peasant institutions. With public choice we can begin to analyze the effects of incentives on villagers as they make their decisions about economic activity in nonmarket and market settings.

This paper discusses two aspects of public choice theories which illuminate patterns of rural relations. First, the free rider problem in collective action; and second, the nonmarket responses to the problem of obtaining information about quality or effort in exchanges. The anonymity of the idealized market would make it impossible for an individual to evaluate the quality of some products or some work efforts. This problem helps us understand why some exchanges have personalized relations and why some crops have more personalized production relations than others.

Free Riders and Collective Goods

The basic question for successful organization is how, and under what conditions, can the resources for a collective project be gathered together and applied? Any attempt to organize for group action must recognize the distinction between individual interests and group interests and provide effective leadership, as well as sufficient incentives, to over-come individual resistance to collective action (Popkin, 1979, Chapter 5).

Many collective projects benefit an individual whether he contributes or not. When weighing his contribution, a peasant can be expected to take account of several factors relating to costs and benefits. First, ex-penditure of resources, that is, if a peasant contributes to a collective action, he must expend valuable resources. If a project fails, the

peasant loses his investment; additionally, he may be punished for participating if the action (such as rebellion) fails. Second, positive rewards,
that is, the value of the direct and indirect benefits. Third, probability
of his action leading to reward (efficacy), that is, the effectiveness of
a contribution depends on its marginal contribution to the success of
the endeavor. This, in turn, depends on how other actions aggregate,
whether they bring the effort sufficiently close to success to make a
contribution worthwhile. Fourth, leadership viability and trust, that is,
when estimating the probability of success, a potential contributor takes
into account not only the volume of resources mobilized but the leadership
skill with which they are mobilized as well.[2]

Given these considerations, whenever there is coordinated action to
produce collective goods, individuals may calculate they are better off
not contributing. As long as they cannot be excluded from the good, there
is the potential for free riders, individuals who do not contribute to
the provision of goods because they believe they will receive the gain
or security even if they do not participate. This divergence between the
interest of the group to complete a project and the interest of an individual to benefit without contributing suggests that an individual who
attaches no special personal (psychic) benefits to the act of participation
and who does not view his contribution as necessary will not contribute
without an incentive to do so.

There is a marked proclivity for individual level adptations to
common problems whenever the only result of group action is common advantage. As long as the only results of contributing to the common goals

----

[2] Editor's Note: See the closely related discussion in the context of
developed societies and environmental groups in Mitchell (1979).

are common advantages, a peasant may leave the contributions to others
and expend his scarce resources in other ways. Collective action requires
more than consensus or even intensity of need. It requires conditions
under which peasants will find it in their individual interests to allocate
resources to their common interests -- and not be free riders.

The structure of peasant society and the failure of so many development
schemes -- in market and nonmarket settings -- reflects the problems of
coordinating mechanisms for the provision of collective goods. In many
situations there are arrangements for providing goods that could, if en-
acted, leave all better off, but that will not be successful because of the
problem of free riders. There are times when many collective goods by
small groups, although large groups could do better -- because neither
the necessary skills nor incentives systems exist to maintain larger groups,
or because peasants, seeking to avert the risk posed by concentrating
resources in the hands of another peasant, are unwilling to invest their
resources in large-scale projects.

Under what conditions can resources for collective endeavor be
aggregated? Olson (1968, p. 2) has stated the argument in its classic
form, "Unless there is coercion or some other special device to make individuals act in their common interest, rational, self-interested individuals will not act to achieve their common or group interest."

This formulates the collective-action problem in its most elegant
and straightforward fashion. If an individual assumes that his contribution to a collective good has no perceptible impact on the contributions
of others, and if the collective good is so expensive that an individual's
contribution will have no perceptible impact in the level of the collective
good supplied, then special incentives are needed to produce any action

toward group goals (the by-product theory of collective goods). The by-product theory is best illustrated by the (simplified) example of the American Medical Association (AMA). The AMA produces major collective goods, particularly political power, for the medical profession. Since the results of the AMA's influence on tax and health legislation, for example, are available to all doctors, membership in the AMA is not required to receive its collective benefits. But a doctor receives selective, noncollective benefits from his membership that justify payment of dues. If the AMA can provide members with valuable information about new medicines or tax loopholes, or if it can monopolize the services of malpractice specialists, then it is in the individual doctor's interest to join the organization. Thus, no one pays anything for collective goods; they are provided by the organization as a by-product of the sale of memberships for individual benefits (Olson, 1968, pp. 137-141).

As framed by Olson, the by-product theory implies that efforts to organize for action can succeed only when the leadership provides selective incentives from whose proceeds the collective goods are financed. However, even for nonexcludable goods, this formulation is too restrictive. Contributions can occur (1) because persons contribute for reasons of ethics, conscience, or altruism; (2) because it pays to contribute on a pure cost-benefit basis; (3) because of selective incentives (excludable benefits), which can either be positive or negative; or (4) because it pays to contribute, given that the contributions of others are contingent on one's own contribution (Frohlich and Oppenheimer, 1971; and Frohlich and co-authors, 1975).

When persons have decided to contribute on the grounds of ethics, altruism, or conscience, a would-be leader need offer no selective incentives. Instead, what must be offered persons searching for the best way to expend their contributions is efficacy. That is, a leader must be able to convince persons that making the contribution through a particular organization or a particular form of participation is the most beneficial.

Selective incentives to include participation also are not needed whenever it pays to contribute on a straight cost-benefit calculation. Olson deals with the pure case of collective goods that benefit all equally and from whose benefits no one can be excluded. Thus, while implicit in Olson's analysis, excludability is separate from the pure problem of collective goods. There are also many collective projects where some benefits can be restricted to participants. In this case, no special selective incentives beyond those tied to the collective project are needed to induce participation. One can contrast an insurance scheme, a planting or harvesting cooperative, or a blood bank -- all of which have collective goods aspects _and_ whose benefits can be restricted to members -- to an expedition to kill a marauding tiger, to plot to kill a landlord, or construction of a dike, the benefits from which accruee to participants and nonparticipants alike. _Ceteris paribus_, maintaining membership is easier if to be exlucded from an organization is to lose valuable benefits.

Excludability is related to the problem of self-enforcement and to situations in which selective incentives, either positive or negative, are needed for leadership to overcome free rider problems. A group is not self-enforcing when a member gains more benefits by dropping out than by voluntarily remaining in the group. If an immediate benefit can be derived from defection, an organization formed to pursue a goal can survive only if there is sufficient coercion available to the leadership to enforce

discipline, or enough resources to make defection less valuable than remaining in the group.[3] An insurance scheme, for example, is self-enforcing:
when a member fails to pay or do his share, he loses his benefits. In
direct contrast is the problem of organizing a work stoppage among laborers
in order to raise their wages. If all the laborers in an area were to
simultaneously withhold their labor from their fellow villagers who are
tenants or smallholders, the laborers' share of the crop could be increased.
But such coordinated action is not self-enforcing, for there is an incentive for any individual laborer to defect and offer his labor. He will
reason that if everyone else withholds his labor, wages will inevitably
rise; he will therefore receive the future benefits of the collective
action as well as the wages he receives as a strikebreaker.

Where defection brings benefits, a second consideration is the ease
with which defections can be monitored. It is easy to detect defectors
during a labor boycott, and when resources are available the defectors
can be dealt with. Similarly, if every villager is responsible for clean-
ing (or digging) a specified section of a canal, and if all villagers are
to do their work on the same day, defections will be more easily monitored
than if villagers were not assigned specific sections or if the villagers
did not all do their work on the same day.[4] There are many times, however,
when it is difficult to detect defections and to apply sanctions to maintain group solidarity. This applies to the problem of interest rates.
It is common for writers on peasant society to refer to exorbitant,

---

[3]Editor's Note: For a comprehensive examination of this Prisoner's
Dilemma situation, see Hardin (forthcoming).

[4]The discussion of issues pertinent to quality monitoring is enlarged
in the section on "Political Entrepreneurs."

"usurious" interest rates. If all peasants could agree to borrow only at
a given rate and at no higher rate, the interest rate would come down,
and nonmarket methods would govern the allocation of credit.

Directly affecting the amount of resources needed to prevent defection
is the extent to which opposing interests and resources can be mobilized
against nascent organizations. Whereas an insurance scheme or a well-
digging group are unlikely to generate immediate, local opposition, attempts
to raise laborers' wages do have a built-in opposition from all tenants
and smallholders. Tenants and smallholders are financially able to hold
out more easily than laborers, and they are in a better power position
because they control more resources. Similarly, tenant movements to
destroy or weaken landlords are likely to be more successful in areas
where there is no class of permanent laborers for the landlords to use
against the tenants.

People will also contribute whenever they believe their contribution
will make a big enough difference. There are two main variants to consider:
(1) a contribution which might influence other persons to contribute and
which therefore has an important perceptible effect on the overall level
of contributions, and (2) situations where every little bit is seen as a
crucial step in a long process. If a large overall goal can be broken into
many small independent pieces, all of which are necessary, the free rider
problem can be overcome, for if each person has a monopoly on a necessary
factor for the final goal, all contributions are essential.

Effective leaders may provide only selective incentives, but by
coordination of contributions, by manipulation of information, or by
breaking up a large overall goal into numerous steps with critical

thresholds, they may also elicit contributions not tied directly to selective incentives.[5] Olson's tidy formulation, therefore, can be expanded from a situation where collective goods are financed solely from funds raised by leaders through selective incentives to situations where collective goods are financed by convincing persons that their contributions will have a perceptible effect.

For pure incentive situations or for contributions justified on grounds of perceptible effects, participation (be it a purchase or a contribution) is a gamble. The value of a contribution to a peasant depends not just on the value of the collective good, but also on how likely it is that others will contribute. Yet other situations also often involve gambles. For example, with selective incentives there are cases where peasants must estimate the probability of actually receiving the selective incentive.

Risk is involved both in purchasing incentives and in contributions; peasants can be expected to evaluate their actions as they would evaluate lotteries. This means consideration of success or failure of the collective good being supplied with or without the individual's contribution. This means weighing the risk of trading the status quo for a lottery between successful action and failure. (Of course, no contribution is also a risky situation with lottery elements.)

In all situations, then, collective action involves risk and uncertainty. It is logically incorrect to equate intensity of need with the likelihood of

---

[5] These two situations, of course, merge together as an organization becomes institutionalized. When there is long-run faith in an organization's survival, strict reciprocity and immediacy of connection between contribution and incentives will become relaxed as persons come to believe that contributions and selective returns will even out over time.

collective response without also considering the ability of individuals to gamble on an improvement in the status quo. A peasant with a small surplus can more readily afford to take risks than can a peasant truly against the margin.

Political Entrepreneurs

When a peasant makes his personal cost-benefit calculations about the expected returns on his own inputs, he is making subjective estimates of the credibility and capability of the organizer (Frohlich and Oppenheimer, 1978; Frohlich, Oppenheimer, and Young, 1971) "the political entrepreneur," to deliver. The problem of the supply of collective goods and the choice among alternative patterns of supply make "mechanisms for coordination of expectations and the pooling of resources" a central issue (Frohlich, and coauthors, 1971, p. 25). Hence, the importance of the leader as a political entrepreneur -- someone willing to invest his own time and re-sources to coordinate the inputs of others in order to produce collective action or collective goods -- cannot be underestimated.

Leadership itself has aspects of collective goods (and bads) for a group. Even when an organization produces divisible goods for individual consumption, there are collective goods aspects to the organization itself. Systems of incentives or mechanisms for sharing costs are collective goods which leadership can supply to the benefit of the leader and peasantry. When improved leadership makes possible the incentive systems or cost-sharing mechanisms for self-help projects such as insurance programs or breeding cooperatives, it is possible to produce benefits for the peasants as well as a surplus which can be applied to broader organization objectives.

Consideration of leadership leads to an enlargement of Olson's central formulation. Discussions of collective goods usually address the problem of whether a particular good will or will not be provided to a group. In practice, many collective goods can be provided in many different ways. Improving the quality of available leadership, for example, can change the way the good is provided, increase benefits for all participants, and supply large amounts of "profit" for the organizers.

Whether the entrepreneur is directly exchanging immediate individual benefits for peasant inputs, providing cost-sharing arrangements or trying to convince the peasant that his actions can have a perceptible and profitable impact on the collective good, he must be concerned with increasing the peasant's estimates of the efficacy of his contribution to secure the promised returns. This means that the peasant's subjective estimates of the would be entrepreneur's capability and credibility will directly influence the entrepreneur's ability to organize peasants, and that, ceteris paribus, a situation with more credible organizers is likely to be a situation with more effective organizations. A would be organizer must also convince a peasant that his goals are credible, that not only can he and will he do what he promises with the peasant's contribtuions, but that if he does what he promises, the peasant's lot will be bettered. One way of increasing the credibility of the goals may be to use leaders already well known to the group in contrast to urban officials cum carpetbaggers.

When an entrepreneur approaches a group of peasants, what features of possible issues are crucial? And how does the "organizability" of an issue vary across areas or social structures? By examining relevant properties of different local issues we can begin to answer this question.

First, examination of examples of successful organization indicates
that one crucial consideration is a focus on local goals and goods with
immediate payoffs. This suggests that an important way to increase the
peasant's estimate of success and, therefore, the probability of contribution is to decrease the scope of the project for which he is being recruited
-- and thus shorten the interval before benefits are received. The profits
can then be directed by the leadership to goals and projects, which take
longer to pay off.

Second, there is the timing of contributions. The start-up costs of
a project and whether peasants are required to pay before or after collective ends are achieved (that is, whether or not there is outside
financing) may determine the potential value of a local issue to organizers.
Poor peasants might find their individual benefits from an undertaking very
high and might be willing to pay enormous amounts to achieve the benefits,
but only if they are able to pay after the fact ("on time") out of the
profits.[6]

Third, there is the size of the group that the leadership can manage.
Many of the collective goals within peasant society can be achieved,
furthermore, within groups of widely varying sizes and structures. Thus,
insurance and agricultural efforts can be organized so as to supply benefits with or without exclusion, either inside or outside of a market
mechanism. With little savings and money, with a lack of trained leadership, and with costly and unreliable mechanisms for enforcing contracts,
it is not surprising to find insurance and agricultural cooperatives
supplied on a quasi-collective basis rather than on a market basis. Large

---

[6] Editor's Note: This solution threatens to exacerbate the free rider
problem.

groups are workable, given problems of excludability and defection, only when there is skilled leadership or enforceable contracts. Almost all the small, insurance-type organizations found among peasants can be organized by very small groups of peasants. But the security and viability of the insurance can sometimes be improved immeasurably if a larger group were also involved. That is, a large insurance company is more likely in the long run to provide the promised benefits than is a small company with few members. Although they may be erratic and offer low-quality insurance compared to villagewide or even intervillage associations, the small group arrangements have the virtue of requiring less capable leadership and are often the only organization possible. As Olson (1965, pp. 33-34) has noted, small groups need few if any special incentives or leadership because there is such a notable effect of each member's contribution on the overall output of the group. In a small mutual aid group, if one member gains a free ride, the loss of his contribution will be perceptible to all and the group will dissolve.

Without skilled leadership or enforceable contracts, exclusion is only possible in small groups. In an eight-man planting cooperative, if a peasant drops out of the group after the other seven have spent the day helping him plant his crops, he will be blackballed from all similar groups as unreliable. So, while small groups may be far less rewarding over a number of years than larger groups, they are viable when there is little or no trusted leadership because there are minimal problems of coordination and incentives. If a skilled leader can convince peasants to join a larger mutual aid group, there is a potentially substantial profit both for the peasants and the leader.

Further, there is the type of reciprocity on which the organization is based. Cooperation can be based on strict or general reciprocity. Peasants make exchanges where it is certain that all (both) parties will be able to maintain a long-run balance. Colson (1974, p. 50) reports, for example, "exchanges and contracts are likely to be either highly specific, with an understanding of just what it is each party is expected to do, or they involve people who are in constant contact so that giving and return can be balanced at short intervals and the advantages to each partner easily assessed." In other words, as Potter (1976, pp. 163 and 171) found in Thailand, if reciprocal obligations are not to be evaded, "records must be kept and sanctions exerted; there is nothing loose or informal about this at all." Strict reciprocity is required for large groups; complex interchanges (general reciprocity) take place among small groups of four of five households. If there is to be general reciprocity in a large group, the demands on leadership will be severe.

Next, schemes can have either fixed or variable returns. The exchange systems common in peasant society, such as labor exchanges or burial societies, have fixed returns. In these groups each peasant receives exactly what he has put into the scheme. Such organizations derive their value from "utilities of scale" in peasant life: eight days of labor at once by many men in a field make a better rice crop than one man working for eight days, and a few coins from many persons when a parent dies are more valuable for meeting religious obligations and avoiding debts than are a few coins on the many occasions when someone else's parent dies. Schemes also can have exact exchange or equivalent exchange -- labor for labor, part of someone's pig this month for part of someone else's pig

next month, or money for money -- rather than exchanges where contributions
and payout involve agreeing on a rate of exchange on more than one item.
It is easier to begin cooperation with fixed, exact exchanges and the less
exact and specific the exchanges become, the greater the need for higher
quality leadership and record keeping.[7]

Cooperative efforts also vary in the extent to which there is a risk
of someone absconding with the assets. A plan can require centralized or
decentralized holding of assets, and the assets can be liquid or illiquid.
Most peasant cooperation, organization and insurance generally do not
concentrate abscondable assets -- peasants seldom give another peasant
money to hold for the future because the peasant can always run away with
the money or spend it on himself or his family. Instead, contributions are
held by the members and given to the bereaved on the death, or the labor
is given to the farmer on the agreed upon day. To concentrate liquid
assets, a would be leader must convince a peasant that he is not going to
take his money and run, supplying neither the collective goods nor the
promised incentives. One solution (although it raises distributive questions) is to use villagers with fixed assets for leadership positions. As
Potter (1976, p. 52) found in Thailand, "Villagers prefer to have wealthy
men as village leaders on the theory that, since they already have money,
they are less likely to run off with funds entrusted to them." And in

---

[7]There can be large groups with little management required for tasks
with large economies of scale, like a bucket brigade, or where only low-
quality labor is required, that is, so-called festival labor. Agricultural
development and refinement of techniques often lead to smaller exchange
groups because higher quality labor input, and thus more vigilance
against slackers, is required.

Vietnam during the 1960s, the National Liberation Front for the same reason generally gave positions requiring the handling of large sums of cash to landowning peasants.

Finally, we can also distinguish among schemes where everyone has a chance of benefiting and those in which many persons have little or no probability of any return. Old age, widow, and orphan support are likely to have some potential value for all villagers, whereas subsidies for poor households are less likely to be of benefit to all villagers and thus may require coercion to establish and maintain.

There are, however, some dramatic occasions when collective action can occur without leadership or organization. There can be collective action such as slowdowns, wildcat strikes, protest marches, or field clearings with little or no formal leadership to supply incentives or even to provide information.[8] This is most likely when there are few internal conflicts of interest over a goal within the group, when the potential participants' job requires some particular skill or the area is isolated so that strikebreaking is difficult, when persons live together in one community so that they can communicate easily and decide on "the last straw," and defections can be monitored easily; and when work can be put off without destroying the product so that crucial wages will not be lost. The demands expressed by such collective action, however, will be limited to highly visible, universal demands and thus are likely to reflect the lowest common denominator of a group, not the full range of interests of its members or even the most important preferences

---

[8]These conditions are most obviously met among rubber plantation workers (Paige, 1978, pp. 50-58; Jayawardena, 1967-68, pp. 418-423. It should be also noted that Cesar Chavez started with vineyard workers in California.

of the members. Thus, when a group engages in collective action and
protest, one should not infer from such demonstrations will be able to
cooperate easily in the more mundane areas of village life. As a colonial
newspaper (quoted in Gran, 1973, p. 523) noted in Vietnam in 1896:

> A whole village comes to an admirable understanding in order
> to pillage a convoy of Chinese junks or to plunder the house
> of a rich neighbor. Discretion will be well guarded even in
> the case of success. But ask this same village to group to-
> gether to store their rice in one central warehouse and assure
> themselves of quick and certain benefits. Disorder and bicker-
> ing will quickly breat out in the midst of the group. In a
> week they will be calling each other thieves.

Lemons

One factor which influences the forms of rural collective action and
economic organization -- information -- has not received the attention
it deserves. Often individuals have to assess the <u>quality</u> of other
people's work or collective contribution. Information about quality is
in many circumstances costly, or uncertain, or even impossible to obtain
without long time lags. This information problem has a profound influence
on forms of collective action and on production relations and the organization of markets as well.

Whereas the work of Olson has provided the starting point for the
analysis of collective action with respect to publc goods and free riders,
the starting point for our preliminary attempts to analyze the impact of
information problems on structure of production, marketing, and profit
in agriculture is Akerlof's (1970, 1976) lemon market.

Akerlof's lemons are found not on trees but in the hands of used car dealers. He coined the phrase the "market for lemons" to deal with problems of information cost and information availability between the two sides in economic exchanges. Akerlof's ideas are a natural complement to the considerations of institutional design which arise when there are problems of divisibility or excludability, for they go to the very heart of agricultural economics, the linkage of work quality and reward. They can help us explain why different commodities have different market, labor and production structures, and why the distribution of profits between producers and middlemen can vary so much among commercial crops.

Akerlof is specifically concerned with situations where there were difficult-to-overcome asymmetries of information between the two sides of an economic exchange. The most obvious example of this occurs whenever a car is sold to a used car dealer. Whatever make and model of car you bring the dealer, the dealer has available a certain amount of general information, subjective or objective, about the general value of all such cars. Your particular car, however, can be either a peach, that is, a car in very good condition with few problems, or a lemon, that is, a car in poor condition with many inherent defects. It is extremely difficult without extensive driving or costly testing for the dealer to ascertain with precision -- except for the most obvious cases -- whether the car is a peach or a lemon. Because the dealer cannot easily evaluate your car, your information advantage both works to your immediate disadvantage and has a detrimental effect on the entire used car market as well.

If a dealer is unable to accurately rate the product, he is unable to pay differentialy for peaches and lemons. Your car may be a peach, but since it is possible you have a lemon, the dealer is unable to reward you for the care with which you have treated your car. Therefore, the dealer pays for a particular car the average value of all such cars on the used car market. This means that if your car is a peach you have an incentive to drive it into the ground, since you will never get its full value from a dealer, and if you have a lemon there is an incentive to trade it in early. Therfore, the information asymmetry between seller and buyer not only deprives the seller of "peach bonuses" but it also leads to a market place dominated by goods of lower quality than if the seller's information advantage could be eliminated and the information shared with the buyers. Thus what the buyer cannot know hurts the seller and the market, not just the buyer.

It is sometimes difficult to collect timely information about quality, and peasant organizations reflect this difficulty. For example, it is very rare in peasant society to find plough teams shared among families, or to find instances where plough animals can be rented without a driver. This is an instance where information problems prevent a form of market from emerging. When plough animals are returned to the owner (or to the collective), it is difficult to determine immediately if they have been overworked, abused, or otherwise damaged. If the water buffalo were overworked or if it has stepped in a hole and cracked a bone, the damage may not show up for several days by which time other persons who had used the animal could therefore have been responsible for the damage. It is easy to tell if the animal has been whipped and lacerated, but beyond looking for these external damages (like kicking fenders and checking the finish) it is difficult to tell if the animal was fed adequately, was not overworked, and has had no bones damaged. So it is virtually unheard of to see plough animals rented without a driver or plough animals owned cooperatively. There have been, however, times when villagers have owned stud animals cooperatively because the problem of damage caused by overwork or abuse is apparently not so serious. (The amount of work the stud animal will do is roughly proportional to the number of females in the pen.)

The same principle helps to predict which crops will be grown with wage labor on plantations or haciendas and which will be dominated by tenancy systems or small holdings.

When labor quality matters a great deal but is very easy to monitor, then it is possible to use wage labor and reward it with piece rates. If it is hard to measure or assess labor quality directly, the quality can easily be inferred from output, it is also possible to easily monitor wage laborers with piece rates. In one case the workers are watched, and in the other their output is sampled. And, of course, if labor quality matters little, then it is also easy to use wage labor and time rates. There are also times when labor quality matters, but it is both difficult to assess the labor quality directly and to infer the quality from output because there are other uncontrolled factors which also affect total output. Then wage labor systems will not successfully link effort and reward, and there will be a tendency for quality shrinking, or "easy riders" to dominate the work force.

Rice, for example, is a crop where labor quality matters greatly and where it is difficult to use wage labor for the entire production process because of the difficulty of inferring labor quality from output or of inferring labor quality directly. Large scale rice plantations have never been as profitable as tenancies on the same land because so much supervision of effort and quality are required. It is more profitable for large landowners to divide a large holding into tenancies than to farm the entire holding with wage labor. What the salesman's commission is to markets that are sporadic or undertain, tenancy is to agriculture -- a way of providing an incentive to perform quality work when direct superivision is unfeasible.[9] Sharing the output with a tenant, rather than paying the same person as a laborer, gives the worker an incentive for self-monitoring when supervised monitoring is too costly and expensive.

The new procedures that are developing for self-monitoring of labor in rice fields planted in the high yielding varieties, illustrate a similar development of incentives for self-monitoring. In the past, for example, in parts of the Philippines, harvesters were paid one-sixth of the harvest as their wage. Now, for two reasons, farmers are trying to pay harvesters less than one-sixth of the harvest. One is that because of the population growth, there is more cheap labor than there used to be as well as laborers who will work for less than one-sixth of the harvest (which, of course, means intraclass conflict among the laborers). Second, high yielding varieties are easier to harvest. A laborer can do more work in a day because all the grain ripens at the same time and the grain is of uniform height. The same percentage, therefore, would mean a higher daily wage.

----

[9]Note the occasions where wage labor is attempted for large scale agriculture and then abandoned for tenancy, as in the American South after the Civil War.

There are two ways of changing the wage structure which looks equivalent to the outsider. One way is to simply cut the harvest wage from one-sixth of the crop to one-eighth of the crop (and then prepare to fight off the laborers if they try and burn you out the first year). The other way is for the tenant to pay one-sixth of the crop to harvesters, but only allow those to harvest who have weeded the same area for free during the year. The cost of weeding plus harvesting is the same price as cutting the harvest wages from one-sixth to one-eighth, and paying for weeding, so that the two systems are equivalent. But, especially where there are high yielding varieties, the tendency has been towards free weeding and one-sixth of the output. Because the pay for weeding is not a day's pay but a share of the harvest, the weeder has an incentive to self-monitor the weeding because total pay now depends on how much rice comes up two months later. The laborer is absorbing risk because hail could come in the meantime, but the laborer also has a strong incentive now not to kick the rice during weeding because the laborer will harvest that same plot (Kikuchi and Hayami, 1977). These changes are also very similar to the reforms that are being tried in China within communes to ensure that the same person plants, weeds, and harvests the same area, so that the incentives for self-monitoring are as high as possible for work that cannot be easily monitored directly or indirectly for quality.

The ease or difficulty of determining quality also affects the market structure for different crops, in the particular form of relations between producer and middleman. There is a tendency to take for granted the problem of measuring agricultural output -- to assume it is easy to determine the value of the commodity a producer has for sale. It is straightforward, after all, to weigh rice or count lemons. In some commodities, however, it is not only the quantity that matters, it is the quality of the product. Furthermore, among producers where the quality matters there are some products where it is very easy to quickly determine the quality of the product being offered for sale, such as by a taste test, and others where it is difficult.

That the relative ease or difficulty of determining quality affects the structure of marketing can be illustrated by contrasting rice and rubber.[10] Quality matters enormously in rice, but it is extremely easy for a potential purchaser to assess it. By rubbing a few grains of rice between two blocks of wood, a prospective buyer can determine moisture content and the size of the grain and get a rough estimate of broken grains.

With rubber, quality cannot be determined immediately. A prospective buyer can weigh the unsmoked sheets of rubber and get the quantity accurately (except, of course, if there is a rigged scale), but the quality of the rubber is not apparent until several months later after further processing of the raw, unsmoked rubber. A smallholder who produces high quality rubber by using quality acid and carefully removing impurities, can only get the "peach bonus" for rubber quality by developing a reputation as a man who produces "peachy" rubber as opposed "lemony" rubber. That requires a good reputation with a buyer, something which is possible only with ongoing relationships. Since quality is easy to assess instantaneously, rice markets are generally auction markets, immediate, relatively impersonal transactions. Or what Adam Smith thought all capitalism was like -- information easily and readily ascertainable, easy switching of buyers, little reason for loyalty to any marketer or to any

---

[10]The following section is based on an extremely stimulating paper by Siamwalla (1978); see also Siamwalla (1980).

buyer. The growers' reputation matters relatively little since direct quality assessments are so easy to perform. Rubber (which is supposedly more modern, more commercial, more capitalist) is the commodity dominated by customer markets, where reputation -- hence ongoing relations -- matters. The difference between rice and rubber is not the difference between traditional and modern, or between capital intensive and labor intensive; it is a characteristic of the crop -- the cost and availability of timely information quality -- determining whether there are customer markets or auction markets.

Does the difference between customer markets and auction markets matter to the producers? Siamwalla's research suggests that the difference in market structures affects the profit structure, and his reasoning and preliminary results are worthy of further attention. Middleman margins in Thailand, he has found, are much lower in auction markets than in the more personal markets with agent-client relationships. At any time a rice buyer can compete for a grower's rice against the grower's previous buyer; timely, low-cost quality assessments mean no entry barriers for middlemen at the lowest levels of the rice trade. But a new rubber buyer has a barrier to entry; last year's buyer will not identify the "peaches," and the growers are not going to admit to "lemons." So a grower who switches buyers can get only the lemon price for his raw rubber. Thus, there is a "shifting cost" for growers and a concomittant advantage for the buyer of previous years. Consequently, a grower who switches to a new buyer can receive an increased base price for his rubber, but the shift will cost him his "peach" bonus. Rubber marketing is less competitive at the lowest levels and the middleman's profits are higher than in rice.[11]

It is at points in the agricultural cycle where shifting costs are highest, Siamwalla implies, that cooperative arrangements have the most potential. It is so easy for competing rice buyers to react to the slightest fluctuations in rice prices that their nearly simultaneous adjustments to price information look like collusion to growers (and noneconomist observers). But the very small margins made by buyers in customer markets like the rice market leave little leeway for cooperative marketing to increase the grower's share of the final rice.[12] In the personal, friendly rubber market where there is no appearance to the growers of collusion because buyers cannot respond as quickly to new price information, there is more room for cooperative marketing. By collectively keeping records of each grower's quality or by selling processed rubber, all the growers profit by recapturing the advantages which now accrue to buyers from a high shifting cost.

Where work quality matters, there is a similar shifting cost for laborers. An employer bidding for new laborers does not know whether a laborer is a peach or a lemon. Laborers may not earn their full value then because the shifting cost gives their old employee a hold over them. In this context there is potential profit to be made from the formation

----

[11]Once the raw latex has been processed by initial buyers, profits along the rest of the marketing chain are no higher than for rice despite the small number of exporters (Siamwalla, 1978, p. 17).

[12]The price farmers receive for their rice immediately after the harvest may be 18 to 20 percent lower than the midseason price, but storage costs are likely to run 13 to 14 percent (Siamwalla, 1978, p. 14).

of teams of laborers. Team members can monitor each other as the same
tasks are done time and again on numerous farms. Even though the identity
of the team members may change from year to year, the team leader's reputation can provide continuity.[13]

Conclusion

In this chapter I have laid out implications for the study of rural
institutions which follow from two issues that have been raised in nonmarket economics.[14] Both the free rider and the lemon are problems which
can require nonmarket solutions. But nonmarket does not mean noneconomic.
Effective institutions are institutions which are free rider proof, not
free rider prone; and appropriate divisions of labor can minimize problems
with lemons. Old dichotomies between public and private, between market
and nonmarket, between economic and noneconomic are as outmoded as the
distinctions between traditional and modern. Rural development requires
linkage between effort and reward. It is necessary to recognize the limits
of markets to provide collective goods and deal with lemon problems, and
it is necessary to recognize the role of economic rationality in nonmarket
settings as well.

---

[13] Roumasset and Uy (1979 provide evidence from the Philippines. In
Vietnam, teams were most likely to emerge when farmers were dealing with
migratory laborers -- who would be less well-known personally -- or when
they were hiring laborers for planting -- work that is harder to monitor
than harvesting.

[14] There are a number of other areas of institutional economics in
which work is also proceeding at this time. The exemplary articles for
the study of rural development are listed in the References.

References

Akerlof, George. 1976. "The Economics of Caste and of the Rat Race and Other Woeful Tales," *Quarterly Journal of Economics* vol. 90 (November) pp. 599–617.

_____. 1970. "The Market for 'Lemons': Quality, Uncertainty and the Market Mechanism," *Quarterly Journal of Economics* vol. 84 (August) pp. 488–500.

Alchian, A.A. and H. Demsetz. 1973. "The Property Rights Paradigm," *Journal of Economic History* vol. 33 (March) pp. 16–27.

Arrow, Kenneth J. 1969. "The Organization of Economic Activity: Issues Pertinent to the Choice of Market Versus Nonmarket Allocation," Joint Economic Committee, 91st Congress, 1st Session, pp. 58–73.

Bailey, F.G. 1971. *Gifts and Poison* (Bristol, England, Blackwell).

Bardhan, Pranab K. 1978. "Interlocking Factor Markets and Agrarian Development: A Review of Issues" (unpublished paper).

_____ and T.N. Srinivasan. 1971. "Cropsharing Tenancy in Agriculture: A Theoretical and Empirical Analysis," *American Economic Review* vol. 61 (March) pp. 48–64.

_____. 1974. "Cropsharing Tenancy in Agriculture: Rejoinder," *American Economic Review* vol. 64 (December) pp. 1067–1069.

Bates, Robert H. 1974. "The Issue Basis of Rural Politics in Africa," *Social Science Working Paper*, no. 102 (October) (Pasadena, California Institute of Technology).

_____. 1976. "Political Science and Anthropology: The Study of Rural Politics in the Developing Areas," Social Science Working Paper, no. 112 (February) (Pasadena, California Institute of Technology).

_____. Forthcoming. *States and Markets in Tropical Africa* (Berkeley, University of California Press).

Bell, Clive. 1977. "Alternative Theories of Sharecropping: Some Tests Using Evidence from Northeast India," *The Journal of Development Studies* vol. 13 (July) pp. 317–346.

_____ and Pinhas Zusman. 1976. "A Bargaining Theoretic Approach to Cropsharing Contracts," *American Economic Review* vol. 66 (September) pp. 578–588.

_____. 1980. "A Bargaining Theory of Marketing Contracts and the Choice of Distribution Channels — The Case of a Simple Agricultural System" (unpublished paper).

_____. 1980. "On the Interrelationships of Tenancy and Credit Contracts" (unpublished paper).

_____. 1980. "Towards a General Bargaining Theory of Equilibrium Sets of Contracts -- The Case of Agricultural Rental Contracts" (unpublished paper).

Braverman, Avishay and T.N. Srinivasan. 1979. "Interrelated Credit and Tenancy Markets in Rural Economies of Developing Countries" (unpublished paper).

Buchanan, James M. 1971. The Bases for Collective Action (New York, General Learning Press)

Colson, Elizabeth. 1974. Tradition and Contract (Chicago, Ill., Aldine).

Day, Richard H. 1967. "The Economics of Technological Change and the Demise of the Sharecropper," American Economic Review vol. 57 (June) pp. 427-449.

Demetz, Harold. 1967. "Toward a Theory of Property Rights," American Economic Review vol. 57, pt. 1 (March-June) pp. 347-373.

Frohlich, Norman. 1974. "Self-Interest or Altruism, What Difference?" Journal of Conflict Resolution vol. 18 (March) pp. 55-73.

_____ and Joe A. Oppenheimer. 1971. "I Get By with a Little Help from My Friends," World Politics vol. 23 (October) pp. 104-120.

_____ and _____. 1974. "The Carrot and the Stick: Optimal Program Mixes for Entrepreneurial Political Leaders," Public Choice 19 (Fall) pp. 43-61.

_____ and _____. 1978. Modern Political Economy (Englewood Cliffs, N.J., Prentice-Hall).

_____ and _____ and Oran Young. 1971. Political Leadership and Collective Goods (Princeton, N.J. Princeton University Press).

Frohlich, Norman, Tom Hunt, Joe Oppenheimer, and R. Harrison Wagner. 1975. "Individual Contributions to Collective Goods: Alternative Models," Journal of Conflict Resolution vol. 19 (June) pp. 310-329.

Gran, Guy. 1973. "Vietnam and the Capitalist Route to Modernity: Village Cochinchina 1880-1940." Ph.D. dissertation, Department of History, University of Wisconsin.

Hallagan, William. 1978. "Self-selection by Contractual Choice and the Theory of Sharecropping," The Bell Journal of Economics (Autumn) pp. 344-354.

Hardin, Russell. "Collective Action" (unpublished paper).

_____. 1978. "Game Theory and the Nature of Man" Paper prepared for de-
livery at the 1978 Annual Meeting of the American Political Science
Association, New York, September.

_____. 1977. "The Contractarian Provision of Group Goods" The Papers of
the Peace Science Society (International) vol. 27.

_____. 1975. "The Economics and Politics of Collective Action," Fels
Discussion Paper, no. 66, University of Pennsylvania. Prepared for
presentation at the Foundations of Political Economy Conference,
Austin, Texas.

Hirshman, Albert. 1970. Exit, Voice and Loyalty (Cambridge, Mass.,
Harvard University Press).

James, William E. 1979. "Agricultural Contracts, Public Land Settlement
and Settler Security," Paper prepared for East-West Center Conference
on Food Security, Hawaii.

_____. 1978. "An Economic Analysis of Public Land Settlement Alternatives
in the Philippines," Agricultural Economics Department Paper no. 78-30,
(Los Banos, Philippines, International Rice Research Institute).

Jayawardena, Chandra. 1967. "Ideology and Conflict in Lower Class Communities," Comparative Studies in Society and History vol. 10,
pp. 413-446.

Kikuchi, M., Dozina, G., Jr., and Y. Hayami. 1978. "Economics of Community Work Programs: A Communal Irrigation Project in the Philippines," Economic Development and Cultural Change vol. 26 (January)
pp. 211-225.

_____ and Yujiro Hayami. 1977. "Inducements to Institutional Innovations
in an Agrarian Society," International Development Center of Japan
Working Paper Series no. A-07 (Tokyo, Japan).

Lewis, W. Arthur. 1962. "Foreword," in T. Scarlett Epstein, Economic
Development and Social Change in South India (Manchester, England,
Manchester University Press).

Lipton, Michael. 1977. "The Technology, The System and The Poor: The
Case of the New Cereal Varieties," Paper presented at the Workshop
on Analysis of Distributional Issues in Development Planning
(Bellagio, Italy, Development Research Center, World Bank) (April).

_____. 1968. "The Theory of the Optimizing Peasant," Journal of Develop-
ment Studies vol. 4 (April) pp. 327-351.

Loehr, William and Todd Sandler, eds. 1978. Public Goods and Public Policy, Comparative Political Economy and Public Policy Series, vol. 3 (Beverly Hills, Calif., Sage).

McCloskey, Donald N. 1976. "English Open Fields as Behavior Toward Risk," in Paul Uselding, ed., Research in Economic History vol. 1 (Greenwich, Conn., JAI Press).

Mitchell, Robert Cameron. 1979. "National Environmental Lobbies and the Apparent Illogic of Collective Action," in Clifford S. Russell, ed., Collective Decision Making (Baltimore, Md., Johns Hopkins University Press for Resources for the Future).

Mueller, Dennis C. 1976. "Public Choice: A Survey," Journal of Economic Literature vol. 14, no. 2, pp. 395-433.

Newberry, D.M.G. 1974. "Cropsharing Tenancy in Agriculture: Comment," American Economic Review vol. 64 (December) pp. 1060-1066.

North, Douglass C. 1978. "Structure and Performance: The Task of Economic History," Journal of Economic Literature vol. 16 (September) pp. 963-978.

_____. 1977. "The New Economic History After Twenty Years," American Behavioral Scientist vol. 21 (November/December) pp. 187-200.

Olson, Mancur. 1965. The Logic of Collective Action (Cambridge, Mass., Harvard University Press).

Paige, Jeffrey M. 1978. Agrarian Revolution (Glencoe, Ill., Free Press).

Pauly, Mark. 1968. "The Economics of Moral Hazard: Comment," American Economic Review vol. 58 (June) pp. 531-537.

Popkin, Samuel. 1979. The Rational Peasant: The Political Economy of Rural Society in Vietnam (Berkeley, University of California Press).

Posner, Richard A. 1980. "A Theory of Primitive Society, with Special Reference to Law," Journal of Law and Economics vol. 23 (April) pp. 1-53.

Potter, Jack. 1976. Thai Peasant Social Structure (Chicago, University of Chicago Press).

Reid, Joseph D., Jr. 1976. "Sharecropping and Agricultural Uncertainty," Economic Development and Cultural Change vol. 24 (April) pp. 549-576.

Roumasset, James A. 1976. Rice and Risk: Decision Making Among Low-Income Farmers (New York, North Holland).

_____ and Marilou Uy. 1979. "Piece Rates, Time Rates, and Teams: Explaining Patterns in the Employment Relation" (unpublished paper).

Ruttan, Vernon W. 1978. "Bureaucratic Productivity: The Case of Agricultural Research," Staff Papers Series no. P78-16 (November) (St. Paul, Minn. Department of Agricultural and Applied Economics, University of Minnesota).

_____. 1969. "Equity and Productivity Issues in Modern Agrarian Reform Legislation," in Ugo Papi and Charles Nunn, eds., Economic Problems of Agriculture in Industrial Societies, Proceedings of a Conference held by the International Economic Association (New York, St. Martin's Press).

_____. 1966. "Tenure and Productivity of Philippine Rice Producing Farms," The Philippine Economic Journal vol. 9, no. 1, pp. 42-63.

Schelling, Thomas C. 1957. "Bargaining, Communication, and Limited War," Journal of Conflict Resolution vol. 1, pp. 19-36.

Schultz, Theodore W. 1964. Transforming Traditional Agriculture (New Haven, Conn., Yale University Press).

Siamwalla, Ammar. 1978. "Farmers and Middlemen: Aspects of Agricultural Marketing in Thailand," Economic Bulletin for Asia and the Pacific (June) pp. 1-36.

_____. 1980. "An Economic Theory of Patron-Client Relationships: With Some Examples from Thailand," Paper presented at the Thai-European Seminar on Social Change in Conetmporary Thailand (May).

Spence, Michael. 1973. "Job Marketing Signaling," The Quarterly Journal of Economics vol. 87 (August) pp. 355-374.

Srinivasan, T.N. n.d. "Agricultural Backwardness Under Semifeudalism" (unpublished paper).

_____. 1979. "Bonded Labour Contracts and Incentives to Adopt Yield Raising Innovations in a 'Semifeudal' Agricultural" (unpublished paper).

Stern, Nicholas. 1977. "On Labour Markets in Less Developed Countries" (unpublished paper).

Thompson, Kenneth. 1963. Farm Fragmentation in Greece, monograph no. 5, (Athens, Athens Center of Economic Research).

Williamson, Oliver E. 1975. Markets and Hierarchies: Analysis and Antitrust Implications (New York, The Free Press).

Chapter 4

PUBLIC CHOICE PROCESSES

Robert H. Bates

> One of the characteristics of the modernization process is
> that it involves both aspects of choice: the improvement of
> the conditions of choice, and the selection of the most sat-
> isfactory mechanisms of choice   (Apter, 1965, p. 11).

A central appeal of the political economy approach is that it direct-

ly addresses several of the major themes in development studies . One

such theme is the centrality of choice. Developing societies are soci-

eties undergoing change. They have before them a variety of alternative

social states. And while the range of attainable states is constrained

by the resources at their command and the techniques which exist for

converting these resources into social values, these societies nonetheless

exercise considerable discretion over which future states will prevail.[1]

Author's Note: I wish to thank Robert Forsythe, Clifford Russell,
and Joe Oppenheimer for their comments and to absolve them of all responsibility for the contents of this article. The article was written
with the support of the National Science Foundation, Grant # SOC77-80573.

[1]A major body of scholarship rejects this interpretation. I refer to
the work of the dependency theorists and related scholars. These scholars
view the structure of the international economy as so thoroughly con-
straining the choices available to policymakers in the less developed

Because the political economy approach directly addresses the problem of
how choices do and should get made, it therefore addresses itself to one
of the central problems of development.

A second theme is the centrality of politics. One of the developing
areas' most prominent spokesmen, Kwame Nkrumah, underscored this point
when he enjoined his fellow citizens to "seek ye first the political
kingdom," holding that by so doing, "all things will be added unto it."
Whatever the causes for the politicization of choice making in the developing areas, the fact that most major choices are _policy_ choices makes
Easton's (1953, pp. 103ff) definition of politics as the authoritative
allocation of values highly relevant to the study of development. By
focusing on the way in which nonmarket institutions allocate valued resources, the political economy approach, of all approaches to the study
of politics, advances a mode of political analysis which is mot in keeping
with Easton's definition.

Not only does the phenomenon of development emphasize the centrality
of choice and the degree to which such choices are made via the political
process. It also underscores the degree to which people can and do choose
among the institutions by which these choices are made. Given a scarcity
of resources, methods must be contrived for allocating them among alternative uses. In many of the developing areas, kinship and institutions of

---

countries that it removes any capacity for discretion on the part of the
local elites (see, for example, Wallerstein, 1974). Increasingly, however,
other scholars emphasize the autonomy of local political and economic
elites, their capacity to accumulate significant resources, and their
ability to divert these resources to the fulfillment of local objectives
(see, for example, Swainson, 1977; and Sklar, 1977).

social reciprocity are left to perform this task. In others, competitive
markets perform the function. In still others, people innovate alternative institutions: bureaucracies, administrative structures, state
enterprises and parastatal companies and so forth. In the political
realm constitutions are made, altered, and abandoned with dizzying
rapidity. People in the developing societies are intensely aware that
the structure of the institutions employed in making choices influences
the nature of the outcome selected. And because the political economy
approach analyzes the ways in which procedures determine outcomes, it
directly addresses the problems of institutional design.

Contemporary political economy has a very broad agenda. In the
spirit of rationalism, it regards no subject as sacred. It has therefore
made mistakes and, upon occasion, elicited well deserved incredulity and
revulsion. Nonetheless, it does offer a minimum agenda that should cause
few to recoil and many of us in development studies to pay close attention.
At its center, it focuses on nonmarket mechanisms for the making of
choices. Lastly, it examines the correspondence between procedures and
outcomes and thus offers a basis for engaging in institutional design.
For all these reasons, I feel, political economy should be examined
closely for the insights it can offer to development specialists.

Particular Issues

In discussing the insights offered by the political economy approach
for the subject of revenue and taxation, I can best begin with a synopsis
of several reports from the Agency for International Development (AID).
These portray situations that illustrate several of the characteristic

problems surrounding this subject, issues which I will be discussing
throughout this paper.

1. Yemen lies on the border of Saudi Arabia and proximate to
several of the world's riches oil fields. Young men have left the rural
areas of Yemen and migrated to the more prosperous neighboring states.
They send back millions of dollars a day in private remittances to the
villages of Yemen. Nonetheless, the public sector is starved for resources, and there is an absence of roads, clinics, schools, and water
projects which would unlock the full potential of the rural areas. There
is an undersupply of public goods (USAID, 1979).

2. In the Philippines, attempts have been made to strengthen the
capabilities of local governments to collect revenues with which to
finance public services. There is general agreement that a significant
upgrading of public services is required; those public officials who
promise to provide more roads, clinics, schools, and so forth win broad
support at the local level. Nonetheless, people invest resources in
evading tax collections. And when attempts were made to tax an immovable
resource -- land -- people resisted with violence. People demand public
goods, but systematically attempt to evade paying the costs of them
(USAID, 1977).

3. In many situations, there are attempts to decentralize the bu-
reacracy. This is particularly true with respect to rural development
programs.

Centralized bureaucracies are costly. Central departments waste
resources by providing services that are inappropriate to local settings.
They are slow and costly in their decision-making procedures. They are
unresponsive to local needs. When they try to work as teams, the problems are compounded. They provide mixes of services that are inappropriate
to particular local settings. And they mutually impede each others' programs by failing to coordinate their actions.

Not only do centralized bureaucracies thereby inefficiently supply
local services, but also, being centralized, they fail to take advantage
of significant opportunities which exist at the local level. Contemporary research increasingly finds that local people are fully aware of what
they need in order to develop. They are far more rational and intelligent
than has been fashionable to admit. They are willing to invest both time
and money in efforts that yield improvements. And they may well have more
resources at their command than has hitherto been fully appreciated. Being centrally funded and centrally directed, most public programs in the
developing areas fail to capitalize on these properties of local populations.

These considerations have led development practitioners to suggest
the decentralization of development programs. To secure a better level
and mix of services -- to make the provision of public goods sensitive
to the needs of the people -- public services should, they contend, be
decentralized to the local level. Proposals for popular participation

in the selection and funding of public services are thus prominent features of the proposals for the decentralization of development bureaucracies (see USAID, 1979). They have been included in programs of bureaucratic decentralization in Egypt (USAID, 1978a), Thailand (USAID, 1979), Indonesia (USAID, 1978b), and the Philippines (USAID, 1977), and also, of course, in countries where USAID is less deeply involved, such as Tanzania.

In many developing areas there is an undersupply of public services. People want and demand public services, but seek to evade the costs of their provision. And public officials increasingly advocate the devolution of the supply and financing of public services to the local areas. If an approach to development studies is to be taken seriously, it should offer insight into these matters. And part of the appeal of the political economy approach is that it does so.

Public Goods, Markets, and the Necessity for a State

All of the above subjects relate to a central issue: the conditions under which an optimum quantity of public goods will be supplied. Basic to all discussions of this issue is the distinction between private and public goods. A public good is a good for which consumption is nonexcludable and nonrivalrous. If the good is consumed by one person, then it can be consumed by another, and the quantity available to others is not diminished by that person's consumption of it. An example of a private good would be a sandwich; if I eat it, you do not. An example of a public good would be a road. If I build a road in a farm community, it would (within limits) be impractical for me to exclude other people from using it; and (again within limits) if I use it, I do not diminish your use of it.

People desire public goods. They also desire private goods. But they have only a finite quantity of resources with which to acquire them.

The question then arises: How will they allocate these resources so as
to fulfill their wants? Assuming an institution which we call a competitive market, we can answer that question for private goods. In the
competitive market, prices will adjust and persons responding to these
prices will make choices that will yield them the maximum utility feasible
given their incomes. Through the "invisible hand" they are led to reallocate resources until they arrive at a competitive equilibrium. Moreover, we know that that equilibrium will be efficient. All resources will
be used to the point where no person can increase his utility from the
consumption of private goods without diminishing the satisfaction secured
by another.[2] These are the classic and well-established theorems of
welfare economics.

Welfare economics is equally insistent, however, that the market
peforms far less satisfactorily in the case of public goods. And it is
precisely the failure of markets in this case that leads us to examine
alternative institutions and to determine how they might perform.

The reason for the failure of decentralized mechanisms such as the
market to perform satisfactorily in the case of public goods is straightforward and uprising; it is also fundamental. Behaving as individual
decision makers, people will take into account solely the satisfaction
which they alone derive from the consumption of that good and not the
satisfaction which their acquisition of the good would provide for others.
Failing to take into account the effect of their choices on others, people
will tend to underestimate the good's true value and will therefore make
choices which lead to an undersupply of the good.

---

[2]We also know that any efficient allocation can be obtained as an
equilibrium in the market through a suitable redistribution of endowments.

To illustrate the failure of decentralized institutions, let us take an example. Supose two farmers wish to build a dam. The dam would cost $60 to build; its benefits to one farmer would be $40 and to the other $50. For this "society" as a whole the dam <u>should</u> be built. Its total benefits (490) exceed its costs ($60). But let each farmer look only at his own private costs and benefits. Then it can readily be seen that the decentralized system of choice will fail to provide appropriate incentives for construction of the dam.

Let (V_1, V_2) be the net benefits to farmers 1 and 2, respectively, where $V_i = B_i - C_i$). When farmer 1 builds the dam, then he secures benefits; but, because the dam is a public good, so too does farmer 2. The <u>net</u> benefits to the two farmers are:

$$V_1 = 40 - 60 = -20$$
$$V_2 = 50 - 0 = 50.$$

And when farmer 2 builds the dam, farmer 1 gets benefits as well. The net benefits then are:

$$V_1 = 40 - 0 = 40$$
$$V_2 = 50 - 60 = -10.$$

When neither pays for the costs of the dam, the net benefits are identically zero. And when both contribute, then their benefits depend on how they share the costs. If they split the costs 50/50, then:

$$V_1 = 40 - (1/2 \times 60) = 10$$
$$V_2 = 50 - (1/2 \times 60) = 20.$$

Or if they split the costs proportionately with the benefits, then

$$V_1 = 40 - (4/9 \times 60) = 13.3$$
$$V_2 = 50 - (5/9 \times 60) = 16.7.$$

How, then, will the farmers behave? The choices facing the two farmers can be summarized in tabular form (Tables 4-1 and 4-2). Let C and $\overline{C}$ be the alternatives available to each farmer. C stands for the decision to contribute to the costs of the dam and $\overline{C}$ for the decision to evade the costs by not contributing. The cells contain the net benefits to each farmer, the benefits to farmer 1 being listed first. I give two tables. Table 4-1 represents the payoffs when, if both farmers contribute, then they split the costs 50/50; Table 4-2 represents the payoffs when, if both farmers contribute, they then share the costs proportionately to the benefits they recieve.

Table 4-1. Payoff Matrix for the Decision to Build the Dam: Costs
Shared (1/2, 1/2) When Both Contribute

		Farmer 2	
		C	$\overline{C}$
Farmer 1	C	(10, 20)	(-20, 50)
	$\overline{C}$	(40, -10)	(0, 0)

Table 4-2. Payoff Matrix for the Decision to Build the Dam: Costs
Shared (4/9, 5/9) When Both Contribute

		Farmer 2	
		C	$\overline{C}$
Farmer 1	C	(13.3, 16.7)	(-20, 50)
	$\overline{C}$	(40, -10)	(0, 0)

For society as a whole, the benefits of the dam exceed the costs; the dam should be built. But, as shown in the tables, the incentives governing choices in this decentralized situation lead to a failure to supply the dam. We can see that in either table, no matter what one farmer does, the other does better <u>not</u> contributing to the costs of building the dam. For each, choosing $\bar{C}$ is a dominant strategy; because the dam is a public good, each farmer does better letting the other bear the costs of supplying it while enjoying its benefits for free. But when both farmers adopt their dominant strategies, the dam does not get built. As a consequence of the incentives to "free ride" the only equilibrium is $(\bar{C},\bar{C})$, and the dam is not constructed.

To summarize: using a market-like institution of voluntaristic, decentralized choice in situations involving public goods, an equilibrium may well exist but it will not be efficient. And the principal reason for this is that public goods generate "inappropriate" incentives. Evasion of the costs of the good and a failure to supply it are thus expected results under this kind of decentralized institution.

Recognition of this problem commonly forms a justification for rejecting the market as a mechanism for securing public goods and for introducing nonvoluntaristic procedures into social life. Where individual choices lead to behavior which imposes costs on others, then, it is asserted, such behavior may justifiably be curtailed. Evasion of the costs of supplying public goods is precisely the kind of behavior which affects others in this manner and which therefore calls for such remedy. Moreover, people may voluntaristically consent to the regulation of their own choice making; they may allow themselves to be coerced so as to be better off. Such reasoning applies to the farmers above. Choosing individually, both choose $\bar{C}$; each acting this way, they make themselves worse off. But could the farmers form an agreement to share the costs of the dam, then they could both benefit from the public good and both be better off. Splitting the costs 50/50, for example, they could secure the payoff of (10, 20) which both would prefer to that of (0, 0). To work, however, these agreements must be <u>binding</u>; to secure the superior outcome, each party must, in effect, consent to be coerced. The social institution specializing in the application of coercion is, of course, the state. To secure the supply of public goods people may thus well prefer the state to the market.

The Welfare-Maximizing State

A prominent theory of the state is that it is an agency which can use coercion to overcome the deficiencies associated with purely self-interested behavior. In this section, I will illustrate the arguments in support of this institution. I will do so in the context of our example. And I will show how the theory of what I will call the social-welfare-maximizing state is seriously flawed.

Rather than illustrating my argument with payoff tables, I will do so with diagrams. In Figure 4-1 the verticle axis can be interpreted as dollars by which to measure benefits and costs; the horizontal axis represents the quantity of public goods supplied. I graphically exhibit two functions. One (TC) shows the total costs of supplying the public good; it increases throughout and marginal costs are constant. The other set of curves represents the benefits derived from the public good. There are three such curves: one for each of two people (b_1 and b_2) and a third (TB) which represents the total benefits to society. This last is the (vertical) sum of the other two, and all are increasing but at a diminishing rate. They are subject to decreasing returns.

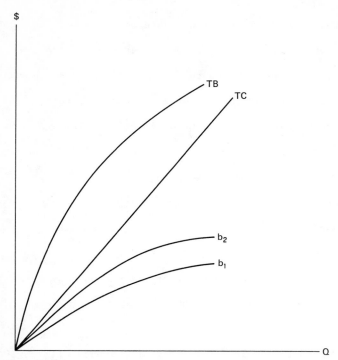

Figure 4-1. Total costs and benefits from public good.

This diagram can be taken to represent the situation captured in the example of the two farmers. The total benefits exceed the total costs. But for both farmers, the private benefits (as shown in b_1 and b_2) are less than the costs (as shown in TC). For each, marginal benefits and marginal costs are equal at only $Q = 0$, and this equilibrium results in the good not being supplied.

But say there is some disinterested third party which is concerned not with individual self-interest but rather with the interests of "society as a whole." This agency therefore pays attention to the sum of the benefits to all members of society rather than to individual benefits. It is classically held that the state, as the safeguard of transcendent

social interests rather than parochial individual interests, is such an
agency. In our example, total social benefits, as represented by the
total benefits curve (TB), everywhere lie above total costs, as represented
by the total costs curve (TC). Insofar as the state is concerned with
the interests of society as a whole it will make decisions in terms of
these total benefits and total costs curves. And as the benefits exceed
the costs, the state will decide to produce the good.

Individual self-interest leads to the failure to supply the public
good. As we have seen, such an outcome is inefficient. But an agency
concerned with the sum of the benefits to all members of society choses
to supply it. The case for the state can be further strengthened by
looking at the level of the good supplied and the price charged for
its provision.

Seeking to maximize the net benefits to society, the agency will
supply that quantity Q of the public good where the distance between
the total benefits and cost curves is greatest, that is, where the slopes
are equal, indicating that the marginal benefits to society equal the
marginal costs. In Figure 4-2, we label the point Q^*. How is the agency
to secure the resources to pay for the cost of supplying Q^*? Through a
tax; more particularly, through a tax where the price charged each individual for the public good exactly equals his marginal benefit from
that good when it is provided at the level Q^*. These "tax prices" are
shown as t_1, and t_2 in Figure 4-2, the slopes of the individual benefit
functions at Q^*.

Being motivated by a concern for the total benefits for society
rather than by a concern with the private benefits for individuals the

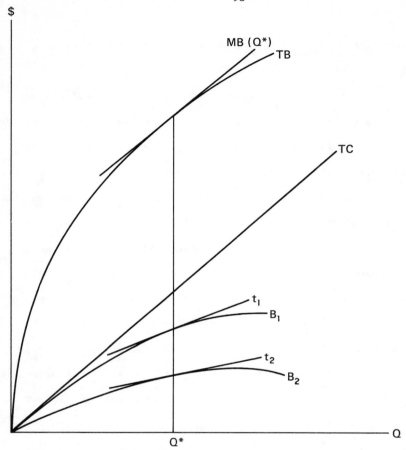

Figure 4-2. A social-welfare-maximizing equilibrium.

state can thus determine an optimum level of supply of the public good; and by using its power to coercively levy resources in the form of taxes, it can set tax prices in a way that will finance that optimum level of supply. This reasoning suggests that a centralized mechanism with its powers of coercion does better than do the decentralized market like mechanisms which rely on voluntary consent. In essence, this reasoning suggests, the state acts as an institution which can perform for public goods the function performed by the market for the allocation of private goods: the elaboration of (tax) prices which would yield equilibrium allocations which are also efficient.[3]

This defense of the state runs afoul of two principal difficulties, however. The first and most obvious is that the mechanism fails to provide any credible motivation for the behavior of the state. What incentives does the agency have to choose optimum allocations? Why should the state seek to maximize the interests of all members of society as opposed to the interests of some segment of them or of the holders of public office themselves? Such a fear of "faction" on the one hand of "tyranny" on the other concerned those most sober minded practitioners of institutional design, the Founding Fathers of the United States. Those in charge of public institutions will, they counseled, have particular interests of their own. Therefore, ambition must be made to counteract ambition .... It may be a reflection on human nature that ... devices should be necessary to control the abuses of government. But what is government itself but the greatest of all reflections on human nature? If angels were to govern men, neither external nor internal controls on government would be necessary (Madison, 1961, p. 322).

The notion of the centralized state contains a second major weakness. Ironically, it falls afoul of the very problem which led to its proposal: the problem of inappropriate incentives at the level of the members of

---

[3]These taxes differ from market prices in one significant respect. In the market, all people face the same price while consuming goods in different quantities. In this case, the good is a public good and people all consume it to the same degree; but the price each pays is equal to his marginal valuation of the quantity supplied, and this of course will vary with differences in tastes. It should be noted that, under the assumptions used in the text, the quantity of taxes paid precisely equals the costs of the good; using this mechanism, the state will neither run a surplus nor go bankrupt.

society. For the institution fails to provide incentives for people to disclose the information required for the state to select the correct set of tax prices. How was the state to learn each person's evaluation of a public good, and thus his willingness to pay the tax price? No one has an incentive to correctly reveal his willingness to pay. For the ghost of the public good remains at large. If the good were provided to one person, it would be provided to all people, and each person therefore has an incentive to avoid contributing to the cost of its provision. Each is better off getting the good for free. The publicness of the good and the fact that each person's costs are proportionate to his stated willingness to pay thus lead to a reemergence of the free rider problem and to the failure to supply the public good. This problem was recognized in the early expositions by Samuelson and by others who explored the feasibility of such Lindahl-like taxing mechanisms (see Samuelson, 1955a, 1955b, and the discussion in Musgrave, 1959). As I will show in a later section, it is just now being solved.

Majority Rule Elections

Thus far we have examined two institutions for the provision of public goods: the market and the state. As a decentralized system, the market fails; it founders on the problem of the incentive to free ride. As a centralized system, the welfare-maximizing state also fails, ironically for some of the same reasons as the market. In this section, we look at a third institution: electoral mechanisms and, in particular, majority rule.

Of all the institutions which we examine, majority rule is perhaps the most topical. Efforts to increase popular participation in governmental decision making, to render public services more appropriate to local needs, and to decentralize public services -- all tend to lead to the advocacy of elections. The movement toward decentralization and popular participation has led to strong efforts to disseminate this institution and to incorporate electoral procedures into public services and programs.

Perhaps one of the most important contributions of the political economy literature is the critical assessment it provides of these proposals. Rarely does scholarship generate so unanimous a conclusion. The dominant message is one of caution. For investigations suggest that, in general, majority rule fails to provide equilibrium outcomes; that the mechanism is manipulable in perverse ways; and that there is little reason indeed to expect the outcomes generated by this institution to be inefficient. Any proposal for decentralization via the promotion of elections must take these criticisms into account.

In the sections that follow, I first demonstrate the concept of an equilibrium under majority rule. I then present examples which illustrate the very special conditions under which such an equilibrium will hold. I conclude the discussion of majority rule by illustrating the way in which the procedure is open to strategic manipulation.

An Equilibrium Under Majority Rule

Assume that we have three farmers (labeled 1, 2, and 3) and assume as well that they seek to select the location of, say, a clinic. There are three alternative locations (call them a, b, and c) and the farmers have different preferences for these locations. In Table 4-3, I represent these preferences in terms of rankings, the alternative which is most preferred being listed at the top.

Table 4-3. The Preference Orderings of Three Farmers (1, 2, 3) Over Three Alternatives (a, b, c).

Farmers

1	2	3
a	b	c
b	a	b
c	c	a

How would a majority rule, electoral mechanism work? It would select an outcome which would be binding on all members of society. In particular we can require that it select that outcome which commands a majority against every other alternative. In the example portrayed in Table 4-3, b is the majority rule (Condorcet) winner. It is prefered two to one over a (farmers 2 and 3 prefer it to a; only 1 prefers a to b) and two to one over c (farmers 1 and 2 prefer b to c and only 3 prefers c to b). It thus commands a majority against every other alternative. By the same token, this is not the case for c or a.

For purposes that will become clear later and because of the fame of the result, it is useful to recast the above example in an alternative form. Say that the preferences of the citizens can be represented along a single dimension and that they take the form represented in Figure 3. In interpreting this Figure, we note that citizen 1, for example, prefers a and that his satisfaction declines as he moves to alternative b and thence to c.

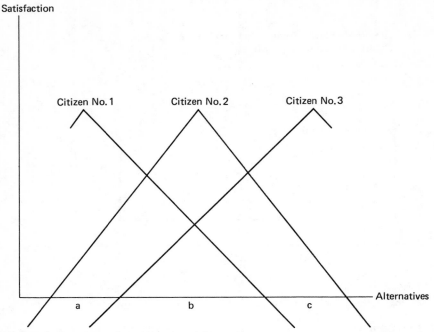

Figure 4-3. A representation of preferences in a single dimension.

Figure 4-3 can be construed as protraying a three person electorate. Let someone propose alternative a over and against alternative b and let that person then call for a vote. As can be seen from the curves representing the citizens' preferences, b will be preferred to a by persons 2 and 3, and a will be preferred to b by person 1. By majority rule, b prevails. Similarly, let alternative c be set against b. Then citizens 1 and 2 will vote for b over c and only 3 will vote for c over b. By majority rule, b again prevails. Under majority rule, the atlernative most preferred by the person occupying the mid point of the issue dimension thus becomes the outcome selected. Very loosely, this is the median voter result popularized by Downs (1957) and Black (1971) (see also Barry, 1970).

The Nonexistence of an Equilibrium

The fame of the median voter results has often disguised the fragility of the majority rule procedures. For a great difficulty with majority rule is that, in general, it cannot be counted on to secure an equilibrium outcome.

The existence of an equilibrium is contingent upon the structure of preferences. To illustrate, we can alter the preferences represented in Table 4-3, to conform to those exhibited in Table 4-4. Whereas a majority rule equilibrium existed under the previous set of preferences, now it does not. Alternative b commands a majority against c but loses out to a. And while c defeats a, it is in turn defeated by b. No alternative commands a majority against every other.

The existence of an equilibrium is also sensitive to the dimensionality of the issue space. More explicitly, while majority winners may exist for single issues, they do not in general exist when there is more than one issue in the election.

Table 4-4. Another Set of Preferences Over the Three Alternatives

1	2	3
a	b	c
b	c	a
c	a	b

To illustrate this point, consider Figure 4-4. It can be considered a two-issue analog to Figure 4-3. The preferences of the citizens now

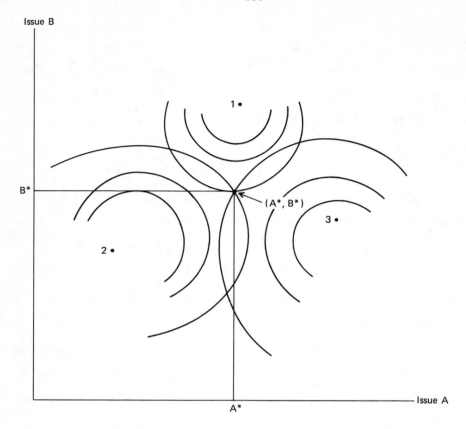

Figure 4-4. Preferences over two issues, with median points indicated.

pertain to two issues (issues A and B), their positions being specified
with respect to the horizontal and vertical axes. Each citizen's most
preferred position with respect to these two issues is indicated by a
point labeled with that citizen's number. The farther a position on an
issue departs from that point, then the less satisfaction that citizen
obtains. We indicate movement to lower levels of satisfaction by movements to further outlying indifference curves; these are represented as
circles.

    Our argument is that while majority rule could generate an equili-
brium in single-issue elections, it will fail to do so in elections

involving a greater number of issues. To illustrate this argument, first
consider an election involving issue A; then, by our earlier reasoning, we
see that the median position (labeled A*) will be the majority rule winner.
An election involving B would yield B* -- the median position in the
vertical axis -- as the majority rule winner. But while A* and B* are the
winners in single-issue referenda, we can easily see that the point (A*,
B*) is not the majority rule winner for an election involving the simultaneous consideration of both issues.

Why should this be the case? The reason is that there are points
which will be preferred by two-person coalitions (which in this context
are majorities) to the point (A*, B*). In Figure 4-5, all points falling
in the crosshatched areas are closer to the most preferred points of two
of the three citizens and so would defeat (A*, B*) under majority rule.
Points in region R, for example, are preferred by citizens 2 and 3 to the
point (A*, B*), for they lie on lower indifference curves. The majority
rule equilibrium for the single-issue election is thus lost when the
election involves the simultaneous consideration and more than one issue
and no other single equilibrium replaces it.

Without restrictions on the structure of preferences and in the
presence of multiple issues, the existence of a majority rule equilibrium
is thus not assured. Investigations reveal a host of other special conditions for the existence of these equilibria. So restrictive are these
conditions that the presumption of the nonexistence of majority rule
equilibria is the dominant expectation deriving from work in the
field (see Plott, 1967; and Arrow, 1951).

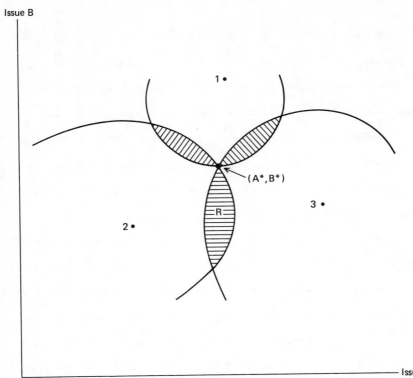

Figure 4-5. Regions of points which defeat (A*, B*) under majority rule.

The Manipulability of Majority Rule Procedures

A second major characteristic of majority rule procedures is that they are vulnerable to political manipulation. Persons can secure a privately desirable outcome, for example, by manipulating the agenda, that is, the sequence in which alternatives are considered. Examine, for example, the social decision problem outlined in Table 4-4. Consider two possible agendas (Figure 4-6). By the first, a is set against b and then the winner of that contest is set against c. By the second agenda, b is set against c, and the winner is then pitted against a. If people vote according to their preferences (as represented in Table 4-4), then the first agenda secures the selection of c; the second, the selection of a.

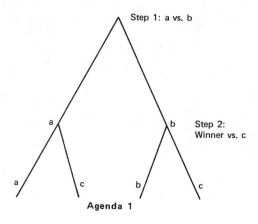

Step 1: a vs. b

Step 2:
Winner vs. c

Agenda 1

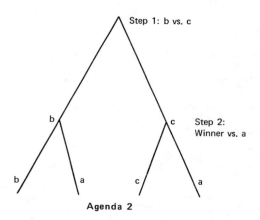

Step 1: b vs. c

Step 2:
Winner vs. a

Agenda 2

Figure 4-6. Two agendas for the decision among a, b, and c, with
preferences as in Table 4-4.

Naturally persons 2 and 3, who prefer c to a, will maneuver to secure
the adoption of the first agenda; person 1, who prefers a to c, will seek
the adoption of the second.

   Influencing the selection of agendas is not the sole form of political manipulation that confounds majority rule. The procedure is also
sensitive to the misrepresentation of preferences. In short, it is

manipulable by lying. This can be illustrated by using agenda 2. As we have seen, under agenda 2 the majority rule outcome is a. This result assumes, however, that people vote truthfully, that is, according to the preferences represented in Table 4-4. For person 2, the selection of a is disastrous; a is his least preferred alternative. But person 2 can improve his situation, and he can do so by lying. Let him, for example, exhibit the preferences ordering of (c > b > c) instead of his true preference ordering (b > c > a); the new ordering is exhibited in Table 4-5. If he votes according to his new ordering, then under agenda 2 majority rule will yield c instead of a as the outcome; this can be verified by seeing (from Table 4-5) that persons 2 and 3 would vote for c over b and persons 2 and 3 would also vote for c over a. By voting in the first round in a manner that does not accord with the true preferences, person 2 has exploited the majority rule procedure and moved the social choice away from his least preferred alternative.

Table 4-5. Preferences Employed When Person 2 Manipulates Agenda 2

Person 1	Person 2		Person 3
	True Preferences	Preferences Exhibited	
a	b	c	c
b	c	b	a
c	a	a	b

This discussion of majority rule should, at a minimum, lead to a reevaluation of proposals for the provision of public goods through the introduction of electoral procedures. There may well be no majority rule equilibrium. The outcome selected may be the result of accident -- for example, the accidental adoption of one agenda as opposed to another -- or the strategic introduction of procedures. In many situations, the institution encourages the misrepresentation of true preferences and the relationship between the social outcome and people's wants is therefore difficult to ascertain. Given these properties of majority rule, it is difficult to defend the alternative which it selects as being socially best.

Alternative Mechanisms

In the provision of public goods, the market fails us. As an alternative, the centralized state fails us, ironically for many of the same reasons as the decentralized market. The conventional alternative to the centralized state, majority rule elections, also leaves much to be desired. The challenge is thus to design new systems which can avoid many of the fundamental problems in public goods supply.

In this section of the paper I would like to introduce one such system, which is often referred to as the pivotal mechanism. Like the majority rule, this mechanism is decentralized; people vote to select the level of public good which they desire. Unlike the market, the mechanism induces people to take into account the impact of their choices upon others. Moreover, unlike the situation that prevailed under the centralized state, the prices people pay are independent of the evaluation they place on the good; they have no incentive to misrepresent their preferences and the mechanism therefore offers no incentives to free ride. The mechanism is a voting mechanism; but unlike the majority rule, it possesses an eqilibrium and it offers no gains from lying.

The best way to describe the mechanism is again by giving an example; the example is adopted from Tideman (1977). Let us assume that we have five farmers; assume as well that they are attempting to determine the location of a feeder road, and there are three feasible locations for the road, (in Table 4-6, options A, B, and C). Each farmer has at least preferred option; in Table 4-6, we assign 0 as the worth of at each least preferred option and we indicate in the other columns the incremental net benefits over the worst option yielded by each alternative. According to Table 4-6, the sum of the incremental benefits is greatest for option C. The question is; Can we devise a mechanism that will create incentives for the farmers to reveal their willingness to pay for each option, with the result that the socially desirable option -- C -- will be supplied?

Table 4-6. Differential Dollar Values for Options

Farmer	A	B	C
1	$ 0	$35	$40
2	50	0	30
3	10	55	0
4	0	20	65
5	45	0	25
TOTAL	$105	$110	$160

Source: Arithmetic example from T. Nicholas Tideman, "Introduction," Public Choice vol. 29, no. 2 (Spring 1977), pp. 1-14.

The answer is yes, and the mechanism is based on the following pro-cedures. Let votes be taken on each of the proposals by all farmers but

one; the votes take the form of bids or statements of evaluations of different options and willingness to pay for them. The option will then be
chosen which commands the highest evaluation. Then let the last farmer
place his bid. If his bid changes the option selected, he is then pivotal
and he is charged a tax which is equivalent to the change in the benefits
to all other farmers produced by his vote. The tax thus privatizes the
social costs of his behavior. Moreover, the level of the tax is not a
function of his own willingness to pay; rather, it is a function of the
worth of the public good as articulated by others.

This procedure can easily be illustrated. In each row of Table 4-6,
the bid of the farmer occupying that row is deleted; the sum of the bids
of the other farmers for each option is recorded in the columns occupied
by that option in Table 4-7. Thus, in row one in Table 4-7, we see that
the sum of the bids for option C by all farmers other than farmer 1 is
$200. It exceeds the sum of the bids for option A and B, and so route C
would be chosen by farmers 2 through 5. Now let farmer 1 cast his bid.
As we can see from Table 4-6, he most prefers C and would bid highest
for it. His behavior does not change the outcome. He is not pivotal.
And so, as seen in Table 4-7, he is therefore subject to no tax.

By contrast, look at row 4 of Table 4-7. In the absence of farmer 4,
the sum of the bids by other farmers would lead to the selection of route
A; it commands $105 of contributions as opposed to $95 for its nearest
competitor, route C. As seen in Table 4-6, however, farmer 4 evaluates
the benefits of route C as being $65 greater than the benefits of route A,
and when he places his bid -- if he bids honestly and his bid alters the
outcome -- route C then commands $160 in bids, as opposed to $105 for
route A. Because he is pivotal and his behavior alters the choice,

Table 4-7. Total Reported Evaluation in the Absence of Bid by Farmer i
            for Options A Through C

Without farmer	Total bids for			Tax on farmer i
	A	B	C	
1	$105	$ 75	$120	$ 0
2	55	110	130	0
3	95	55	160	0
4	105	90	95	10
5	60	110	135	0

Source: Arithmetic example from T. Nicholas Tideman, "Introduction,"
         Public Choice vol. 29, no. 2 (Spring 1977), pp. 1-14.

farmer 4 is made to pay a tax equivalent to the change in the benefits
experienced by others as a consequence of his vote; they would have got
$105 in benefits, but now only get $95, and so, as shown in Table 4-7,
farmer 4 pays a tax of $10.

How does this mechanism alter the incentives faced by decision makers?
Clearly, it privatizes the social costs of their decisions; when their
behavior alters the social outcome, they are made to pay a price -- the
cost of that change to others. But also, it modifies the incentives to
misrepresent preferences; communicating true evaluations of a public good
becomes a preferred strategy. This can best be seen by examining the
options open to one of the losers. As can be seen from Table 4-6, for
farmer 3, the social choice, C is his least preferred alternative; he
would most prefer B. To secure his preferred outcome, let him bid more
for B than it is, in fact, worth to him; by way of illustration, let his
bid be $110. B is then chosen. The value of the deception to farmer 3

is his true valuation of the chosen alternative, or $55. The costs of
his deception come in the form of the taxes he must pay and can be computed
from Table 4-8. In being compelled to switch from an option (c) worth
$60 to an option (B) worth $55, the other farmers loose benefits valued at
$105. These costs are transferred to farmer 3 in the form of a tax; he is
taxed for being pivotal. The net benefits to farmer 3 gained from lying
are thus negative ($55 in benefits - $105 in taxes = $150). Farmer 3 does
better bidding his true valuation and consuming C, the social outcome,
even though it is his least preferred alternative. His net benefits would
then be $0 instead of -$55. If any farmer bids falsely and so changes the
outcome, he too has to pay a tax. And as the amount of the tax depends
on the valuations of other people, it is totally out of each farmer's
control. Each thus does better bidding truthfully. Indeed, under this
mechanism, the truthful revelation of preferences becomes a dominant
strategy.

By privatizing social costs, and by eliciting a correct revelation
of preferences, the mechanism thus avoids many of the problems that bedevil
the market and the centralized, tax-setting state. In addition, it secures
an equilibrium -- the selection of route C -- where majority rule would
fail to do so. To illustrate this, we note from Table 4-6 that option B
would defeat A (3 votes to 2); C would defeat B (4 votes to 1); and A
would in turn defeat C (3 votes to 2). As is so often the case, there
is thus no majority rule equilibrium. But because the pivotal mechanism
makes use of information concerning the intensity of preferences, it
avoids the problem of cyclic majorities and yields a determinant outcome.

Table 4-8. False Representations of Different Values for Options

Farmer	A	B	C
1	$ 0	$35	$40
2	100	55	0
3	100	0	0
4	0	20	65
5	100	0	0
TOTAL	$300	$110	$105

Table 4-9. Computations of Tax, Given False Bids: Total Reported Evaluation in the Absence

Without Farmer	Total bids for			Tax on farmer i
	A	B	C	
1	$300	$ 65	$ 65	0
2	200	55	105	0
3	200	110	105	0
4	300	90	40	0
5	200	110	105	0

Several caveats should be registered, however. The first is that the mechanism assumes no income effects. Second, while it obtains an equilibrium, the equilibrium is not necessarily efficient; the tax is kept by the fisc, and were it redistributed to the farmers, then the system would again provide incentives for people to behave strategically. Not being redistributed, some resources are left idle, and the system fails to attain a point on the Pareto frontier. Moreover, under this system, there is no protection of the taxpayer, in the sense that his endowment of private goods may be confiscated by the state. He may be assigned a tax bill that exceeds his assets. Such possibilities are, of course, notoriously open under other systems as well. Lastly, the mechanism is susceptible to coalitional behavior.

This last point is sufficiently important to warrant illustration. As we have seen, under the pivotal mechanism the potential infliction of taxes furnishes the incentives to bid truthfully; and the magnitude of the taxes is a function of other people's statements of their valuations. Were others to collude with a particular player in misrepresenting their preferences, then the mechanism could be undermined; for then no single individual's misrepresentation need be pivotal and so no tax penalty need be incurred for lying. In Table 4-8, I illustrate a set of bids in which the three farmers who prefer A to C (farmers 2, 3, and 5) collude to secure the selection of A. As seen in Table, 4-9, no taxes are levied. And, as seen in Table 4-10, assuming that C is the status quo, the result of the collusion is a redistribution of income from the noncolluding farmers and a decrease in the total benefits to society.

The pivotal mechanism thus solves some problems but runs afoul of others. Efforts have therefore been made to analyze the properties of analogous mechanisms. These examinations have involved the use of formal theory (see, for example, Hurwics, 1979; Groves, 1978; Groves and Ledyard, 1977), experimental methods (Smith, 1978; Ferejohn and coauthors, 1977, 1979), and research in real life settings (Ferejohn and coauthors, 1977, 1979). The work of this last group can be used to illustrate these investigations.

Table 4-10. Change in Net Benefits from Collusion

| Farmer | When true valuations drive pivotal mechanism and C is chosen: | | | When false valuations drive pivotal mechanism and A is chosen: | | | |
	True valuation of C	Tax	Net benefit	True valuation of A	Tax	Net benefit	Change in net benefits
1	40	0	40	0	0	0	−40
2	30	0	30	50	0	50	+20
3	0	0	0	10	0	10	+10
4	65	10	55	0	0	0	−55
5	25	0	25	45	0	45	+20
TOTAL	160	10	150	105	0	105	−45

The particular problem Ferejohn and his coauthors examined was the selection and financing of programs by the public broadcasting network. Because television programs that are acquired by a network can be broadcast virtually costlessly to any member station, they constitute public goods. The public broadcasting network sought a procedure by which it could choose which programs to acquire for network dissemination and the prices to charge member stations for them.

Commencing at the theoretical level, these authors posited a series of criteria which such a mechanism should satisfy. These criteria are based upon practical considerations and notions of economic desirability. To be acceptable to the networks and to its member stations, the mechanism should never impose upon a station costs for programs which exceed its budget -- that is, it should never inflict bankruptcy. Nor should the procedure require the network to run deficits -- that is, the charges levied the member stations should cover the costs of providing the programs. The mechanism should yield (weakly) efficient outcomes. And it should elicit true evaluations as a dominant strategy.

Ferejohn and his coauthors found that these criteria were mutually inconsistent. No procedure could, in fact, secure all of them; a solution to the problem of institutional design as defined by these requirements was infeasible. As the author (Ferejohn and coauthors, 1978, p. 11) states: "Any institution that could be constructed would necessarily have shortcomings that might in view of some be critical. One has to be prepared to trade-off one [feature] against the others when trying to design institutions." Examination of the nature and extent of the tradeoffs therefore became a critical element of their research.

These authors, among others, have proposed weakening the requirement that the true valuation of preference be a dominant strategy. In particular, they proposed examining mechanisms where Nash rather than dominant stragegy equilibria obtained. Under "Nash" demand-revealing mechanisms, when all other players are revealing true preferences, then an actor does best by himself reporting truthfully and the outcome associated with this equilibrium is efficient. An important practical difference between Nash and dominant strategy mechanisms is the costliness of the procedures. Dominant strategy mechanisms yield quick results; each player has a strategy which is unconditionally best. By contrast, mechanisms which possess Nash equilibria may require repeated "plays of the game," as players calculate their best strategies and reevaluate them in response to the actions of others. Arriving at equilibrium points therefore can consume resources. And one of the tradeoffs examined by Ferejohn and

and his coauthors was the amount of resources consumed by the procedures
given the relaxation of the strict requirements for the truthful revelation
of preferences.

As a first step, Ferejohn and coauthors examined the properties of two
alternative systems. Both were designed to guarantee the avoidance of
deficits by the network and to safeguard against the bankruptcy of member
stations. They were compared in terms of the amount of strategic behavior
which they generated, the degree to which the outcomes they secured approximated efficient outcomes, and the speed with which the systems arrived
at equilibria. These investigations were conducted in laboratory settings.
Second, the group examined the procedure actually employed by the public
broadcasting system and evaluated its performance. While formal analysis
had suggested fundamental weaknesses in the mechanism and the danger
of perverse outcomes, empirical investigation of the actual functioning
of the procedure revealed that it worked at relatively low cost (consuming
less than 5 percent of the networks' resources), that it neither bank-
rupted member stations nor forced the network into deficits, and that it
minimized strategic behavior by member stations. Nonetheless, it was not
efficient. Incentives therefore remained to design and to implement
more satisfactory procedures.

Obviously, the problems facing the members of a broadcasting network
are not identical to those facing a group of rural farmers. But the
elements of commonality are sufficient that the work done in elaborating
social choice procedures for the one should be illuminating for efforts
to design procedures for the other. The supply of electricity to a rural
electrification cooperative or water to a rural irrigation district pose

problems similar to those faced by the broadcasting network. Those
interested in the design and implementation of institutional reforms in
rural development prorgrams could therefore benefit from work being done
in this seemingly disparate area.

Conclusion

The study of development leads us to explore how institutions can be
structured so as to allow the making of choices which will authoritatively
allocate the resources of society and thereby help people to attain social
objectives. The study of political economy gives us a means for analyzing
institutions and for securing insight into the way in which they perform.
In this paper, I have examined what the literature in political economy
teaches us about the ability of the market, the centralized state, and
majority rule to attain one social objective: the provision of public goods.
I have also discussed a less classic institution, the pivotal mechanism
and some of its analogs, all of which are designed to resolve one of the
basic problems that confounds the performance of most institutions seeking
to supply public goods: the incentives to misrepresent preferences and
thereby to free ride on the contributions of others.

While the study of development convinces one of the importance of
institutional design, the literature in political economy underscores the
difficulty of this endeavor. Some of the most famous results in the
literature are impossibility theorems (Arrow, 1951); and the conditions
specified for the securing of "positive" results are often so strong that
the prospects for securing them in real life appear most doubtful (Plott,
1967). Moreover, each of the major institutions examined in the literature
exhibits major flaws; while a given institution may resolve certain

difficulties, it falls afoul of others. A primary contribution of the political economy literature to the study of development is thus that it forces the analyst to confront the problems inherent in the task of institutional design, while supplying the tools with which to correctly specify, and in some few cases, to resolve them.

References

Apter, David E. 1965. The Politics of Modernization (Chicago, University of Chicago Press).

Arrow, Kenneth. 1951. Social Choice and Individual Values (New York, Wiley).

Barry, Brian M. 1970. Sociologists, Economists and Democracy (London, Collier-Macmillan).

Black, Duncan. 1971. The Theory of Committees and Elections (Cambridge, England, The University Press).

Downs, Anthony. 1957. An Economic Theory of Democracy (New York, Harper & Brothers).

Easton, David. 1953. The Political System (New York, Knopf).

Ferejohn, John A., Robert Forsythe, and Roger G. Noll. 1977. "Implementing Planning Procedures for the Provision of Discrete Public Goods," (Pasadena, California Institute of Technology Social Science Working Paper, Number 154).

_____, _____, and _____. "Practical Aspects of the Construction of Decentralized Decisionmaking Systems for Public Goods," in Clifford S. Russell, ed., Collective Decision Making (Baltimore, Md., Johns Hopkins University Press for Resources for the Future).

Groves, Theodore. 1978. "Efficient Collective Choice with Compensation," The Economic Series, Technical Report Number 258 (Palo Alto, Calif., Stanford University Institute for Mathematical Studies in the Social Sciences).

Groves, Theodore and John Ledyard. 1977. "Some Limitations of Demand-Revealing Process," Public Choice vol. 29, no. 2, pp. 107-114.

Hurwicz, Leo. 1979. "Outcome Functions Yielding Walrasian and Lundahl Allocations at Nash Equilibrium Points," The Review of Economic Studies vol. 42(2), no. 143, pp. 217-226.

Madison, James. 1961. "Federalist Paper Number 51," in Clinton Rossiter, ed., The Federalist Papers (New York, The New American Library).

Musgrave, Richard A. 1959. The Theory of Public Finance (New York, McGraw-Hill).

Plott, Charles R. 1967. "A Notion of Equilibrium and Its Possibility Under Majority Rule," American Economic Review vol. 57, no. 4, pp. 787-806.

Samuelson, Paul. 1955a. "The Pure Theory of Public Expenditures," The Review of Economics and Statistics vol. 36, pp. 387-389.

_____. 1955b. "Diagrammatic Exposition of a Theory of Public Expenditure," The Review of Economics and Statistics vol. 37, pp. 350-356.

Sklar, Richard L. 1977. "Socialism at Bay: Class Domination in Africa," Paper prepared for the Annual Meeting of the African Studies Association, November 2-5.

Smith, Vernon L. 1978. "An Experimental Comparison of Three Public Good Decision Mechanisms" (Mimeographed, University of Arizona).

Swainson, Nichola. 1977. "Foreign Corporations and Economic Growth in Kenya" (unpublished manuscript).

Tideman, T. Nicholas. 1977. "Introduction" Public Choice vol. 29, no. 2, pp. 1-14.

_____ and Gordon Tullock. 1976. "A New and Superior Process for Making Social Choices," Journal of Political Economy vol. 84, no. 6, pp. 1145-1159.

U.S. Agency for International Development. 1977. Project Paper, Real Property Tax Administration (Philippines).

_____. 1978a. Project Paper, Development Decentralization (Egypt).

_____. 1978b. Project Paper, Provincial Development Program II Indonesia).

_____. 1979a. Project Paper, Local Resources for Development, (Yemen Arab Republic).

_____. 1979b. "Managing Decentralization," mimeo, U.S.A.I.D. Development Support Bureau.

_____. 1979c. "Report of the Study Team in Provincial Planning and Administration in Thailans; Office of Rural Development, Development Support Bureau.

Wallerstein, Immanuel. 1974. "Dependence in an Interdependent World" African Studies Review vol. 17, no. 1, pp. 1-26.

Chapter 5

PUBLIC CHOICE ANALYSIS OF INSTITUTIONAL CONSTRAINTS ON

FIREWOOD PRODUCTION STRATEGIES IN THE WEST AFRICAN SAHEL

James T. Thomson

This essay presents a public choice policy analysis of firewood production possibilities in the West African Sahel, the arid southern fringe
of the Sahara Desert.

Demand for firewood has outstripped supply in much of the contemporary Sahel. Arid areas and urban hinterlands now face the worst pinch, but
population growth will soon create scarcities in many regions where supplies remain temporarily adequate. Since firewood will amost certainly
continue to be the staple cooking and heating fuel of most Sahelien
families, sustained severe shortages will sharply reduce many Saheliens'
living standards.

Author's Note: Research upon which this article is based was undertaken in Niger and Upper Volta during 1979, with funding provided by the
International Relations Fellowship Program of the Rockefeller Foundation
and by the Junior Faculty Leave Program of Lafayette College, Easton,
Pennsylvania. I wish to acknowledge my appreciation for this support.
I am also grateful to the governments of Niger and Upper Volta for
authorizing the research. My greatest debt, however, is to all those
Saheliens who willingly bore with countless questions about renewable
resource management possibilities in their difficult environment.

The pertinent problem thus becomes identification in particular settings of best strategies to prevent serious firewood shortages. Using standard public choice assumptions about human nature, this analysis highlights technical, legal, political, and economic impediments to reforestation and then suggests several strategies to reduce or overcome them. Drawbacks as well as advantages of individualist, collective, and mixed approaches to woodstock management are considered.

Arguments and analysis are presented in the following sequence: (1) assumptions and an outline of seven problems to be considered; (2) a particularly fictionalized account of one individual's frustrating attempt at fuelwood production, which illustrates some of these problems in a Sahelien local context; (3) consideration in detail of each problem; and (4) conclusions.

Assumptions and Problems

The people whose behavior is here analyzed and who must implement any solutions are assumed to be self-interested, rational maximizers who make decisions under conditions of uncertain information (and therefore often satisfy rather than maximize). They do so within a basic legal framework which varies from place to place but establishes in any local context parameters of their decision-making processes. People are also assumed to be capable of learning over time as new information becomes available (Ostrom, 1974, pp. 50-52).

Constraints on Firewood Production

Assume that a Sahelien state wants to promote local participation in firewood production. Then assume home and market demand suffice, all else being equal, to encourage peasant production. Certain constraints may nevertheless hamper sustained yield management of the local woodstock. Major problems are concerned with:

1. The availability of seeds or seedlings, or both, and whether there is nursery stock or natural regeneration, of appropriate species. In land-scarce and food-short areas, "appropriate-ness" will reflect species' compatibility with crops, effects on soil fertility, and valuable by-products.

2. Land tenure, tree tenure, and associated residential patterns which may blunt farmers' interest in wood production if they do not own land they farm; and affect the ease with which trees are protected, thus causing choices to be made between woodlot and on-field production schemes.

3. The feasibility of protecting trees from foraging livestock.

4. The feasibility of protecting trees from unauthorized cutting by humans.

5. The enforceability of property rights in land, which influence the risks entailed and the advisability of going into such a slow-maturing crop as trees.

6. The enforceability of property rights in trees; that is, how can damage be claimed when protection fails?

7. The collective action capabilities at the local level, given distribution of political (rule-making) authority there and in overriding regimes.

Each of these issues may affect an African peasant's calculations about whether tree farming can fit in with his and others' goats and crops, that is, how desirable is it to undertake agro-sylvopastoralism in any particular Sahelien setting? In the following section I will highlight some relevant constraints.

Hedging the Law -- A Bad Example by Way of Elucidating Wood Production Problems

Abdu Issa runs a peasant farm on ten arid acres of the West African Sahel. One recent dry season he decided to start a fuelwood plantation/

windbreak through the middle of his sandy field, reducing wind erosion by planting the break counter to prevailing east-west winds.

Abdu put in Commiphora africana, a small tree often used for live fencing because it can be started from cuttings of existing stock in the dry season without using irrigation. Trimmed hedges become dense and grow up without shading adjoining crops. Modest nutrient requirements further reduce the hedge's competition with crops. The trimmed branches burn nicely and, though slow growing, the wood is hard enough for saddle-making. Finally, C. africana is not on the protected species list in Abdu's country. He could cut it without fear of being fined by a forester, as he might be were he to opt to plant Acacia albida or any of fourteen other species on the endangered list. Nor would he need permission, available for a fee (or a small bribe), each time he wanted to trim the hedge.[1]

As his field lies close to his village home, Abdu figured the hedge would make life easier for his wife who gathers all the household's firewood.

Unfortunately, other villagers at first took too little, then too much interest in the hedge. Livestock roam freely here after the harvest. Once fields were bare, goats browsed the C. africana leaves and tender twigs in the daily struggle to fill their stomachs, thereby stunting the

---

[1]The forestry code in this country in fact vests ownership of planted trees in those who planted them. But peasants are often reluctant to formally establish title, because they are afraid of foresters, because foresters are so few as to be hard to contact, and because the process by which title may be established is vague, cumbersome, and of uncertain efficacy. In the absence of firm title, many forestry guards see an illegal opportunity to increase fines or bribe income ... and take it.

little trees. Many villagers saw animals chewing on the hedge, but no one shooed them away: after all, local rules allow animals to rove freely during the dry season.

Local interest picked up, however, when the hedge put out burnable branches. Village women, too busy to comb surrounding fields for fuel, lopped off many for firewood. They all knew Abdu had planted the hedge but rationalized their actions by claiming the right as local residents to cut any unprotected species. Since hedges are by national law un-regulated common property unless title has been established to specific trees. Those who did not cut Abdu's hedge never told him the names of those who did for fear of being labeled troublemakers.

Abdu's wife complained; and when he caught a woman "trimming" his hedge, he became angry enough to call a case against her before the canton chief. Since he lived in the same town, time and court costs were minimal. Had Abdu lived ten miles from the canton seat in a village with no local moot, such court action would have been much more expensive in time and money.

Abdu presented his complaint in court. In reply the woman's husband publicly ridiculed him for being so petty as to haul an honest housewife to court over something so minor as a piece of wood. Moreover, he as-serted, there really was no law preventing local people from trimming unprotected trees.

The canton chief, as judge, tried to decide after hearing the parties. The case perplexed him: what did Abdu expect? The woman had taken wood all right, but it was worth practically nothing. Did he want two cents' worth of compensation? Embarrassed, Abdu said he did not care about

<u>that</u> piece of wood, but he did want an end to unauthorized trimming of
his hedge. He asked for the equivalent of a two dollar fine. The chief
declined. He had no legal authority to impose such a fine. Nor could he
legislate new rules, even were they to apply solely within his canton.
Only his administrative superiors at the national level could make such
decisions; at most he could merely conciliate the parties.

True, he might have let Abdu pronounce a Quranic oath to prohibit
further hedge trimming without permission. But the penalties violators
would face (leprosy, poverty, etc.) were too draconian for the value
involved. Moreover, he knew his superiors would rebuke him if he con-
sented to the oath. It really offered no solution to Abdu's problem.

The chief's admonitions finally convinced the husband his wife should
give Abdu fifty cents in damages. She did; and after all the fuss, Abdu
had to accept. For his troubles, he made himself a laughing stock of
village gossips. Damages did not even cover court costs, to say nothing
of his loss of face. Worse still, the amount would not deter future
trimmers, the more so because everyone knew Abdu could not afford, in
personal terms, to call another such case. Nor were others likely to
do so, after this debacle.

Later somebody cut two good trees out of the windbreak. Abdu ignored
the incident (though he could have used the wood), but the hole chan-
neled strong air currents through the trees and severely eroded topsoil
on both sides of the opening.

Fuelwood windbreaks have not become popular items in Abdu's village.
Implications of this example for firewood production using other unprotected species are only too clear. On the other hand, to raise

protected species for fuelwood would require the regional forester's written consent. Otherwise a standard permit would be needed to authorize cutting or even trimming above the three meter level.

This account suggests _some_ of the social, legal, political, and technical constraints which may affect firewood policy and production schemes. Systematic examination of these and other obstacles to sustained yield management is now in order.

Constraints on Fuelwood Production

Appropriate Tree Seeds or Seedlings

To pervert a proverb, great oaks from little oaks grow .... only. Seeds, seedlings, or saplings, from natural regeneration, direct seeding, or transplanted private or government nursery stock constitute the starting point of reforestation. Without them, it will not happen. They must be adapted to the job at hand, that is, reproduction must be technically and economically feasible, survival rates adequate in rainfed (or irrigated) plantings, and wood must be adequate as fuel. All else being equal, where demand is strong, faster growing species will be preferred. But other things are not equal. Species vary. Some produce good construction as well as firewood, or valuable by-products such as foods, medicines, gum, tannin, and fibers.

Nonconsumptive uses served by various species also vary markedly, and these may sharply influence a farmer's decision to grow one rather than another, or to grow trees at all. In land rich areas, crop competitive characteristics -- space, light nutrients, and water requirements -- may be immaterial. But in infertile, land scarce areas villagers will

be extremely sensitive to these aspects: fuelwood for cooking is a basic
necessity only if there is food to cook. Thus, undeniable advantages are
offered by species which fertilize crops through nitrogen fixation, reduce
wind or water erosion, or act as nutrient pumps in bringing soil chemicals
leached below the reach of crop roots to the surface again as do leaf
mulch or manure (Poulsen, 1979a, p. 4, and 1979b, pp. 9-10). These on-
site uses as well as growth characteristics will influence farmers'
decisions to go into fuelwood or stick exclusively to crops.

If disseminated to farmers, improved varieties could tip the balance
in favor of more wood production. Greater cash income from tree by-products and replacement of market by homegrown items might well compensate
for less cropland. In this regard, much remains to be done in appropriate
species research, development, and dissemination.

Land Tenure, Tree Tenure, and Residential Patterns

Land tenure. Land tenure can be succinctly defined as "those legal
and contractual or customary arrangements whereby people in farming gain
access to productive opportunities on the land" (Dorner, 1972, p. 17).
Land tenure systems allocate productive opportunities. Those who firmly
control land they farm can plan accordingly. But the tenant who expects
his landlord to evict or shift him to another plot after several years
to prevent him from establishing title by prescription is not able to
plan improvements with the same security. He may be perfectly aware
that terracing, live fencing, or windbreaks eventually improve land and
yet be certain that he will gain nothing thereby. Thus he may rationally
opt for short-term investments in greater fertility. The use of manure
or chemical fertilizer promises a return to investment at the next harvest,

assuming he gets a reasonable share of the crop produced. Although such
attempts to maintain soil fertility are probably inadequate in the long
run, given undiminished wind or sheet erosion, the farmer who expects to
move on will find them preferable to longer term, more fundamental
improvements.

This logic applies with equal force to wood production schemes,
since trees take at least four or five years to reach usable size. The
potential fuelwood farmer whose view of the long term is cluttered with
land tenure related risk factors cannot be faulted for hesitating to
plant trees.

Tree tenure. Sahelien tree tenure terms often add another risk,
thus inhibiting investments in fuelwood production. Land ownership and
tree ownership do not always concede. In pre-colonial times he who planted
a tree usually owned it. If he also owned the land under the tree, either
might be sold without parting with the other. Trees growing wild in the
bush by contrast often counted as "free goods" (or "bads," since they
had to be cleared before the land could be cultivated).

It is probably that few rural Saheliens were initially disturbed by
deforestation. Accustomed for centuries to slash-and-burn agriculture,
they judged woodstock levels by the availability of free bush land.[2] So
long as forested lands remained for colonization, a frontier mentality
prevailed. When the farmland and surrounding bush failed, migration or
colonization commonly offered the easiest way out. Under such circum-

---

[2]Political boundaries drawn along ethnic or state lines clearly put
some "available" lands off limits to aliens of the political communities
involved. Such humanly imposed land shortages induced active conservation
practices in many areas (Ware, 1977, pp. 174-175).

stances it made little sense to actively manage renewable resources. Renewable resources. Positive conservation measures to permit continuous use -- windbreaks, sheet erosion control terraces and dikes, and so forth -- demand sustained effort. They require more labor input than does clearing forested, fertile lands which can be fallowed when worn out while the farmer opens new fields elsewhere. Given sufficient land, passive conservation -- fallowing fields well before they were totally exhausted -- adequately restored soil fertility and trees to the landscape, and the Saheliens knew this.

The colonial conquest brought a European style forest service and forestry regulations to most Sahelien areas by the 1930s. Modifications in tree tenure followed. Colonial officials, fearing deforestation, imposed forestry codes. These generally tried to freeze demand rather than promoting sustained yield management. Particularly in the French colonies codes restricted use of valuable species by establishing a protected species list and creating extensive forest reserves, without regard to customary African land and tree tenure rights (Raeder-Roitzsch, 1974). Upholding these regulations against popular resistance required suppressive police action, ever since a hallmark of Sahelien forestry. With foresters spending the greater part of their time chasing illegal cutters, opportunities for a cooperative approach to forestry were few indeed.

In many Sahelien states today deadwood and unprotected live species remain effectively unregulated common property. In supply tight situations of the sort becoming increasingly common in the Sahel, this arrangement, often underwritten through local level misinterpretation of national forestry codes, discourages wood production. Where wood is available for

the taking, wood ownership is established by appropriation, not by investment in planting, nurturing, and protection. Despite an urgent need for
reforestation, working rules of tree tenure in such cases render the
activity virtually pointless from the perspective of individual conservers.
Significantly, deadwood is becoming increasingly privatized in the evolving
common law of many African locales (for example, Zinder Department, Niger,
and Yatenga Department, Upper Volta). This development reflects peasant
dissatisfaction with forestry code rules as they are locally (and often
incorrectly) interpreted. Research to determine villagers' perceptions of
this situation should be a priority item in programs focusing on incentives
and deterrents to increasing fuelwood supplies.

Do shrinking firewood supplies make conservationists of peasants?
If so, policy implications are far-reaching. Popular readiness to innovate,
to experiment, and to do added work necessary to use new techniques successfully may sharply reduce efforts needed to "sensitize" people. Peasants
who want to reforest because they foresee shortages should make a willing
audience for forestry extension workers. Conversely, premature efforts
to make active conservationists of villagers not yet convinced by personal
observation of a resource crunch may merely waste everyone's time and
money. Scattered fragmentary evidence suggests this is the case (Thomson,
1979a, 1979b), but more research on the question is indispensable. In
the meantime, a caveat is in order.

Pro-conservation attitudes by no means lead automatically to conservation activity. Intervening variables shape farmers' final estimates
of feasibility of sustained yield management, whatever their desire for
same. Three of these -- availability of appropriate stock, effective land

and tree tenure rules -- have just been examined. The remaining variables will be analyzed in the sections that follow.

Residential patters: closely settled versus dispersed. Some Sahelien peasants live in villages at the center of the community's fields. Others live in dispersed family units, each on its own field. If trees have to be protected -- as seems likely -- from grazing livestock and illegal trimming, dispersed settlement cuts surveillance costs for scatter-sited trees (windbreaks, live hedges, and trees interplanted with crops). Close-settled communities, with many more eyes and ears, can better patrol village woodlots located close to population centers. But such sites are often hard to come by: the richest fields constantly fertilized by compound sweepings, manure, and nightsoil lie in the first circle of land around the village (Raynaut, 1978).

Assume that only protected seedlings survive. Thus raising them in sites beyond range of costless surveillance implies either hiring a guard, enduring unauthorized depredations, or giving up. Because most locations in dispersed-settlement communities can always be seen by someone, such localities may enjoy a tactical advantage in wood production over closely settled villages.

Trees Versus Livestock

Many knowledgeable observers maintain that Sahelien reforestation is feasible only if trees receive adequate protection from browsing livestock, particularly goats, while others, such as Poulsen (1979c, pp. 6-8) argue the contrary. The issue is thus problematic; research should seek data to help decide when and where what species must be fenced to prosper. Given cross-Sahelien variations in grazing pressure and tree species auto-defense mechanisms (thornless, with thorns, and so forth), few sweeping generalizations about fencing are likely to be valid.

Major interdependencies in traditional sylvo-agro-pastoral systems. Symbiotic relationships between highly productive herding, farming, and tree-growing activities unquestionably exist (compare, for example, Funel, 1979; Nicolas, 1962; Souleymane, 1978; Swift, 1976; and Thomson, 1977). Trees, crops, and livestock in properly balanced relationships enrich and protect each other to the great benefit of the entire community. To maintain this system of mixed farming under a tree canopy at peak productivity interrelationships must be managed in mutually reinforcing ways. When this fails to take place, a desert may well result.

Controlling grazing pressure. If livestock can destroy natural regeneration of trees, reforestation depends on controlling livestock. In most Sahelien countries animals forage during the rainy season only under guard, but after the harvest livestock often roam at will. This cuts feeding costs, and investments in herding, enclosures, and fodder stocking are avoided.

Treating dry-season fields as common property lays the groundwork for an eventual tragedy of the commons because it encourages overstocking. Each additional animal means more profit for the owner. But when the carrying capacity of a pasture is exceeded, each additional animal marginally reduces the food supply for every other animal. Hunger drives them all from the lush to the rough grasses and eventually to saplings, thus curtailing natural regeneration of the woodstock. This is the classic tragedy of the commons, in which a once valuable renewable natural resource is reduced to dust or hardpan laterite by uncontrolled overgrazing (Hardin, 1968, and 1977).

Two kinds of solutions exist to prevent overgrazing: privatization, which encourages each owner to take account of the full costs of over-stocking his own land; or political controls, which keep grazing at or under carrying capacity. Both involve problems.

Short of privatization or grazing controls, fuelwood resources can be protected from livestock by regulating livestock movements or somehow protecting trees, whatever happens to pastures.

Herding requires pasturage, herders, and returns to investment to support the latter. Full-time migrant herders, who regularly move through the Sahel, for the example, the Fulbe and Twareg, are harder to control in terms of protecting the woodstock from abusive cutting of woody browse than are sedentary herders who have a greater incentive to respect local regulations concerning exploitation of tree forage. For herders, keeping hungry animals from gardens and woodlots is easier than protecting scat-tered natural regeneration. Local goats, however, often are not herded: their limited value frequently does not justify the labor input.

Fencing is difficult because it is expensive, and traditional fencing materials -- thorns, mats, and live hedges -- may be scarce, either be-cause it is protected by forestry code provisions (Thomson, 1977, pp. 64-65; and Felker, 1978, pp. 118-119) or because population pressure has largely eliminated free bushlands. Enclosing larger areas reduces per unit cost, as some ethnic groups who maintain consolidated forms of land tenure have found (Nicolas, 1962; Souleymane, 1978; Thomson, 1977, pp. 261-264). Typically, however, this cannot be achieved when fields are small and scattered.

Stabling requires substantial labor inputs to collect fodder. Gen-erally this is feasible only during the growing season, when grasses and

foliage are plentiful near at hand. Tethering on pastures is again only
feasible when forage is plentiful, that is, when trees need no particular
protection from livestock.

Where lack of appropriate sites precludes informal policing (above,
pp. 160, 161), seedling survival may depend upon active guarding. Local
funds (rates or voluntary contributions), money from overriding governments,
or international aid donors may permit hiring guards. Or, guard duty
might be shared on a rotating basis within the village, assuming that
effective local political institutions exist that can resolve problems
associated with enforcing equitable participation in guard service.

Woodlots can be fenced given sufficient tradiational materials or
units large enough to reduce wire fencing costs to acceptable levels, per
unit area. Reusing materials on other sites once trees have outgrown
stock pressure will further reduce costs.

Scatter-site, in-field wood production may also be possible using
browse-resistant species, or on a fenced basis, only if tree growers are
committed to protecting saplings and if they have legal access to enough
thorns from mature trees.

Trees Versus People

Doubts may exist about when, where, and how much foraging animals
threaten wood production. But people unquestionably cut innumerable
trees while harvesting fuelwood and other forest products. Whether the
woodstock as a renewable resource will be run down depends on institutional incentives to balance supply and demand. As suggested, Sahelien trees
may be private or common property, or a mix of the two. Theoretically,
if trees are private property a wood shortage should stimulate individual

investment in supply. Evidence from rural Niger and Upper Volta suggests this in fact happens. Indeed, forest service heads in Niger, Upper Volta, and Mali are all currently interested in exploring this option along with collective approaches to reforestation.

By contrast, where trees are common property, wood will be harvested on a first come, first served basis (Thomson, 1977). This reduces incentives to produce, since the tree planter has no guarantee he will reap the benefit of his investment. To overcome this dissociation between investment in supply and reward inherent in all common property systems, special management capabilities must be developed. Some political community must control use and promote supply. Conceptually this is always possible; practically it is often difficult and costly -- often, but not always.

Trees as private property; protecting and producing to guarantee supply. Where trees are private property, tree owners either protect them or bear losses occasioned by theft. Two consequences flow from privatization: first, a "do to others as you would have them do to you" ethic is implicit, that is, don't steal wood if you don't want yours stolen. Second, tree owners and their dependents function as an informal local polic force. Community members thus help enforce tree tenure rules instead of leaving the job entirely to foresters. Perfect policing will not result. Some, preferring to avoid "meddling," will not report observed wood thefts to owners. But the incentive to do so is there: to protect one's own trees, one protects others' and hopes for reciprocity.

Privatization of trees also motivates individuals to produce trees for their own use. Where all trees are privately owned, he who does not provide for his future wood needs by growing now will later pay the going price for lumber and firewood. Because trees cannot be harvested on a first come, first served basis, the option to avoid investment in wood production no longer eixsts. Privatization brings home directly to the individual consequences of nonconservation, and so encourages planting and protecting future firewood supplies. While maturing, trees protect the environment.

<u>Unregulated common property trees: consumption without production.</u> The first come, first served rule governing exploitation of unregulated common property woodstocks promotes consumption but not production. Demand can exceed supply without automatically pressuring individuals to act in their enlightened self-interest by investing now in supplies to meet future needs and thus avoid total deforestation and environmental degradation.

The Sahelien peasants are often admonished to become aware of environmental degradation. By implication, ignorance or plain stupidity underlie peasants' current failure to take better care of the land and trees that support them. But it is highly unlikely that peasants fail to see the ecological breakdowns occurring around them. They may be aware and concerned, yet simultaneously immobilized by inappropriate rules.

What pushes an individual to ensure regeneration of an unregulated common property woodstock threatened by excessive demand? Very little, in fact. The peasant who values trees on his field as windbreaks, forage sources, soil fertility regenerators, and the like will at most try to get his firewood eslewhere. If free bush exists nearby he will use that. But once bush goes, the desire for trees on his own field goads him to harvest those on his neighbors' fields to meet his own construction and firewood needs (Thomson, 1979b). Given excessive demand, the unregulated common property system leads to a "cut anywhere but home" ethic of forest exploitation. Instead of encouraging each landowner to invest in future supply, this ethic leads peasants to cut their losses by not investing in regeneration of common property woodstock which somebody else will most likely consume. Instead, people spend more time, energy, and money meeting daily needs from the everdwindling supply.

Spontaneous privatization of the woodstock. Assume that the woodstock is formally unregulated: that is, any tree is legally fair game for anybody. Given resource scarcity, will privatization replace the first come, first served rule? Economic theory argues that the commons will be parceled into private units when it is both technically feasible to enforce property rights and economically advantageous to do so (Demsetz, 1967). Field data from a rural region of Upper Volta not patrolled by the national Environmental Service support the prediction. Parallel developments -- privatization of formerly common property crop residues (peanut vines, millet stalks, and the like) -- in parts of Niger and Upper Volta, where destruction of bush has made livestock forage a scarce commodity, likewise support the prediction. This change lays one kind of groundwork for greater individual investment in wood supply. But other alternatives exist.

Common property woodstock: formally regulated, effectively unregulated. Assume that a woodstock is formally but not effectively regulated because of inadequate enforcement. Even though demand exceeds supply, incentives here still discourage better wood supply management through informal privatization. Everybody is in the same boat: all have to cut protected species illegally to satisfy urgent needs for wood. It is therefore difficult for anyone to protect his "own" trees by preventing others' cutting on his own land.[3] Even worse, nobody can morally afford to assist foresters in protecting trees except where such "collaboration" is the only way to avoid unjust punishment for others' illegal cutting on one's own land.

This leaves the forest service with total responsibility for defending the woodstock. Even assuming that foresters manage adequate policing with minimal peasant support, individual investments in regenerating the woodstock still will not occur. This conclusion follows from the continuing lack of direct connection between investment in new supply and expected reward, so long as the permit system effectively authorizes regulated cutting of protected species anywhere: tree planters still have no assurance they will harvest wood they grow.

Reducing disincentives to invest in supply of common property woodstock. Disincentives to producing common property trees can be reduced by subdividing common property woodstocks into exclusive units allocated to specific user communities (which might be larger than, equal to, or smaller than village jurisdictions). Formalizing local control should encourage village investment in policing and increasing the woodstock, by explicitly allocating management responsibility to village residents. This strategy seems especially attractive where some fields are already

---

[3]Given a formal permit system an individual could in principle acquire one and then legally cut trees on his own land. But since foresters are thin on the ground, it is expensive in time and energy, at which point one must pay for the permit; and since they are thin on the ground it is usually possible to get away with illegal cutting. When this becomes everybody's least-bost solution, unregulated deforestation proceeds apace.

treeless: it would reduce potential hardship some would otherwise suffer through privatization of trees currently maldistributed on village lands and should ease the transition to sustained yield management, by calming fears of those community members less well endowed with wood.

Village governments or quarter committees could regulate access. Local management units would be empowered to exclude nonresidents.[4] By reducing information costs and facilitating the consensus required to maintain a local regulation system, such units might well cut policing and investment costs involved in building collective supply.

Adequate collective management decisions depend on accurate knowledge about who is doing what with the woodstock. Wood must presumably be distributed under some locally acceptable formula which would equitably apportion supply and hardships associated with short supply. Details of distribution formulas appear to be an intimately local matter, defined by each local unit's consensus about what is right and proper. Two general conditions hold, however. First, such formulas must be enforceable to be effective. If those who run short are permitted to raid the collective woodstock, the now inappropriate first come, first served rule will replace group management.

Second, a formula will only work if it is seen by villagers to achieve equity. Inequitable arrangements will be violated by aggrieved peasants

---

[4]Where scattered quarter or village landholdings interpenetrate each other, interesting boundary problems can be expected. If they are sufficiently intractable and collective management is considered a must, special woodstock management districts not necessarily contiguous with existing villages or quarter boundaries might offer a solution. Each district would regulate wood on a group of contiguous fields no matter where field owners resided or were registered for census and tax purposes. The approach is not without problems; however, they will not be explored here.

pressed for fuel. Accurate information gathered in ways which local people consider reliable can avoid this. Considerable room for local experiment exists here, but the smaller the user group and the greater their daily interaction the lower information costs will be (Olson, 1965). It may be possible to control use only of guarded woodlots: monitoring wood gathering from on-field trees simply may be too expensive. If so, privatization of trees not in woodlots may be the only workable way to manage them on a sustained yield basis.

Consensus on distribution formulas and investment in new wood supplies will be easier where the quarter or village is accustomed to taking collective decisions, if the same process and persons can handle woodstock management. Otherwise organizational difficulties must be surmounted before local collective management will be feasible. This may be both expensive and time-consuming. Given a consensus, users have some incentive to help with policing as a means of protecting their own shares. But the incentive is weakened because losses are spread over the entire group rather than being borne only by the one who sees illegal harvesting. To overcome this handicap, consensus will have to be very solid.

Local collective management for sustained yield assumes sustained investments in new supply. Planting trees and protecting natural regeneration require labor, perhaps money.[5] Management units thus require authority to impose user charges, labor service or taxes on group members.

---

[5]Acquiring access to woodlot sites poses fascinating problems. Location of sites, terms of cession (sale? loan? rent? conditions of reversion to owner?), possible effects on distribution of product must all be examined. Local political authority seems indispensable. Overriding regimes should offer a dispute resolution process only to settle intractable local deadlocks.

In many parts of the Sahel, such authority does not now exist, at least
for purposes of collectively producing trees.

User fees might provide a way to sensitize users to the social impact
of their individual demands on the woodstock. They could promote conservation by adding a price to the time and energy invested in harvesting
fuelwood. They could also generate funds to pay for additional fuelwood
in the form of woodlots or by protecting natural regneration (fences,
guards' or herders' remuneration). Again, adequate information and effective enforcement would condition feasibility. If total reliance on
user charges would strain budgets of the pooerst persons it might be
advisable to adopt either graduated fees (that is, to tax heavier users
disproportionately more) or a mixed system, coupling fixed-ration distribution of the indespensable minimum amount of firewood with user charges
for any additional amounts. Again, what will work depends on local
institutions.

Enforcement of Property Rights in Land

This section treats the critical problem of rule enforcement. It
builds on our earlier discussion of protection problems, particularly
arguments about informal policing mechanisms and local collective action
organization. Analysis of land tenure enforcement problems here will lay
the groundwork for briefer comments in the next section about enforcement
of collective or individual property rights in trees.

Enforcement: the indispensable minimum. Laws are man made artifacts
designed to organize human conduct for certain ends. Effective laws,
by restricting the choices open to individuals, raise odds that desired
actions will occur.

Laws, however, are not self-enforcing. Formal laws only become effective when individuals and officials uphold them in cases of dispute or violation. Without enforcement, laws remain mere formal orderings, paper rules, without capacity to shape realities of human conduct.

Commons's (1959, pp. 65-142) concept of working rules of going concerns provides a useful framework for analyzing enforcement issues. For Commons, any institution can be viewed as a going concern. Members' conduct is patterned by working rules -- effective laws, which reflect officials' decisions of whether to enforce formal rules. Any set of working rules creates opportunities, in the form of rights and liberties which encourage certain actions, and deterrents, duties and exposures, which discourage other activities (Ostrom, 1976).

Rights and liberties, however, are only desirable, duties and exposures only onerous if they are enforced when challenged. Whether officials command the necessary power is problematic. Assuming they do, whether they will use it to uphold formal laws depends on whether their decisions are subject to review by superior officials (and if so, how those officials exercise their powers). And, if their decisions are not subject to review, that is, if they have the last word, whether they consider a particular law should be upheld in light of their own analysis of the situation. Where an official has the last word, or determining power, danger always exists that the indispensable capacity to enforce laws by legally imposing "bads" on individuals and so coercing them to act in desired ways may be abused to promote the official's interests at the expense of at least some members of the going concern.

Where abuses are possible one can be sure officials and other members of the concern will find ways to manipulate the legal process to their mutual advantage. In the Sahel as elsewhere land tenure laws often become prime objects of manipulation as uncontrolled officials seek to promote their own interests in greater income, control over more land and power over people. Information about working rules, and the enforcement process that underlies them, is thus indispensable to achieving an accurate understanding of why people act as they do.

Legal costs. Legal costs include time and energy necessary to litigate, official and personal costs of coming into court, lawyers' fees and illegal payments to court personnel.

Configurations of working rules are frequently much influenced by costs of legal action. All else being equal, the lower these are the more vigorous one can expect litigants to be in protesting rule violations and perceived unjust rulings. How officials' exercise their powers will thus face greater scrutiny, and as a result abuses will diminish.

Village moots to resolve disputes and maintain local rules probably offer the most efficient, low-cost solution to enforcement problems. Village moots by no means guarantee a just legal process. Yet appeals are usually possible to courts of higher jurisdiction. This provides a partial check on local court-holders and makes rule manipulation less attractive in their eyes if superiors consistently correct abuses. However, appeals, though necessary as a control measure, can threaten integrity of the local legal process if used too frequently. They may then make rule enforcement impossible at the village level (Thomson, 1977).

Enforcement of Property Rights in Trees

The question this section addresses may be simply stated; where excessive demand threatens the woodstock, are trees valued enough by somebody

so that rules promoting sustained-yield management can be upheld by enforcement when necessary? This can be followed immediately by another
question; What are the costs and, therefore, the likelihood of enforcement?

Increasing land shortages in most contemporary Sahelien communities,
and the critical importance of land as a basic factor of production in
Sahelien peasant families' farming economy ensures that most will vigorous-
ly litigate, even in the face of high legal costs, when their land claims
are challenged. Trees are another matter. Where supply exceeds demand
peasants will not likely complain about cutting. Who cares? There is
enough left for everybody. Even when the balance changes, it may be some
time before people perceive the loss of a tree as a loss they suffer.
Sooner or later, however, the lack of wood will bring the point home.
Once people become aware of the loss, fundamental questions of tree tenure
and enforcement processes become pertinent. Who owns what? What kinds of
policing deter violators? When formal rights are violated, what kinds
of recourse are available and at what costs?

Policing: a first-order solution. Policing is an indispensable start
towards management. It demonstrates somebody's direct concern with trees
and puts potential violators on notice that they are illegally infringing
collective or individual interests in the woodstock.

State control and policing of the woodstock to the exclusion of all
local involvement in management is a major weakness of many contemporary
Sahelien reforestation schemes. It dissociates policing and harvesting
interests: foresters police alone, and everybody else harvests on the
sly. Financing now available to Sahelien forestry agencies is insufficient
to permit massive staff increases. Therefore, exclusive state policing

as a control system seems doomed to severely suboptimal performance, and
sustained-yield woodstock management by such means is unlikely.

Local policing, where trees are collectively owned by local units
or held by individuals, appears to offer a useful alternative. However,
it must resolve the enforcement problem or witness a return to the working
rule governing unregulated common property woodstock exploitation: "cut
anywhere but at home."

Local enforcement: calculations. Incentives to demand enforcement
of tree tenure rules will be heightened if clear remedies exist when illegal cutting occurs. Restoration in kind or cash of wood value taken
seems essential to indemnify community or individual owners. If user
fees are enforced (above, pp. 172, 173), violators should pay the appropriate fee for wood taken. Additional damage payments also seem
advisable, both as a further deterrent and to compensate owners for loss
of nonconsumptive uses they suffer when live trees are felled.

Note that combined sanctions must be adequate to deter but not so
draconian as to hinder their application. Only the local sense of equity
can set appropriate standards. Local autonomy in this respect is a
necessary element in effective local management, as is the authority to
modify penalty structures in light of changing definitions of equity.

As with land tenure enforcement, judicial costs to the litigant
will affect his willingness to prosecute violators of tree tenure rules
for restitution and punitive damages. Judicial costs -- time to get to
court and have the case heard, legal or illegal court costs, lawyers'
fees -- all represent outlays which somebody has to support. Unless legal
costs are expected to be less than the value of the wood taken, wood
owners are unlikely to bother with litigation. Again, through their

proximity, availability, and informality, village moots will tend to cut costs, which is a great point in their favor. Individual owners may then have enough incentive to defend their part of the woodstock and so contribute to overall management.

Collective ownership, because it spreads any loss sustained over all group members, probably means the management unit will have to designate an enforcer to represent the community in proceedings against violators. He should not be expected to shoulder the task on a voluntary basis: self-sacrifice for community good is fine, but expecting one person to bear the entire burden of providing community benefit -- maintenance of wood-stock management rules -- is asking a bit much.

Issues of Collective Action

For sustained-yield woodstock management to occur, supply and demand levels have to be balanced. Certain control measures noted above are indispensable to achievement of this goal. Even privatization involves local collective action in fixing and upholding tree tenure rules; otherwise enforcement costs will likely dissuade peasants from investing in wood production. Collective approaches to wood production, harvesting and distribution require correspondingly more elaborate local government capabilities.

Many villages in contemporary Francophone Sahelien areas lack legal authority necessary to sustain local management activities. Governments or external donors funding woodlot programs often "solve" the problems of collective organization that are associated with running such wood-stock management projects by simply _assuming_ that villages will handle them. Indeed, some villages can. Residual traditions of collective action, maintained by social pressure, permit them to impose necessary constraints. But many others cannot; traditions have eroded, informal collective action capability has greatly weakened or expired, rules governing use cannot be upheld locally over the long run; and without collective discipline, costs of management are simply prohibitive. Programs fail for lack of attention to critical issues of local government organization.

Note also that erosion of traditional forms (and their replacement by informal modern alternatives in some instances, for example, religious communities, voluntary associations, and the like) is extremely variable across, but also within, ethnic groups. Organizational capacity is a village-specific (or quarter-specific) phenomenon. Dramatic differences manifest themselves within villages and among quarters as well as among communities of the same ethnic group located in close proximity.

While project designers may ignore such problems, peasants cannot afford to do so. Nigerien Hausa community action is difficult: while some are farting with effort, others get new shirts." As many Hausa see it, those who voluntarily contribute money or effort for the public good (whatever the specific good) will find others "free-riding" on their sacrifices. Without enforcement free-riders will not bear their fair share of costs of producing goods. Hinging development efforts on willingness of people to get together for the community good will work well only where the village or groups within it are effective going concerns capable of organizing requisite efforts through a working system of rules. But where there exists no going concern -- or one whose membership is limited to a small subset of the community population -- the costs of getting together may be prohibitive, and people may have to opt for getting separated even though they know such a strategy may leave them worse off in the long run.

Projects should be designed to take account of this local complexity, by drawing on villages' organization strengths where possible and respecting others' limits by not arbitrarily imposing collective forms on those which now lack such capacity. Designs should build in local options to choose reforestation strategies from a range of possibilities. For certain kinds of reforestation programs it will be necessary in some locales to invest time and energy in reconstituting or creating local autonomous government capability.

Collective action costs. One can identify two kinds of costs associated with collective action: (1) costs of taking collective decisions, for example, acquiring land for woodlots or imposing user fees; and (2) costs flowing from decisions taken, for example, land loss sustained by group members whose fields may be expropriated for community woodlots or user fees which people may be required to pay. (For a more formal treatment of these concepts -- "opportunity" and "deprivation" costs -- see Ostrom, 1968, and literature therein cited.)

These costs vary with degrees of effective local autonomy and organization in any particular community. Where local structures can achieve consensus and uphold decisions with or without official authorization to enforce rules, the time and effort required to establish a woodstock management structure may be relatively low. But in consequence some people may bear substantial costs. They may lose land, or have to buy wood, or invest in new supplies when they would prefer to do other things with their time or money.

On the other hand, where local government is weak, consensus may be extremely difficult to achieve and decisions impossible to impose. In consequence, people may escape immediate costs associated with decisions they do not like. It is probable, however, that failure to manage wood-stock for sustained yield will lead ultimately to desertification in the Sahel, the costs of which are probably enormous.

If to manage their woodstock local communities require authorization from higher government levels, for example, district, county, state, or national jurisdictions, in general one can expect costs of getting author-ization will rise as the authorizing level becomes more remote. As juris-dictions increase in size, problems they deal with typically become more numerous. Since officials only have as much time as anyone else they typically cannot deal with all problems presented, but only with those they consider most important. A village petitioning for permission to manage its own woodstock (in the absence of special enabling legislation) is likely to face great difficulty acquiring the requisite authority. Thus one can expect villages to be uninterested in formulating and present-ing such petitions. The problem will be dealt with, if at all, in a top-down manner by officials who view it as serious enough to merit their attention.

Conclusions

This analysis of firewood production problems in the West African Sahel has addressed tehcnical and institutional problems which may impede woodstock management once dwindling wood supplies commit local residents to active conservation practices (Thomson, 1980a). Clear possibilities exist in the region for greater tree production and sustained-yield woodstock management, but realizing these will depend on the awareness of and ability to overcome problems discussed.

Technical advances -- more appropriate species, production techniques, and so forth -- remain critical: peasants already hard-pressed to survive will shun species and projects they know to be unproductive or threatening to short-term crop production possibilities.

Land and tree tenure rules, and political organization capabilities sharply influence the kind of woodstock management strategy that is appropriate for any particular user community, as do judicial process and woodstock protection possibilities. Some villages or village quarters can master both individual and collective approaches to wood production. Others, lacking appropriate local instituions, are restricted to individual enterprises. Probabilities that either will succeed can be heightened by legal changes, particularly in Sahelien national forestry codes. Reforms should give villagers greater incentives to participate in woodstock management by authorizing local communities to make and enforce management rules necessary and relevant in light of local conditions. Reforestation project designs should likewise address these critical issues as the most efficient way of promoting effective reforestation and environmental management in Sahelien states.

References

Commons, John R. 1959. Legal Foundations of Capitalism (Madison, University of Wisconsin Press).

Demsetz, Harold. 1967. "Towards a Theory of Property Rights," American Economic Review, vol. 72 (May), pp. 347-359.

Dorner, Peter. 1972. Land Reform and Economic Development (Baltimore, Md., Penguin).

Felker, Peter. 1978. State of the Art: Acacia albida as a Complementary Permanent Intercrop with Annual Crops (Riverside, Calif., Department of Soil and Environmental Sciences, University of California at Riverside, for USAID, Grant No. AID/afr-C-1361).

Funel, J.M. 1979. "Espace physique et développement rural en Afrique sudano-sahélienne: quelques variations sur ce theme," in Ph. Couty et a., eds., Maîtrise de l'espace agraire et développemnt en Afrique tropicale; Logique paysanne et rationalité technique, Actes du colloque de Ouagadougou (4-8 decembre 1978) (Paris, Editions de l'Office de la Recherche Scientifique et Technique Outre-Mer) pp. 229-238.

Hardin, Garrett. 1968. "The Tragedy of the Commons," Science, vol. 162, pp. 1243-1248.

_____. 1977. "Ethical Implications of Carrying Capacity," in Garrett Hardin and John Baden, eds. Managing the Commons (San Francisco, Calif., W.H. Freeman) pp. 112-123.

Nicholas, Guy. 1962. "Un village bouzou du Niger: étude d'un terroir," Cahiers d'outre-mer, vol. 40, no. 58, pp. 138-165.

Olson, Mancur. 1965. The Logic of Collective Action: Public Goods and the Theory of Groups (Cambridge, Mass., Harvard University Press).

Ostrom, Elinor. 1968. "Some Postulated Effects of Learning on Constitutional Behavior," Public Choice, vol. 5, pp. 87-104.

Ostrom, Vincent. 1974. The Intellectual Crisis in American Public Administration, rev. ed. (University, Ala., University of Alabama Press).

_____. 1976. "John R. Commons' Foundation for Policy Analysis," Journal of Economic Issues, vol. 10, pp. 839-857.

Poulsen, Gunnar. 1979a. "Woodlots in the Sahel -- Is That the Solution?" Sylva Africana, no. 4, pp. 3-4.

_____. 1979b. "Agroforestry before the Word," Sylva Africana no. 4, pp. 9-11.

_____. 1979c. "Is Fencing of Plantations Necessary in the Sahel?" Sylva Africana no. 4, pp. 608.

Raeder-Roitzsch, J.E. 1974. "Institutional Forestry Problems in the Sahelian Region" (New York, United Nations, Secretariat, Special Sahelian Office [ST/SSo/32]).

Raynaut, Claude. 1978. "Rapport de synthèse" (Bordeaux, France, Universite de Bordeaux II [Analysis of environmental problems in Maradi Department, Niger, undertaken by a multidisciplinary team based at Universite de Bordeaux II]).

Souleymane, Diarra. 1978. "Les Stratégies spatiales des éleveurs-cultivateurs peul du Niger central agricole," on Ph. Couty et al., eds., Maîtrise de l'espace agraire et développement en Afrique tropicale; Logique paysanne et rationalité technique, Actes du colloque de Ouagadougou (4-8 decembre 1978) (Paris, Editions de l'Office de la Recherche Scientifique et Technique Outre-Mer) pp. 87-81.

Swift, Jeremy. 1976. "La Désertification et l'homme" (Contribution lors de la Consultation CILSS/UNSO/FAO sur le rôle de la forêt dans un programme de réhabilitation du Sahel, Dakar, Senegal, April 26-May 1, 1976).

Thomson, James T. 1975. "Law, Legal Process and Development at the Local Level in Hausa-Speaking Niger: A Trouble Case Analysis of Rural Institutional Inertia," (Ph.D. dissertation, Department of Political Science, Indiana University, Bloomington, Indiana).

_____. 1977. "Ecological Deterioriation: Local-Level Rule-Making and Enforcement Problems in Niger," in Michael H. Glantz, ed., Desertification: Environmental Degradation in and around Arid Lands (Boulder, Colo., Westview Press) pp. 57-79.

_____. 1979a. Interviews with Inuwa District (pseudonym) villagers during field research, Inuwa District, Mirriah Arrondissement, Niger, February-May 1979.

_____. 1979b. Interview with the Black Drummer, Kwari (pseudonum), Inuwa District (pseydonym), Mirriah Arrondissement, Niger, April 7, 1979.

_____. 1980a. "Rapport préliminaire de fin de mission; Les Programmes nationaux et internationaux pour l'amenagement des forêts, des pâturages et des bas-fond sahéliens: les influences sur la mise en oeuvre des structures locales au Niger et an Haute-Volta" (Easton, Pa., January 25, 1980).

_____. 1980b. "Preliminary Evaluation: OXFAM Microcatchment Project, Ouahigouya, Upper Volta" (Unpublished report, Ouahigouya, Upper Volta, March 15, 1980).

Ware, Helen. 1977. "Desertification and Population: Sub-Saharan Africa," in Michael H. Glantz, ed., Desertification: Environmental Degradation in and around Arid Lands (Boulder, Colo., Westview Press) pp. 165-202.

Chapter 6

SOCIOLOGICAL ANALYSIS OF IRRIGATION WATER MANAGEMENT --
A PERSPECTIVE AND APPROACH TO ASSIST DECISION MAKING

David M. Freeman and Max K. Lowdermilk

The technical input required to improve water management is
relatively simple. The problem is to formulate practical
programs on a large scale which will allow for the technical,
social, legal and political factors....(World Bank, n.d.)

The Problem

Irrigation water is of sociological interest because people must

organize collectively to secure it, transport it, divide it into usable

shares, enforce rules for its application, pay for it, and dispose of

unused portions. The kinds of social organizations, the patterns of

power, decision making, conflict, and cooperation which people create

and maintain for the social control of water intimately affects the

productivity of its use. Attempting to comprehend physical and agronomic

problems of irrigation without probing into surrounding social organiza-

tional webs is like attempting to understand deficiencies in plant growth

without reference to conditions of climate. When water moves efficiently

from rivers, through a network of canals, to plant root zones, it is

because people have effectively organized a decision system capable of

enforcing technically sound rules for pursuing the collective interest.

Defects in the delivery and application of irrigation water are typically associated with deficiencies in social organization. Many engineering and agronomic technologies of irrigated agriculture must be exercised through the medium of farmers organized for collective action. Lack of organizations for sustaining such collective action, or their breakdown, will seriously hinder development of irrigated agriculture. The central premise of this paper, therefore, is that programs to improve the management of irrigation water -- either in existing or newly constructed systems -- must center on the design and improvement of irrigation organization at local, regional, and national levels.

The objective of this paper is to define the types of sociological research problems encountered in irrigation management by sorting out social properties of irrigation water management technologies -- a task complicated by the fact of their multiple dimensions. The technologies which supply, control, divert, and convey water have different properties than do the technologies employed by farmers in applying water to the fields, for leveling land, or for tilling, planting, and harvesting. This bundle of highly diverse irrigation technologies needs to be analytically broken down so as to clarify sociological research approaches.

For example, earnest discussion has taken place about the potential contribution of sociological research to improved water management. One central question seems to be, Why research sociological factors associated with farmers if one thinks that farmers are "rational" in response to economic incentives? If a technology can be designed which can be demonstrated to have a favorable economic benefit-cost ratio, will it not be employed by substantial numbers of farmers regardless of whatever interesting sociological factors may be at work? After all, did not many farmers, even smaller ones to some extent, adopt the technologies of the Green Revolution? It will be contended that the "economic man" approach is viable given certain properties of the technology, but the sociologist's "organizational man" analysis is an essential companion to economic analysis. Social organizations are the central vehicles through which water management technologies are delivered, utilized, improved, and maintained. The point is to demonstrate that the nature of sociological research must shift as the properties of water management technologies shift. A sociological research and action approach, which is highly useful to the decision maker for one kind of technological system constraint, will be most inappropriate when the technological dimensions of the problem have shifted into other configurations.

Selective Review of the Literature

The sociology of water management is in a state of infancy; theoretical frameworks to suggest questions, and provide a context of meaning, remain undeveloped. Nevertheless, some initial work in the field is highly suggestive and will be briefly reviewed.[1]

The dependent variable, quality of water management, has generally been measured in terms of either yields per cubic feet per second (cusecs) of water applied, yields per acre or application and delivery efficiencies (Keller and coauthors, 1974; Reidenger, 1974; Cory and Clyma, 1975; and Lowdermilk, Early, and Freeman, 1978). Independent or explanatory

---

[1]The interested reader will find more materials of value than can be reviewed here; see E. Walter Coward, Jr. (1976a).

variables such as communication between farmers and the Phillipine
National Irrigation Administration, cooperation among farmers, farmer fee
payment, farmer satisfaction with yields and with water supply, farmer
evaluation of irrigation administrative services, and adoption of improved
farm practices. Gustafson and Reidinger (1971) and Reidinger (1974)
discuss the inability of farmers to control the timing and quantity of
their water deliveries -- factors which limit farmers' ability to participate in the Green Revolution. These analysts explicitly recognize the
importance of collective action on the part of farmers to secure and
allocate a "community commodity" which irrigation water represents.
Wickham (1972), working in the Philippines, a country which enjoys an
established organizational framework for farmer decision making, assumes
the existence of farmers' associations and studies variables having to do
with their functioning. Reidinger (1974), on the other hand, confronts
in India an irrigation system which is designed to operate with only
minimal linkage to the farmer-user. Reidinger concludes his analysis by
advocating farmer associations on each watercourse to organize distribution
of irrigation water and eventually replace the rigid water share rotational
system so as to increase flexibility and farmer control.

Radosevich and Kirkwood (1975) have reviewed the organizational and
institutional setting of irrigation development in both the United States
and Pakistan. In the United States, as elwewhere, water development and
allocation has been achieved through the building of social organizations
capable of undertaking activities for a range of collectivities -- from
small groups of individual farmers diverting surface flow near a river, to
ditch companies, to large irrigation districts. To have foregone

organization building would have been tantamount to foregoing irrigation development -- a point earlier developed by Smith (1960).

Coward (1976b and 1976c) examines the problems of interaction between local organization and national water bureaucracies and points out our dearth of knowledge about the realities of local indigenous organizations. He also has discussed the diverse, traditional, small-scale irrigation organizations that exist in Southeast Asia and finds three themes reflected throughout: (1) a common concern for accountable leadership, (2) a recurrent necessity to create small-scale local organizations around "mini-units" which are (3) parts of larger canal-based networks extending beyond local village boundaries. Coward contends that important lessons are to be learned from analysis of traditional irrigation organizations and that thought should be given to ways in which local indigenous elements might be integrated into current irrigation development efforts.

Hunt and Hunt (1976) have assembled a most useful and detailed review of several anthropologically oriented case studies with a view toward extracting important questions which need to be pursued by social science students of irrigation systems. Their review of the literature leads them to suggest that future sociocultural studies of irrigation systems should pay more attention to attributes of the physical environment as they condition organizational forms, that the role system for management of water be more carefully articulated to the political role system, and that the larger encompassing social environment (economic, political, religious) be more systematically connected to the analysis of local irrigation management systems. Hunt (1978) also has assessed the influence of two types of water management social organizations --

formal staff management units versus small informal multiplex management units[2] -- on production and distribution, using existing case materials from around the world. He finds a widespread reluctance of farmers to pay for their water and to pay for irrigation system maintenance but does not examine this phenomenon in the light of collective goods theory.

Lowdermilk, Clyma, and Early (1975) have completed a detailed case study of the physical and socioeconomic conditions along one Pakistani watercourse and discuss how farmers informally organize around brotherhood groups to distribute water. In addition, these authors describe the lack of effective linkage between these informal groups and the formal bureaucratic provincial organizations. The lack of adequate organizations is viewed as being related to low delivery efficiencies and poor irrigation practices.

Subsequently, Lowdermilk, Early, and Freeman (1978) issued a six-volume study providing data on sixteen villages encompassing forty watercourse command areas, representing the major agroclimatic zones of the Pakistan Punjab and Sind Provinces. They reported that irrigation delivery efficiencies were uniformly low across all sample watercourses -- approximately 33 percent of the water is lost per 1,000 feet of water-course. After presenting data describing the general village social structure, the key component of which is the biridari (brotherhood) kinship group, the authors report that nowhere are local organizations

---

[2]A "multiplex" management is one in which the farmer-managers are bound together by multiple and mutual sets of obligations stemming from the kinship and religious networks. There is not sufficient specialization of role obligations such that one can act autonomously as an irrigation manager independent of familial and kinship obligations.

to be found which are capable of providing the village collectivity the "public good" of an improved, reconstructed, and well-maintained water-course, even though farmers throughout the sample overwhelmingly reported that lack of water was the most important single constraint on their production.

Although the literature is largely case-study oriented, lacks overall theoretical coherence, and presents an analyst with much noncomparable data, there is consensus that irrigation technologies fundamentally condition, and are conditioned by, patterns of social organization. If we wish to comprehend successes and failures of irrigation projects, we must carefully examine the interaction between physical, economic, and social organizational variables. It is equally clear that there is little con-sensus as to how to go about the process of building a coherent conceptual framework. This is understandable because properties of different tech-nologies have not been adequately delineated; the role of social organiza-tions in helping people obtain and utilize technologies with different properties has not been sufficiently articulated. An analysis of the role of social organization in water management technology is essential. In the sections which follow, we will develop the rudiments of such an analysis.

Diagnosing the Nature of the Sociological Problem in Irrigation Water Management

Six types of technology are distinguished on two important dimensions. First, the dimension of divisibility -- a technological good is said to be divisible if it can be utilized productively in "small" units as well as large. This is to say that productivity of the good is insensitive to scale. For example, seeds, fertilizers, and pesticides are highly divisible because farmers with varying amounts of cultivatable land can utilize whatever amounts of those inputs they need. An indivisible technology, on the other hand, is one which is "lumpy" -- units of some minimum size must be purchased with no possibility of subdividing as in the case of large pieces of machinery. Interest in "fractional" technology has to do with making relatively lumpy technologies more divisible by developing mini-pumps, engines, tractors, and the like. It is worth noting that much water management technology, on the engineering side of things, tends to be relatively indivisible -- for example, aligned and lined watercourses, large water lifts, dams, power generation and transmission facilities. Agronomic technology tends, on the whole, to be highly divisible.

The dimension of <u>collective/public versus private goods</u>. A good is said to be <u>private</u> if its major benefits can be captured by the investor-owner and denied to those members of the community who do not invest in it.[3] A <u>public or collective good</u> is a good, the significant benefit of which cannot be denied to those who do not help bear the costs. For example, an improved watercourse is a collective good because individual village farmers will calculate as follows with regard to potential improvements: if one makes an investment of time, energy, and money to improve the section running through one's land and many other farmers do

---

[3]The problem of collective or public goods received its original formulation, in economic terms, at the hands of Paul Samuelson (1954). Still others (Olson, 1965; Chamberlain, 1974; Frolich and Oppenheimer, 1970) have developed extensions and critiques.

not do so, then the payoff of one's work is negligible. On the other hand, if many others for some reason undertake lining and straightening, one will still enjoy a share of the benefits -- for example, reduced water logging and salinity and increased water supply -- if one does little or nothing. Therefore, the rational calculating individual, in the absence of a disciplining organization, will choose to do nothing either way -- even assuming that he has information about potential benefits, the know-how and resources to make improvements. This situation can only be mitigated by the presence of some social organization with sanctions to control free riders so that each can be assured that one's contributions will be matched by some acceptable proportion of contribution by a sufficient number of others who benefit.[4]

These two dimensions can be combined into a six-cell table (see table 6-1):

Cell One. High divisibility of technology is combined with private goods in this cell. Although small farmers tend to lag behind large farmers in adopting these kinds of technology, smaller farmers can and do respond to economic incentives to adopt them whenever they are (1) aware of them; (2) reasonably certain of their efficacy; (3) able to secure necessary credit and technical assistance; and (4) when there is sufficient supply such that more powerful members of the community do not utilize most of what is available.

If any single irrigation-related discipline can be associated with technologies of this sector, it probably would be agronomy; the Green Revolution was centrally dependent on new technological inputs of this

---

[4] Editor's Note: The recurring Prisoner's Dilemma theme. See Hardin (forthcoming).

type. Several observers (Lowdermilk and Schmehl, 1979; Planning Commission, 1978; pp 9-10; and World Bank, n.d., p. 22) agree that the Green Revolution is now stalled, at least in Pakistan, if not also in several other countries, and that if higher plateaus of production are to be reached, technologies outside of Cell One -- for example, water management -- must be advanced and utilized in conjunction with those of Cell One.

Although technologies with the properties of Cell One are the most likely to secure relatively rapid adoption, there are substantial problems -- even here -- of getting them employed by small farmers. Yet, the economic man model is viable as a basis for understanding diffusion of technologies with Cell One properties. If technologies of this type can be demonstrated to have good cost-benefit ratios and if risks are manageable, chances are that the technologies can be diffused through the market place. The required research here is that of demonstrating technical and economic feasibility combined with sociological diffusion work having to do with communication channels, extension, and of ensuring that the market place is functioning.

Cell Two. This sector presents moderately divisible technologies of a private type. The economic man model applies here only for large farmers who have access to the capital and credit to make these moderately lumpy purchases of items such as large units of farm machinery. Also, these technologies generally require substantial amounts of land to make them productive. Therefore, normal market incentives tend to apply to larger farmers; small farmers are in no position to adopt these kinds of technology, unless they are organized collectively to do so. The central sociological problems associated with Cell Two have to do with equality

Table 6-1. Types of Irrigation Technology

Type of Good	HIGH	MEDIUM DIVISIBILITY	LOW
Private	Cell One Seeds, fertilizers, pesticides, small plows, drills.	Cell Two Large farm implements, (tractors, land scrapers, tubewells, left pumps).	Cell Three Centralized nondivisible production of private products employed as inputs into farming-irrigation operations, for example, fertilizer, machinery.
Public Collective	Cell Four Fractional cusec tubewell located to pump up seepage from watercourse. Sector of small-scale subcommunity social organization.	Cell Five Watercourse improvement (realignment, lining). Sector of social organizational man -- community scale.	Cell Six Centralized nondivisible production of large-scale collective good. Sector of public enterprise; for example, power grids, dams, barrages, major canals.

of power and income and of organizing smaller farmer operators so as to make possible their utilization of lumpy private technologies. For example, Lowdermilk (1972, p. 408) found that approximately 80 percent of all private tubewells in his Pakistan sample were owned by farmers with 25 acres or more of land and that smaller operators obtained the use of tube-wells primarily via joint ownership mechanisms which, in turn, are primar-ily structured by kinship ties. Furthermore, the data suggest that farmers with landholdings of 50 acres or more have little incentive to sell their tubewell water to smaller operators.

Cell Three. Representing a combination of technologies of low divi-sibility but of a private nature, this sector might be exemplified by lumpy centralized factories for providing agricultural inputs such as inorganic fertilizer, chemical pesticides, or agricultural machinery. On the farm output side, such large-scale private organizations might process raw farm products such as cotton, paddy rice, sugar cane, maize, or jute. At the level of any given organization, the sociological problems in this sector are those traditionally defined by industrial sociology -- how to organize the work process such that it is integrated well with needs and perceptions of the work force. The tools for investigating problems of this type are those that have been traditionally developed by industrial sociologists and social psychologists. At the level of the overall in-dustrial sector, the problems are typically those of the state's willing-ness to provide adequate incentives for operation of private industry.

Cell Four. Here one finds a combination of collective goods which are relatively divisible. Since these technologies are bundled up in small projects, it may be that smaller subunits of community (joint family, kinship groups) can undertake to supply them. Since individuals who are rational and calculating will not find it in their interest to invest in projects which produce major benefits for free riding noninvestors, some social organization structure must exist to ensure that the recipients of benefits will also pay an acceptable share. An example of this·kind of technology in the domain of on-farm water management might be the small fractional cusec" tubewell positioned halfway down a watercourse to pump seepage water back into the watercourse -- thereby benefiting upstream farmers by reducing their water logging and salinity and benefiting down-stream farmers by increasing water supplies (see figure 6-1).[5] Although private tubewells have widespread use in Pakistan -- there are presently over 200,000 -- it is no accident that they are not positioned to generate such collective benefits. The sociological problem here is how to create and sustain conditions for small-scale subcommunity organizations espec-ially in a manner that will provide for the needs of small operators.

Cell Five. This sector contains those technologies which have the attributes of moderate divisibility and of collective goods. Rational "economic man" will not invest individually in this type of technology because he will calculate as follows: (1) if any single individual should make an investment and many others do not, then the single contribution

---

[5]The benefits of upper command area reductions in water logging and salinity represent two key aspects of a collective good: (1) non-rivalness of consumption and (2) non-exclusiveness of consumption. Reductions in water logging and salinity can be enjoyed by any given farmer without re-ducing the benefit to others (non-rivalness) and there is no feasible way to deprive a non-paying free rider of the benefit (non-exclusiveness). Furthermore, in the absence of a disciplining organization, there is no way for the investors in such a tube well to exclude the free rider from enjoying the benefits of down stream increases in water supply.

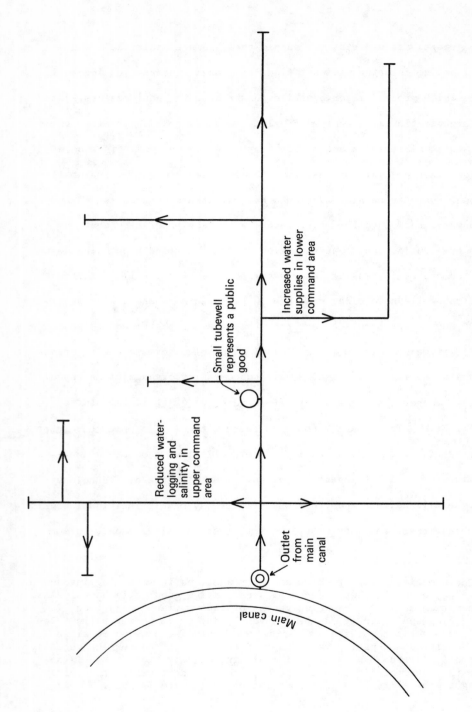

Figure 6-1. Idealized layout of main and branch watercourse system.

comes to naught; (2) if many others make the investment and he does not,
the project will be completed without his relatively negligible contribution. Therefore, the individual will tend to decide to do nothing and
avoid those technologies either way -- unless there is a strong and viable
local social organization which will provide assurance to each member that
his sacrifice for a collective good will be matched by others in some
acceptable proportion. A specific case in point has been documented in
Pakistan where farmers, highly polarized over land and water conflicts,
refused to organize to obtain and maintain a highly valued improved watercourse even though individually all agreed about the benefits these technologies would confer (Lowdermilk, Clyma, Early, 1975). Improved earthen
watercourses are important to farmers in Pakistan because unimproved ones
lose on the average about half the water which enters the watercourse
(see figure 6-1) by the time the flow reaches the farmers field inlet
(Lowdermilk, Early, and Freeman, 1978, vol. 1, p. 4). The seepage water
contributes to salinity and waterlogging. Recovering water lost in poorly
designed and maintained conveyance structures imposes high energy costs
for pumping, degrades water quality, and reduces welfare of farmerw without means to reclaim the lost water. An improved watercourse represents
a collective good because if the benefits of reduced waterlogging and
salinity and increased delivery efficiency can be provided to a few
farmers on the channel, they can be made available to others at little
or no marginal cost. Furthermore, in the absence of any disciplining
formal or informal organization, noninvestors cannot feasbily be kept from
consuming the benefits. Because earthen watercourses even when improved,
are highly vulnerable to burrowing animals and the hooves of livestock,

farmers must not only collectively organize to construct them, they must also organize to continuously maintain them. Water flowing too high will be lost through lateral seepage through holes of burrowing animals, and water flowing too low will be lost because of dead storage below field level. An earthen improved watercourse is not a robust technology; it can only perform under conditions of proper construction and careful maintenance. Yet, why should individual unorganized farmers provide the improved channel and maintain it if they cannot be certain, via the discipline of a reasonably predictable organization, that each other farmer will contribute a fair share toward construction and maintenance. As figure 6-2 indicates, the majority in a sample of Pakistani farmers report that water problems represent a greater constraint to farm production than all other farm problems combined (Lowdermilk, Early, Freeman, 1978, vol. 4, pp. 1-3). Table 6-2, constructed from figure 6-2 data displays ratios by which sample farmers selected water problems versus all other farm problems combined as the most important constraint on increasing their agricultural production. Even farmers located at head positions where presumably water supply problems are less severe, identified water over all other problems combined by a ratio of almost two to one (see table 6-2) and water problems dominate others identified by even greater ratios for sample farmers located at other watercourse positions. Yet, nowhere in sample villages was there any provision of improved water structures.

We suggest that lack of local level farmer-controlled organizations is a major constraint on the provision of this collective good which can potentially increase water supplies at a lower cost than other water sources in Pakistan (Akram and Kemper, 1976) and which addresses problems

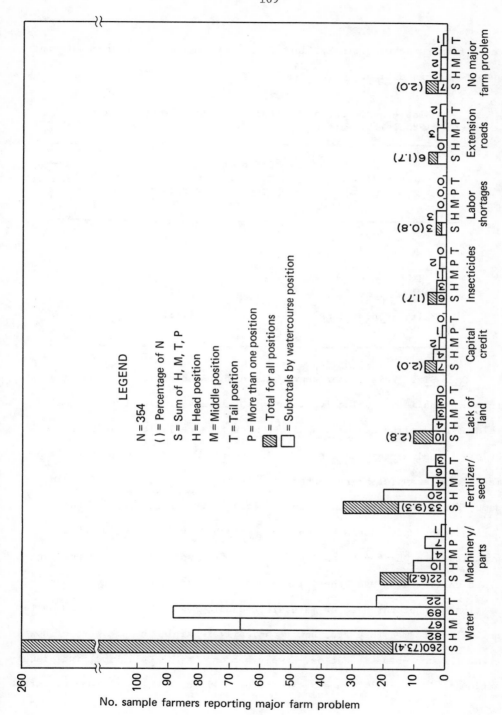

Figure 6-2. Sample farmer perception of major current farm problem by position of landholding on watercourse.

which farmers overwhelmingly identify as their most important constraint upon their production.

Table 6-2. Farmer Perception of Major Current Farm Problem by Watercourse Position

Watercourse position	Ratio of sample farmer identification of water problems as the key constraint versus all other farm problems combined.
Head	1.8:1
Middle	3.5:1
Tail	3.1:1
Multiple positions	4.1:1

Cell Six. This sector represents highly indivisible technologies that are public or collective in nature. If any single technologically related discipline can be associated with this cell, it would probably be civil engineering -- especially in the field of irrigation water management. For example, a great share of the products of civil engineering -- dams, barrages, large canals, and various control structures cannot be purchased by individuals but must be purchased by large-scale public organizations which can capture the costs from socially diverse and geographically widespread benefiting groups. Individuals or private organizations cannot purchase or maintain technologies in this sector no matter how well informed they are, how technically feasible the project, or how great the cost-benefit ratios, simply because, as in Cell Five, individual action is irrational if one's sacrifices will not be met by proportionate sacrifices of each other significant member of a region, province, or nation. The central sociological issues revolve around the analyses of large-scale bureaucracies and their linkages to local organizations.

Conclusion

In sum, it is suggested that the constituent technologies of water management can be usefully divided into six mutually exclusive categories. Each category represents a unique combination of properties which, it is asserted, affects adoption and utilization of the technologies. Each major type of technology implies a different research thrust on the part of social scientists.

In essence, if irrigation problems appear to center in Cell One, the primary problem is to work with economic analyses to ensure that the technological "packages" are attractive from a benefit-cost standpoint, and to do that sociological research which focuses on identifying and resolving problems of communication and other constraints limiting farmer awareness and interest. Also sociological work is needed to identify and overcome problems of maldistribution of power, status, and income which operate undercut small farmers' participation in an equitable market system.

If one has reason to believe that irrigation project problems are those of Cell Two, the focus can be largely economic for the larger farmer, but will have to be "social organizational" for small operators who cannot individually purchase and operate technologies too lumpy relative to their small resource base.

If one sees Cell Three irrigation project problems, the appropriate response would be to ferret out the economic problems preventing private firms from supplying necessary inputs to farmer irrigation operations or processing farm outputs. The role of sociology here would be to (1) perform industrial sociological analysis getting at questions of internal firm organization and operation which affect affect firm productivity, or (2) to examine macrorelationships between state and firm affecting the firm's incentive to produce.

If irrigation project problems are those identified in Cell Four, the problem is to design ways to create local small-scale organizations which can provide collective goods to subcommunity units. No matter how technically feasible or economically attractive, these irrigation technologies will not be provided in the absence of viable local organizations capable of disciplining potential free riders. The task of the sociologists and anthropologists is to understand existing informal organizations and to determine feasible ways of harnessing such organizations to the task of sustaining the needed technology.

If one finds that irrigation project problems center around Cell Five, the analytical problem is to design larger community level organizations to provide collective goods, not just for some sublocal unit but for an entire community command area. Sociological organizational problems here are larger-scale versions of those in Cell Four.

If one views irrigation project problems to be those in Cell Six, the problem is to sociologically examine the problems of intra and interbureaucratic relationships and the linkages of the large-scale regional or national bureaucracies to local organizations.

Irrigation projects can encounter difficulties associated with any one cell or any combination of cells. The tasks of sociological analysis must differ significantly as the diagnosis of irrigation project. Constraints shift from cell to cell. A sociological analysis of farmer "awareness" problems -- highly appropriate to the problems of Cell One -- would be insufficient and misleading if project problems are those represented by Cells Four, Five or Six.

Furthermore, any given technology -- for example, fertilizer -- might present a Cell Three problem at the production stage and a Cell One problem at the application or utilization stage. This is to say that the technologies for production of any given good may have very different attributes than the technologies for distribution or application of that same good. It falls to the sociologist, therefore, to diagnose the types of key constraints upon production in the sociotechnical system and to then devise research and action approaches appropriate to the type of technology required to relay the constraints. Centrally important types of irrigation technologies represent collective goods; provision of collective goods, in turn, requires disciplined social organization. Social organizational factors are left unanalyzed at real risk to irrigation project performance.

DISCUSSION OF SOCIOLOGICAL ANALYSIS

OF IRRIGATION WATER MANAGEMENT

Kathleen O. Jackson

Professors Freeman and Lowdermilk have undertaken an ambitious and largely uncharted venture in their sociological research-development approach to irrigation water management. Their premise that programs to improve the management of irrigation water must center on the organizational frameworks wherein decisions are made to control water is an interesting contribution to planning in this very important area of resource development. They have made a strong case that improvement of water management may not be forthcoming from planning based primarily upon physical irrigation technologies and benefit-cost ratios if there is not a corresponding analysis of the sociological factors that affect the productivity of water use.

While I find myself in general agreement with the authors' view of the importance of understanding the decisions systems responsible for water management, there are a number of points to be made about their conceptual framework. My primary concerns are twofold: first, with their application of the concept of public goods to diagnose the nature of the sociological problem in irrigation water management; and second,

with their view of the role of the organization in providing a solution
to that problem.

In developing their typology of irrigation technology, the authors
distinguish between private goods and public goods on the basis of whether
the benefits to be derived from an investment are exclusive. To the
extent that significant benefit of a good cannot be deined to those who
do not help bear the costs, that good is considered to be a public or
collective good. Most of the irrigation technologies such as improved
watercourses, tubewells, canals, and so forth, are categorized as collective in nature. Freeman and Lowdermilk argue that becuase the benefits
of investment in these technologies are nonexclusive in nature, the
rational farmer will not invest in improvements <u>unless</u> there is some
social organization with sanctions to control free riders. Two points
are germane here. First, the mere lack of willingness to invest in a
good by a potential user or beneficiary does not constitute a solid test
of a public good. An entrepreneur may be willing to invest in an irrigation system as long as he is able to profit therefrom and thus mitigate
the necessity for farmers to organize collectively. Second, the focus
upon the free rider problem leads to a value laden view of the role of
farmer participation in organization building.

If we examine two properties that are used to define the classic
public or collective good, we are led to some other issues relevant to
the management of water for irrigation. One attribute of a public good
is that additional consumption of that good by one individual does not
diminish the amount available to others. This principle, variously
referred to as "collective consumption" (Margolis, 1955), "jointness of

supply" (Olson, 1965), or "nonrivalness" (Chamberlain, 1974) raises an important set of questions about the supply of water relative to demand. One could make the argument that the use of water for irrigation purposes diminishes its use for other purposes; that the diversion of water to rural areas diminishes its supply to urban areas; that the use of water by one member of an irrigation system diminishes the amount available to others.

On the other hand, it has been observed that, "except for the most primitive cases, social action is required in order to construct the works to make water usable" (Peterson, 1966). Thus, we have a situation with water that if it is used for one purpose or by one social group, it may not be available for other purposes or other users, but some form of collective action is necessary to have a useful supply at all.[6]

As various analysts have pointed out, the study of water policy is basically a study of the resolution of conflicts over water resources use (Smith and Castle, 1964; Hartman and Seastone, 1970). This places the organizational aspects of irrigation management within the broader social and political context wherein values are translated into collective goals. A logical question is how irrigation fits into goals such as rural development or economic growth which are set at community, regional, or national levels. What mechanisms exist in a given society for the resolution of competition over limited water? Does competition for water use provide an incentive for collective action or is this phenomenon the result of a particular institutional framework? What criteria are used

---

[6]It should be noted here that multipurpose water development projects such as dams have overwhelming public goods characteristics, for example, flood control, navigation, aesthetics, and so forth.

for the allocation of water among alternative uses, how are standards
for distribution set, and what are the consequences of these choices for
the achievement of goals?

Returning to the nonexclusivity property of a collective good, it
would seem that a case could be made that the benefits derived from irrigation *may* be exclusive in the sense that quantities of water may be
parceled out among different users and may be captured by an individual
farmer to become a factor in his ability to produce. The literature in
this area suggests that the distribution of water for irrigation is highly
susceptible to manipulation and control by both institutional and technological means (Reidinger, 1974; Peterson, 1966; Smith and Castle, 1964).
Water may be provided to users by various types of rationing systems or
through the establishment of property rights which are exchangeable either
through producers and users or between users, for example, a ditch company
in which water users own stock. Further, even commonly owned water
resources may be restricted by laws and regulations setting conditions
for use (Dales, 1968).

Thus it seems that the important organizational issue is *not* whether
free riders are controllable but rather what are the consequences of distribution rules adopted by whatever agency controls them. For example,
are wealthy, large property owners favored by water rates or payment
schedules or by the attachment of use rights to size of holding or
number of irrigable acres? How flexible is the distribution system to
meet problems of scarcity or to reallocate water to meet changing social
goals? What are the legal and administrative constraints under which
an individual farmer makes planning decisions? And would changes in the
distribution system provide more or less control or predictability?

The authors' recommendation for an organization building process which includes active involvement of farmers in all its phases is reminiscent of the model of citizen participation that was very much in evidence during the 1960s' War on Poverty programs in this country. In both cases, one rationale for intensive client involvement was to "give credibility" to the organization forthcoming from that process. In this case, organizational credibility is seen as essential for solving the free rider problem and hence investment problem defined as a major obstacle to irrigation improvements. Leaving aside the issue of the intended purpose of involvement of clients in the design of programs or organizations which deliver goods from which they will presumably benefit, we are left with the very pragmatic concern of whether this approach works.

The underlying assumptions of the authors' client participation model are basically twofold: first, given the opportunity, a rational individual will participate in a decision making entity which will provide him with benefits; and second, that the fact of participation will produce a better outcome for the individual than if he did not participate. In both cases, there are theoretical and empirical grounds for dispute.

The model of farmer participation proposed by Freeman and Lowdermilk presumes a relatively high degree of commitment, interest, information, and time on the part of farmers, which can only be viewed as additional costs to them in making decisions about their farming activities. Using the same reasoning the authors applied to individual decisions to invest in technologies, it could could be argued that it would be irrational for the calculating farmer to invest his time and energy in organization

building unless everyone were compelled to do so.[7] So unless they are
proposing a compulsory system of farmer participation, we are left asking
what incentives are present for involvement? An obvious incentive would
be some degree of actual control over the resources distributed by the
decision-making body. In the absence of actual decision-making efficacy,
involvement becomes a waste of time or, as in the case of some of the
poverty programs in this country, merely a means of cooptation.

Further, the phenomenon of the active few is almost universally the
case in organizations. We cannot assume equal participation any more
than we can assume an equal distribution of societies' resources. Thus,
it would seem that the linkages between the decision-making roles in an
organization established to manage an irrigation system and the existing
power structure is a relevant concern. Insofar as management of irrigation involves rewards and sanctions, it is by its nature a highly political
activity and decision-making roles may be sought as a means of enhancing
personal status or gain.

Of equal concern is the issue of whether or not involvement by
farmers makes a difference. This is essentially an empirical question
which cannot be answered here. However, it does suggest that a study
of existing irrigation systems with varying types of client involvement,
particularly those evolved within different social and political systems,
may provide a sounder basis for this recommendation.

In closing, I would like to comment that the authors have done a com-
mendable job in developing their research-action program. Either of the

---

[7]If compulsory participation meant an increase in the size of the
decision-making group, the result would be a diminished contribution on
the part of a given individual according to the analysis provided by
Olson (1965).

objectives of this paper warrants more intensive analysis and perhaps
even separate papers to further contribute to this new field of inquiry.

References

Akram, Mohammed, and W.D. Kemper. 1976. "Watercourse Improvement:
    Methods, Costs, and Loss Rates," Appendix 6 in Annual Technical
    Report, Water Management Research Project. Submitted to the U.S.
    Agency for International Development Contract AID/ta-c-1100.
    (Fort Collins, Colorado: Colorado State University, December 31)
    pp. 91-104.

Chamberlain, John. 1974. "Provision of Collective Goods as a Function
    of Group Size, American Political Science Review vol. 6, no. 2
    (June) pp. 707-735.

Colorado State University Water Management Team. 1979. Handbook for
    Identification of Irrigated Farming System Constraints (Fort Collins,
    Colorado State University Water Management Research Project, Engi-
    neering Research Center).

Cory, Gilbert L. and Wayne Clyma. 1975. Improving Farm Water Management
    in Pakistan, Water Management Technical Report No. 37 (Fort Collins,
    Colorado State University).

Coward, E. Walter, Jr. 1976a. Irrigation Institutions and Organizations:
    An International Bibliography (Ithaca, N.Y., Department of Rural
    Sociology, Cornell University).

_____. 1976b. "Peasants and the Dilemma of Irrigation Development:
    Bureaucracy and Local Organization," paper presented to the Fourth
    World Congress of Rural Sociology, Torun, Poland, August 9-13, 1976.

_____. 1976c. "Indigenous Irrigation Institutions and Irrigation De-
    lopment in S.E. Asia: Current Knowledge and Needed Research," paper
    prepared for Symposium on Farm Water Management for the Asian
    Productivity Organization, Tokyo, September 7-11.

Dales, J.H. 1968. Pollution, Property and Prices (Toronto, Ontario,
    University of Toronto Press).

Frohlich, Norman and Joe Oppenheimer. 1970. "I Get by with a Little
    Help from My Friends," World Politics vol. 23 (October) pp. 104-120.

Gustafson, W. Eric and Richard B. Reidinger. 1971. "Delivery of Canal
    Water in North India and West Pakistan," Review of Agriculture
    (December 25) pp. A157-A162.

Hardin, Russell. "Collective Action," (unpublished paper).

Hartman, L.M. and Don Seastone. 1970. Water Transfers: Economic Efficiency and Alternative Institutions (Baltimore, Md., Johns Hopkins University Press for Resources for the Future).

Houston, Clyde E. and Michael Grehan. 1974. "A Worldwide View of Implementation of Improved Water Management," in Dean F. Peterson ed., Research Needs for On-Farm Water Management (Logan, Utah State University for U.S. AID).

Hunt, Robert C. 1978. "The Local Organization of Irrigation Systems: Policy Implications of Its Relationship to Production and Distribution," unpublished paper prepared under U.S. AID Contract AID/OTR-141-77-78 (Waltham, Mass., Department of Anthropology, Brandeis University).

_____ and Eva Hunt. 1976. "Canal Irrigation and Local Social Organization," Current Anthropology vol. 17, no. 3 (September) pp. 389-398. See also exchange of comments on pp. 398-411.

Keller, Jack, Dean F. Peterson, and H.B. Peterson. 1974. "A Strategy for Optimizing Research on Agricultural Systems Involving Water Management," in Dean F. Peterson, ed., Research Needs for On-Farm Water Management (Logan, Utah State University for U.S. AID).

Lowdermilk, Max K. 1972. "Diffusion of Dwarf Wheat Production Technology in Pakistan's Punjab," Ph.D. Dissertation, Cornell University, Ithaca, New York.

_____, Wayne Clyma, and Alan C. Early. 1975. Physical and Socio-Economic Dynamics of a Watercourse in Pakistan's Punjab: System Constraints and Farmers' Responses, Water Management Technical Report No. 42 (Fort Collins, Colo., Colorado State University).

_____, Alan C. Early, and David M. Freeman. 1978. Farm Irrigation Constraints and Farmers' Responses: Comprehensive Field Survey in Pakistan, Water Management Technical Report No. 48A-F, vols. 1-6 (Fort Collins, Colo., Colorado State University).

_____ and Willard R. Schmehl. 1979. "The Green Revolution in Pakistan," presented at the Annual Meeting of the American Society of Agronomy, Colorado State University, Fort Collins, Colo., August 5-10.

Margolis, Julius. 1955. "A Comment on the Pure Theory of Public Expenditure," Review of Economics and Statistics vol. 37, pp. 347-349.

Olson, Mancur. 1965. The Logic of Collective Action (Cambridge, Mass., Harvard University Press).

Peterson, Dean F. 1966. "Man and His Water Resource," Utah State University Thrity-Second Faculty Honor Lecture, Logan, Utah.

Planning Commission, Government of·Pakistan. 1978. <u>Research Issues
Affecting Agricultural Development Policy</u>, Report of the Indus
Basin Research Assessment Group.

Popkin, Samuel L. 1979. <u>The Rational Peasant: The Political Economy
of Rural Society in Vietnam</u> (Berkeley: University of California
Press).

Radosevich, George and Craig Kirkwood. 1975. <u>Organizational Alter-
natives to Improve On-Farm Water Management in Pakistan</u>, Water
Management Technical Report No. 36 (Fort Collins, Colo., Colorado
State University).

Reidinger, Richard B. 1974. "Institutional Rationing of Canal Water in
Northern India: Conflict Between Traditional Patterns and Modern
Needs," <u>Economic Development and Cultural Change</u> vol. 23, no. 1
(October) pp. 79-104.

Samuelson, Paul. 1954. "The Pure Theory of Public Expenditure," <u>Review
of Economics and Statistics</u> vol. 36 (November) pp. 387-389.

Smith, Stephen C. 1960. "Legal and Institutional Controls in Water
Allocation," <u>Journal of Farm Economics</u> vol. 42, no. 5 (December)
pp. 1345-1358.

Stephen, Stephen C. and Emery N. Castle. 1964. <u>Economics and Public
Policy in Water Resource Development</u> (Ames, Iowa State University
Press.

Vohra, B.B. 1974. "Implementation of Water Management Programs in
Canal Irrigated Areas," in Dean F. Peterson, ed., <u>Research Needs
for On-Farm Water Management</u> (Logan, Utah State University for
U.S. AID).

Wickham, Gekee Y. 1972. "The Sociology of Irrigation: Insights from a
Philippine Study," <u>Philippine Sociological Review</u> (January/April).

World Bank, n.d., Report No. 922a, PAK. Pakistan Special Agricultural
Sector Review, vol. 3: Annex on Water Management (Washington, D.C.,
World Bank, General Agriculture Division, South Asia Projects
Department). p. iii.

Chapter 7

THE POLITICAL ECONOMY OF AGRICULTURAL

EXTENSION SERVICES IN INDIA

Joel M. Guttman

Social scientists are devoting an increasing amount of attention to
resource allocation by the public sector in developing countries.[1] Part
of this renewed interest can be attributed to the demand for institutional
change -- a demand which increases the social value of research on how
institutions work. Whether the goal of such institutional change is
redistribution of income or increased efficiency in existing government
programs, change will clearly be more effective if it is based on an understanding of the factors promoting or inhibiting it, which are inherent
in the institutional framework of a society. In addition, such an understanding aids us in identifying which changes are demanded.

At first glance, it might appear that economists have little to
contribute to the study of instituitonal change. Economists have focused
attention on the workings of the private sector, not of the public sector.
Institutions are usually taken as given, not as phenomena to be explained.

Author's Note: The Material in this paper was drawn from a more
detailed study (Guttman, 1980). My thanks are due to Kyklos for their
permission to quote from that study.

[1]
See. for example, the work of Hayami and Ruttan (1971), and
Binswanter and Ruttan (1978).

In recent years, however, this trend has reversed itself. A "new political economy" has emerged, with an emphasis on rigorously applying the analytical tools of economics to political and social behavior.[2] But this new political economy has not been extensively used to study institutional change in developing countries. There has been little recognition that, since institutional change is change in public <u>resource allocation</u>, the tools of economics are relevant to its study.

A systematic, analytical approach, such as that of economics, can make a major contribution to our understanding of the possibilities and limitations of institutional changes. Studies of institutions and development often merely describe what occurred in past attempts at institutional change in specific settings, without comparing these experiences to those obtained in other contexts and without deriving generalizations which could guide policy. Systematic, comparative studies capable of producing such generalizations require an analytical framework which is not specific to any one setting. Economic theory, derived from the fundamental concepts of scarcity and maximizing behavior, can provide such a framework. The challenge is to enrich this extremely general theory with the appropriate cultural and institutional data so that the theory can be usefully applied to developing countries.

This study explores the potential of the new political economy as a basis for a more systematic study of institutional change. The setting is the allocation of agricultural extension services in India. The economic principles guiding this study are elementary -- they are the basic concepts of supply and demand, the concept of monopoly (or monopsony)

---

[2]For a summary and critique of this literature, see Posner (1974).

power, and the free rider problem. The application of these principles
to our setting is first discussed, and two alternative theories that
attempt to explain public resource allocation in the agricultural sectors
of developing countries are sketched. Data on the allocation of agricultural extension services in India are then used to test these two
theories.

The economic value of extension services -- whose existence is pre-
supposed by this study -- is well documented. Studies include Welch
(1975) and Huffman (1976) for the United States, Evenson and Kislev
(1975) for India, and Halim (1977) for the Philippines. In addition,
I visited some sixteen Indian villages in 1979 and found that the value
of extension services is widely recognized on the village level.

Economics of Politics in Developing Countries

The Free Rider Problem

Our economic approach to the study of politics takes the individual
member of the body politic as the unit of analysis. We are thus led to
a crucial question which is ignored by studies treating the group or
party as the unit of analysis; Why do individuals act collectively, given
their individual incentives to free ride on the efforts of others? Since
in any group of appreciable size, the individual's effect on the success
of the group is very small, and given that the individual cannot be excluded from enjoying the benefits of the group's efforts, why should he
make a substantial contribution to the collective activity? The solution
of this problem has a decisive bearing on the ability of the group to
act collectively.

There are essentially two sets of solutions to this problem. One set posits some form of coercion which overcomes free riding (see Olson, 1965). The second set postulates individual incentives deriving either from some peculiarity of the specific "collective good" being sought (for example, the collective good is produced most cheaply together with an "excludable" private good) or from matching behavior (see Guttman, 1978b) which depends critically on each individual having complete information of the contributions of other individuals (see also Olson, 1965; and Stigler, 1974). Without such peculiarities in the collective goods (in the political realm, these collective goods are policies sought by the group), and in the absence of such complete information, it is difficult to explain collective action without positing coercion.

In developing countries -- particularly in villages -- coercion is a frequent means of promoting collective action. Notwithstanding reforms which have made land ownership more equal, wealth in such villages is very unequally distributed. Such wealth can be translated into power to coerce, if the less wealthy individuals are dependent upon the relatively wealthy villagers for important commodities and services -- such as loans, access to the bureaucracy, marketing of produce, jobs, and so forth. This "dependence," of course, presupposes market power by the wealthy villagers -- either monopoly or monopsony power, as appropriate to the good in question. This market power requires (1) a small number of wealthy villagers (otherwise, the internal village market would be competitive), and (2) relative isolation from larger, regional markets. Given these prerequisites, the resulting "patron-client relationships" (to use the political scientists' term) can make the village

into a unified political bloc, serving the interests of the wealthy
villagers (whose interests may or may not coincide with those of the less
wealthy villagers).[3]

How do these principles apply to the allocation of agricultural
extension services in India? In India, as in many other developing
countries, land ownership in villages is often highly concentrated. Transportation links to major towns, moreover, are commonly sufficiently weak
that villagers are essentially isolated from regional markets. Given
these two characteristics of rural India, political leverage of the kind
discussed above would be a frequent phenomenon in Indian villages. We
can assess the validity of this view by testing the following hypothesis.

Hypothesis 1. Among villages that are relatively isolated from
regional markets, the higher the proportion of landless villagers, the
greater will be the ability of the village to obtain collective goods
such as agricultural extension services. Thus, among relatively isolated
villages, the proportion of landless farmers in the village will be
positively related to the probability of the village obtaining extension
services. As the remoteness of the village decreases, this relationship
should disappear, because landless villagers in such villages would have
alternatives to those presented by their landowners.

---

[3] As Scott (1972, p. 93) writes, "A locally dominant landlord ... is
frequently the major source of protection, of security, of employment,
of access to arable land or to education, and of food in bad times. Such
services could hardly be called more vital, and hence the demand for them
tends to be highly inelastic ... Being a monopolist, or at least
an oligopolist, for critical needs, the patron is in an ideal position
to demand compliance from those who wish to share in these scarce commodities."

This hypothesis rests on the existence of certain empirical magnitudes which we cannot observe directly; thus, the test of the hypothesis will have to be indirect in the framework of a broader regression anslysis including other predictors of the provision of extension services. One unobservable empirical magnitude is the cost of "buying" the votes, or more generally, the political support of the less wealthy villagers. If this cost is very small, wealthy villagers can buy votes even without market power. If, on the other hand, the cost is very high, then an unreasonably large amount of market power would be required. Hypothesis 1 thus presupposes an intermediate level of this cost of buying political support.

The Supply of and Demand for Agricultural Extension Services

The preceding discussion has emphasized one determinant of the demand for agricultural extension services (and, incidentally, for other collective goods): the ability of the village to act collectively. The ability to act collectively, in turn, was hypothesized to depend on the existence of political leverage or a "dependency structure" which overcomes the free rider problem. This hypothesis must now be placed in a framework which takes into account other influences on the supply and demand for extension services.

The factors determining the allocation of agricultural extension services can be viewed as affecting either the supply or the demand for such services. On the supply side, there are the relative costs of supplying services to different villages -- which may be transportation costs leads to the prediction that villages near large town and served with relatively good roads will be relatively intensively supplied with

extension services. There are also costs of conveying information within
the village. A village with a few large farmers may be more efficient
in "receiving" technical information than a village with with less concentrated landholdings, not only because these few farmers hold a relatively large fraction of the land whose yields are to be improved, but also
because they can relatively cheaply convey information to other farmers.

On the demand side, a number of variables must be considered in
addition to the dependency structure effect discussed above. These
variables include:

1. The percentage of land that is irrigated affects the receptivity
of the land to the new varieties of the crops. Thus (Hypothesis 2) villages with a relatively large percentage of irrigated land would benefit
from extension services more than other villages, and would have a relatively large demand for such services.

2. The education of farmers affects their ability to process new
information, as a number of studies now testify (see, for example, Huffman,
1976; Welch, 1973; and Halim, 1977). These studies, however, indicate
that education is a substitute for, rather than a complement to, extension
services. Thus a village with a relatively large fraction of educated
farmers would have a relatively small economic demand for extension
services. There is, however, also a political effect to be considered.
Education appears to facilitate the ability to use political systems (see
Zagoria, 1972). Thus, if we are correct in viewing the demand for extension services as operating through political channels, the effect of
education on this demand is unclear, depending on whether the political
effect or the purely economic effect is stronger. On the other hand,

if the allocation of extension services is governed by purely economic considerations, the effect of education on the provision of extension services should be negative (Hypothesis 3).

3. Economies of scale in the use of technical information were alluded to above. Thus (Hypothesis 4) villages with relatively large proportions of large farmers are predicted to be relatively well served with extension services, at least on purely economic grounds. But consideration of political effects injects some ambiguity here, as in the case of the education variable. The dependency structure discussed earlier would be expected to be strongest where there are only a few large farmers, because only then would they individually have the market power required for political leverage over smaller farmers. Thus, once political effects are taken into account, the net effect of this variable is ambiguous.

4. The quality of land affects its suitability to new varieties of crops. Since higher-quality land generally has a higher price, the provision of extension services would be expected to be relatively large where the price of land is relatively high (Hypothesis 5).

5. To the extent that capital markets are imperfect, the existence of credit facilities in the village would tend to increase the adoption of new technology and thus increase the demand for extension services. One such form of credit facility -- the cooperative -- can also serve as a fulcrum of political activity (cf. Baviskar, 1968). Thus (Hypothesis 6) the existence of a credit cooperative would be expected to be positively related to the provision of extension services.

6. A further indication of the suitability of the village to new technology is whether the village was selected for a program devised to

demonstrate the potential of that technology, such as the Intensive Agricultural Development Program (IADP). Including this categorical variable
in the analysis will "pick up" unobserved economic variables which determine the demand for extension services. Thus (<u>Hypothesis 7</u>) IADP villages
will be relatively well served with extension services.

7. The distance of a village to the nearest transportation facility
(for example, bus stand) was already mentioned as a determinant of the
cost of providing extension services to the village. Proximity to towns
may also be a substitute for extension services, as a source of technical
information. Thus the net effect of this variable is unclear. Nevertheless, it is included in the analysis as a control variable and as a check
on some alternative hypotheses to be discussed in the next section.

Summary

In the preceding discussion, two alternative models of the distribution of agricultural extension services were implicitly contrasted. One
of these, which we call the "interest group" model, postulates that the
allocation of extension services is determined by political incentives,
which may or may not coincide with economically efficient incentives.
In this model, the dependency structure effect has a clear role, and some
of the other variables in the analysis (such as education and the proportion of large farms) have ambiguous effects. In the alternative,
"efficiency" model, the allocation of extension services follows the
directives of economic efficiency, much as competitive markets in the
private sector are supposed to do under certain idealized conditions.
In this model the dependency structure has no role, and all the economic
variables except distance to transportation facilities have unambiguous
effects.

Table 7-1 summarizes the differences in the predictions of these two theories. A qualification is needed regarding the "proportion of landless villagers" (that is, the percentage of such villagers in the total). As indicated above, the costs of distributing information within a village (which are equally relevant in both theories) may be relatively small where there are a few large farmers who can serve as foci of information distribution ("opinion leaders," to use the term of Rogers, 1969), as opposed to an unconcentrated distribution of holdings. If this were the case, even the efficiency theory would predict a positive effect for the "proportion landless" variable.

This effect, moreover, would be stronger where alternative sources of information (through transportation links to nearby towns) are relatively weak. In principle, therefore, the opinion leadership phenomenon could provide an alternative explanation for a positive coefficient for the proportion of landless variable and an interaction between this variable and distance to transportation facilities. Our preference for the dependency structure argument, presented earlier, must rest on the extensive documentation of this structure in the work of sociologists and political scientists (for example, Alavi, 1971; and Beteille, 1974), as compared to the seemingly more sparse evidence for the opinion leadership effect.

A second alternative explanation of the dependency structure effect would posit that policymakers are trying to equalize income disparities, and that the villages with relatively high proportions of landless villagers tend to be relatively poor -- the disparities being greatest in relatively isolated groups of villages. The main problem with this alternative theory is that it makes no clear predictions for most of the other variables in the analysis. If the allocation of extension services behaves according to either the interest-group theory or the efficiency theory for these other variables, then the income equalizing theory loses much of its force.

Table 7-1. Predictions of the Interest Group and Efficiency Theories

Variable \ Hypothesis	Interest group theory	Efficiency theory
1. Proportion of landless villagers	+	?
2. Percentage of land irrigated	+	+
3. Education	?	−
4. Proportion of large farms	?	+
5. Price of land	+	+
6. Existence of credit facilities	+	+
7. IADP village	+	+
8. Distance to transport facilities	?	?

Note: Key to table symbols

+ As variable increases hypothesis indicates extension effort allocated to village will also increase.

− As variable increases hypothesis indicates extension effort allocated to village will decrease.

? Effect of variable on allocation of extension effort ambiguous.

Empirical Evidence

The Data Source

The data employed in this study are taken from a survey conducted in 1970-71 by the National Council of Applied Economic Research (NCAER) of India. The survey was a three-year panel study of Indian rural households; only the third year of the data was examined because of its greater accuracy. The sample was a stratified sample, in which villages selected for the IADP or an alternative (IIAP) program comprised two-thirds of the selected villages. Geographically, however, the sample covers India quite uniformly.

As with most secondary data sources, most of the variables being used only imperfectly measure the concepts in which we are interested. Thus, for example, data in the existence of other types of cooperatives than credit cooperatives would have been most useful for our purposes, but were simply unavailable. Such lacks in the data source, troublesome as they can be in testing multiple-variable theories, are typical of all empirical work on development problems.

Many of the village-level variables used in this study are specified explicitly in this household-level survey. The others -- average education of cultivators, proportions of landless, proportions of farmers in various size classes, and the overall number of households in the village -- were estimated by forming weighted averages based on the households sampled. Weighted averages were necessitated by the fact that relatively high-income households were oversampled. The relevant weights were provided by the NCAER data. For further details on the construction of these variables, see Guttman (1980).

Empirical Results

The dependent variable in the analysis is a dummy variable indicating whether the village was supplied with an "organized extension program." Such a program could consist of group demonstrations of new technology, seed package programs, and so forth. The ambiguity of this variable, and its categorical (0-1) nature, are clear drawbacks of the data source for our purposes. These drawbacks, however, should not bias our results, but rather will tend to introduce unexplained "noise" into the empirical analysis. The statistical method is probit analysis, which is particularly suitable for the analysis of categorical variables.

Two additional variables are included in the analysis, which do not distinguish between the two models. One of these is the size of the village (in number of families; population "works" equally well); a second is the proportion of cultivators in the village. Clearly, both the economic and the political payoff of serving a village is greater, the larger the agricultural sector being served. The empirical results can be conveniently organized along the lines of eight hypotheses listed in Table 7-1.

Hypothesis 1. Consistent with the interest group theory, the proportion of landless villagers is positively and significantly related to the provision of extension services, where the village is relatively far from the nearest bus stand. In contrast, where the village is relatively close to such transportation facilities, there is no significant effect. (See regressions 1 and 2 in Table 7-2). As indicated earlier, our preferred interpretation is that the dependency structure is relatively strong where a few large landowners have market power over

Table 7-2. Probit Regressions of Extension Services Dummy

	(1)	(2)	(3)	(4)
Proportion of villagers:				
With no owned land	-.249 (1.12)	-.267 (-1.23)	-.178 (-.778)	
Owning land, but < 2.5 ha				-.480 (-2.26)^d
Owning > 2.5 ha				-.606 (-2.95)^e
Who are cultivators	.549 (1.79)^d	.514 (1.72)^d	.637 (1.98)^d	1.02 (3.43)^e
With no owned land X D1^a	.499 (2.61)^e	.494 (2.62)^e	.458 (2.30)^d	
With no owned land X D2^c			-1.74 (-1.07)	
Education of cultivators	.252 (1.99)^d	.307 (2.44)^e	.352 (2.41)^e	.300 (2.38)^e
Distance to bus stand	.069 (.544)	.079 (.641)	.098 (.749)	-.137 (-1.56)
Price of irrigated land	-.189 (-1.43)	-.141 (-1.07)	-.200 (-1.48	-.200 (-1.38)
Percentage of land irrigated	.061 (1.70)^d	.078 (1.99)^d	.057 (1.55)	.082 (2.28)^d
LADP village	.626 (2.80)^e		.612 (2.69)^e	
Credit coop in village	1.11 (3.25)^e	1.17 (3.40)^e	1.05 (3.03)^e	1.16 (3.40)^e
Credit bank in village	-.120 (-.650)	-.155 (-.855)	-.153 (-.804)	-.217 (-1.19)
Factory in village D2			-.213 (-.291)	
Number of households	.220 (2.20)^d	.244 (2.47)^e	.208 (2.05)^d	.218 (2.16)^d

Table 7-2 continued.

	(1)	(2)	(3)	(4)
Constant	−1.39	−.198	−1.43	−2.13
−1 Log L (d.f.)	57.5	49.4	63.3	51.0
	(11)	(10)	(13)	(10)
Number of observations	252	252	250	252

Note: T-statistics are in parentheses. All variables in log form except dummy variables.

[a]D1 = 1 if distance to bus stand > median.

[b]D2 - 2 if factory exists in village; D2 - 1 if factory exists in nearby village.

[c]Distributed as chi-square with (d.f.) degrees of freedom.

[d]Significant at .05 level, one-tailed test.

[e]Significant at .01 level, one-tailed test.

a large number of landless farmers, and that this dependency structure solves the free rider problem which otherwise would impede the ability of the village to act collectively. Where the village is well integrated into regional markets (indicated by closeness to transportation facilities), such a dependency structure cannot exist, because local large landowners would have relatively little market power. Thus the proportion landless variable would be expected to have no effect in such villages.

A further test of this hypothesis -- and one which can distinguish it from the alternative explanation based on opinion leadership -- uses the existence of a factory in the village as a proxy for a relatively competitive labor market, which again would diminish the importance of a dependency structure.[4] Where such a factory exists, we would expect the effect of the proportion-landless variable to be relatively weak. In regression 3 in Table 7-2, the sign of the relevant interaction term is negative, as expected, but insignificantly different from zero. This statistical insignificance, however, may be due to multicollinearity between this interaction term and the factory-in-village dummy variable (included in the regression only for completeness), and also between this interaction term and the proportion-landless-distance-to-bus-stand interaction term. When the latter two variables are omitted from the regression, the interaction term of the factory-in-village dummy with the proportion landless variable rises in statistical significance (the T-statistic becomes 1.7 in absolute value).

Hypothesis 2. The coefficient of the proportion of land that is irrigated is positive, as expected by both theories, but not always statistically significant.

Hypothesis 3. Education receives consistently positive and statistically significant coefficients, contradicting the efficiency theory, which predicts negative coefficients (because education and extension have been found to be substitutes in agricultural production). These positive coefficients are consistent with the interest group theory, and would be interpreted as indications that the political effects of education outweigh the economic effects arising from the substitutability of education and extension.

Hypothesis 4. In regression 4 of Table 7-2, the proportion of landless villagers is omitted, and replaced by the proportions of landowners

------

[4]This, of course, would only be true if the factory was not owned by the local large landowners.

in two size classes, in an effort to test the hypothesis of the efficiency theory that villages with relatively large farms are relatively well provided with extension services. The results indicate that increasing the proportion of large farms would not significantly affect the proportion of extension services. This is consistent with the interest group theory, because in that theory the economic effect is counteracted by a political effect -- the diminution of the dependency structure where large farms are relatively numerous.

Hypothesis 5. The price of (irrigated) land receives negative but insignificant coefficients in the regressions, which does not support either theory. A possible explanation is that the elasticity of demand for farm products is sufficiently low on the village level to make the effect of new technology on producers' surplus (and thus on land values) negative.

Hypothesis 6. Two measures of credit facilities are included in these regressions: the existence of a credit bank and a credit cooperative in the village. As indicated in the previous section, both should receive positive coefficients according to the efficiency theory, and one would not expect either variable to be more important than the other. According to the interest group theory, the credit coop variable carries with it an additional effect, since cooperatives have been found to be foci of political activity. The results are that the two variables both receive positive coefficients, but only the credit coop variable appears to have a significant effect.

Hypothesis 7. The IADP village variable receives positive and significant effects, as predicted by both theories. In regression 2, this variable is omitted, because of an argument that this variable is, in reality, endogenous. Dropping the variable has little effect on the other variables in the analysis.

Hypothesis 8. Neither theory has a clear prediction regarding the direct effect of distance to transportation facilities. This variable, in general, does not receive significant coefficients. The positive and marginally significant coefficient in regression 4 probably results from the omission of the interaction term of distance to the bus stand with proportion of landless villagers.

Conclusions

Where the predictions of the efficiency and of the interest group theory differ, the empirical results consistently support the interest group theory. This does not imply unambiguous support for the dependency structure hypothesis; there is at least one alternative explanation of the observed effect of the proportion of landless villagers. Nevertheless, it may be worthwhile to point out some policy implications of the existence of dependency structures. One implication is that land reforms, which tend to break down such structures, may have the unintended effect of weakening the villages affected, politically, unless they are accompanied by efforts to maintain the ability of the relevant villages to act collectively. One means of accomplishing this end might be increased education, which, according to our results, appears to aid the village in the competitive political marketplace. More generally, our results imply that charges in social and economic conditions which may be caused by government programs -- have subtle effects on the ability of villages to act collectively. This, in turn, will affect the distribution and level of provision of government services to villages.

Our study also appears to have methodological implications. The fruitfulness of using an economic model to predict government behavior in a developing country has been demonstrated. Relatively simple economic and political considerations led to the formulation of hypotheses which could be confronted with empirical data. This approach promises to provide a more systematic and reliable understanding of politics and institutional change in developing countries.

References

Alavi, Hamza A. 1971. "The Politics of Dependence: A Village in West Punjab," South Asian Review vol. 4, pp. 111–128.

Baviskar, B.S. 1968. "Cooperatives and Politics," Economic and Political Weekly vol. 3, pp. 490–495.

Beteille, Andre. 1974. Studies in Agrarian Social Structure (London, Oxford University Press) p. 66.

Binswanger, Hans P. and Vernon W. Ruttan. 1978. Induced Innovation: Technology, Institutions and Development (Baltimore, Md., Johns Hopkins University Press).

Evenson, Robert and Yoav Kislev. 1975. Agricultural Research and Productivity (New Haven, Conn., Yale University Press).

Guttman, Joel. 1978a. "Interest Groups and the Demand for Agricultural Research," Journal of Political Economy vol. 86, pp. 467–484.

_____. 1978b. "Understanding Collective Action: Matching Behavior," AER Papers and Proceedings vol. 68, pp. 251–255.

_____. 1980. "Villages as Interest Groups: The Demand for Agricultural Extension Services in India," Kyklos.

Halim, Abdul. 1977. "The Economic Contribution of Schooling and Extension to Rice Production in Laguna, Philippines," Journal of Agricultural Economics and Development vol. 7, pp. 33–46.

Hayami, Yujiro and Vernon W. Ruttan. 1971. Agricultural Development: An International Perspective (Baltimore, Md., Johns Hopkins University Press).

Huffman, Wallace. 1976. "The Productive Value of Human Time in U.S. Agriculture," *American Journal of Agricultural Economics* vol. 58, I, pp. 672-283.

Olson, Mancur, Jr. 1965. *The Logic of Collective Action* (Cambridge, Mass., Harvard University Press).

Posner, Richard A. 1974. "Theories of Economic Regulation," *Bell Journal of Economics and Management Science* vol. 5, pp. 335-358.

Rogers, Everett M. 1969. *Modernization Among Peasants: The Impact of Communication* (New York, Holt, Rinehart and Winston).

Scott, James C. 1972. "Patron-Client Politics and Political Change in Southeast Asia," *American Political Science Review* vol. 66, pp. 91-113.

Stigler, George J. 1974. "Free Riders and Collective Action: An Appendix to Theories of Economic Regulation," *Bell Journal of Economics and Management Science* vol. 5, pp. 359-365.

Welch, Finis. 1973. "Returns to Scale in U.S. Agriculture," in R. Evenson and F. Welch, "Education, Information, and Efficiency," National Bureau of Economic Research, Working Paper 1.

Zagoria, Donald S. 1972. "A Note on Landlessness, Literacy, and Agrarian Communism in India," *Archives Européennes de Sociologie* vol. 13, pp. 326-334.

Chapter 8

PEASANT BEHAVIOR AND SOCIAL CHANGE --

COOPERATIVES AND INDIVIDUAL HOLDINGS

James Petras and Eugene Havens

Over the past several years the notion has been popularized that
cooperative farming is the most rational, efficient, and equitable approach
to developing agriculture in societies experiencing agrarian reforms or
other forms of structural change. The demise of traditional landlord
systems under the pressure of peasant movements has proceeded apace in a
number of societies. In the face of centuries of exploitation and deprivation, peasant-based movements have either directly taken control of large
landed estates or forced governments, through specialized agencies, to
expropriate landed property. The disintegration of traditional landholding
patterns immediately raises a basic policy question; What system of land
tenure should take its place?

Cooperative farming has been frequently proposed as the most viable
alternative. By combining resources it cuts back on the duplication of
costs, allows the enterprise to take advantage of economies of scale,
facilititates large-scale purchases, and lessens the possibility of social
inequalities, thus promoting collective in place of individual mobility
and sustaining "communitarian" values. Economic rationality (scale of

production and distribution) is supposedly combined with equity (greater social good for the greater number).

Moreover, a number of writers, anthropologists included, stress the continuity between the past precapitalist collectivity and the postreform cooperative, with the latter seen as fitting in better with the cultural-historical traditions thereby ensuring the integrity of the community as against the divisive effects of unmitigated market activities (cf. Erasmus, 1961; and Wolf, 1978). The cooperative thus serves to sustain cultural continuity and promotes social integration while augmenting the levels of production and income.

What has been lacking in a great deal of this literature is a discussion of the larger political and social context which influences the internal structure, social relations of production, and economic exchange all of which in turn determines the viability of the cooperatives and thus the attitudes of their members. The policies and social nature of the state under whose auspices the cooperatives are initiated is crucial to understanding peasant behavior.

Our thesis is that peasants are neither inherently in favor of nor against cooperative or individual holdings but will respond to either according to their own practical experiences and how these experiences affect their everyday calculations of their private interests. If peasants experience cooperatives as agencies through which they can maximize their interests, they will support and participate in them. If they experience them as exploitative or adversely affecting their private interests, they will reject them or act in such a fashion as to undermine their operation.

The Peruvian Case: From Hacienda to Cooperative

We will focus our attention on the recent experience of extensive

and widely publicized land reform and cooperativization initiated in Peru

over the past ten years. The "model" of agriculture promoted by the "re-

formist" military regime was essentially rooted in the notion that the

highland traditional latifundio and coastal plantation systems were

serious obstacles to economic development, social and regional integration,

and political participation. The Peruvian agricultural system had been

characterized by great concentrations of land in the hands of a few domes-

tic and foreign landowners, while the bulk of the rural labor force was

located in tiny plots of land (minifundistas) and Indian communities,

frequently employed as wage laborers or even held in semifeudal obligations

to the landowners.

Table 8-1. Distribution of Total Land Area, Arable Land, Permanent Cropland Natural Pastures by Size of Production Unit in 1961

Size of production unit (hectares)	Percentage of number of production units	Percentage of total land in farms
0–5 ha.	82.9	5.8
5–100 ha.	15.7	10.4
100–500 ha.	0.9	8.8
Over 500 ha.	0.5	75.0
TOTAL	100.0	100.0

Source: Peru, Direccion Nacional de Estadisticos y Censos. Primer Censo
Nacional Agropecuario (Lima, 1965).

The military coup of 1968 brought a reformist military regime with a

different vision of rural society, one which emphasized the centrality of

cooperatives in transforming the rural sector. There were three ideas which informed this vision: first was the notion that the cooperatives were part and parcel of Peru's communal past. This fit in nicely with the search for a nationalist developmental conception that claimed the necessity to adapt processes of social change to "national realities." The second idea (closely related to the first) was that the "Peruvian Revolution" (as its leaders described it) would follow a "third way" between the capitalist market of the West and the centralized collectivism of the East. The cooperative idea was seen as a means of combining features of both worlds in a way that optimized collective work and individual enterprise. The third idea that informed the cooperative vision of the Velasco regime (a nationalist-populist military government led by General Velasco who took over in a coup in 1968, and was in turn overthrown by his more conservative military colleagues in 1975) was rooted in the Catholic-humanist ideology that stressed the notion of an organic community over and against individual gain, in which leaders and followers (government and cooperative members) were bound together by a set of mutual obligations and duties. What was never clear in the ideology was who would decide the distribution of obligations and duties. And in case of conflicts between government and cooperative it was not clear who would serve as arbiter, since the divine spirit could be seen to talk in many tongues -- ranging from state technocrats interested in harnessing peasant production to industrial growth to Marxist peasant organizers encouraging peasants to keep the whole of the social product that they produced.

As the government moved beyond the expropriation of landed estates to the establishment of cooperatives, the crucial question arose as to the organization of the cooperatives. The meaning of the co-ops to the peasants, their role and experiences, were substantially determined by the structure and organization of the coops. The philosophical and vision- ary cooperatives of humanistic thought and communitary ideology were operationalized by military generals and colonels. Thus the ideology of cooperatives was presented as an abstract plan that would stand above class structure and class struggle; but the official who presided over its implementation maintained concrete and tenacious ties to the class structure and the state apparatus.

The Structure and Organization of the Cooperatives

The formative period in the establishment of the cooperatives played a decisive role in determining their long-term operation and ultimate demise. The relation between mass peasant movements and the military was crucial in this period. From the mid 1950s to the mid 1960s large-scale peasant movements developed in many parts of Peru. One indication of this mobilization was the rising number of strikes in agriculture. These movements, sometimes organized by Marxists, frequently took over estates and confronted military and police detachments dispatched to restore land- lord possession. The high point of these movements occurred in Convencion- Lares. Many officers who had witnessed the radicalization and mobilization of the peasants, and not infrequently had participated in the repression, helped form the post 1968 reformist military regime. Notwithstanding their coercive role they were cognizant of the underlying social realities, or so they thought.

A classic example of the intervention of the military in peasant up- risings was that of La Convencion-Lares. When this movement began in the late 1950s, the police were sent in to control it. However, they were

Table 8-2. Strikes in the Agricultural Sector from 1957 to 1968
Officially Recognized by the Ministry of Labor

Year	Total number of strikes in all sectors	Strikes in agriculture Number	percent
1957	161	19	11.8
1958	213	21	12.6
1959	233	31	13.3
1960	285	40	14.0
1961	341	32	9.3
1962	380	55	14.4
1963	442	58	13.7
1964	398	71	17.8
1965	397	36	9.0
1966	394	51	12.9
1967	414	77	18.5
1968	364	69	18.9

Source: Jose Mejia and Rosa Diaz, Sindicalismo y Reforma Agraria (Lima,
Instituto de Estudios Peruanos).

incapable of putting down a movement that was spreading rapidly and was
becoming more and more organized. So, the army was called on to "restore
order." This was the first time that the military became involved in a
popular movement in the interior of the country. They were able to confirm for themselves the precapitalist conditions under which the peasant
had to work and that the demands made by the peasantry were not only
justified but were directed against illegal labor conditions practiced by
the landowners. This experience convinced the more progressive elements
of the military that an agrarian reform was necessary, not only to destroy
the backwardness of a great portion of the Peruvian socioeconomic structures, but also necessary to avoid future popular uprisings (Villaneuva
1973). The success of the Convencion-Lares movement demonstrated to
the military the danger of ignoring the conditions that make a populist
movement possible.

Table 8-3. Land Redistribution in Peru, 1969-79.

	Units	Area distributed (ha.)	Beneficiaries
CAP[a] (excluding sugar)	566	2,096,069	79,354
Sugar CAP	12	128,566	27,783
Peasant Groups	798	1,585,561	43,945
Peasant Communities	408	715,850	110,971
SAIS[b]	60	2,802,435	60,930
Social Property	11	232,653	1,375
Individuals	---	542,794	31,918
TOTALS	1,855	8,103,948	356,276

Source: Direccion General de Reforma Agraria, Lima, Peru.

[a]Cooperatives Agrarias de Produccion (Agrarian Production Cooperatives).

[b]Social Interest Agrarian Societies (Included several haciendas and adjoining small producers, and day laborers in an organized community.

While there were some 356,000 beneficiaries and over half of the total cultivatable land was affected, the reform did not affect the more than 1 million landholders (that is, those holding less than 2 ha.). The origin of the cooperatives was essentially in the hands of the military. They chose the targets, the timetable, the ideas -- clearly this was a case of "reform from above." To "popularize" the idea of "cooperativiza-tion" among peasants, a mobilization agency, SINAMOS, was later established to provide political leadership and to encourage peasant participation (Caballero, 1978a; and Havens and coauthors, 1979).

The organization of the coops was essentially centralized in the military or in civilian officials under their orders (Caballero, 1978b; and Havens and coauthors, 1979). Both locally and nationally, hierarchi-cal patterns of authority, not dissimilar to those of the previous land-owners were pervasive -- even to the point where the "cooperative colonel"

who ran the farm occupied the house of the former landowner. (An apo-
cryphal story circulating in Peru talks of the colonel who, two days
after taking over the Guildermeister estates, spoke with a German accent.)
Centralized control of the management and operation of the cooperative
reflected the concern of the military that change be "ordered" and "controlled," that is, that it would not spill over and challenge their
authority by creating independent bases of social and political activity.
While the military expropriated the landowners, they did not do so to allow
the "Marxists" to take advantage of the changes to gain new adherents.
Lacking a capacity to compete politically with their Marxist rivals, the
military substituted bureaucratic-administrative measures to try to exlude
critics and to "integrate" peasants into their national development plans
through centralized power.

Within the larger scheme of development the cooperatives were es-
essentially subordinated to economic projects elaborated by a regime
primarily concerned with rapid industrial and mineral growth. The agro-
cooperative setup, apart from eliciting political support from the peasants
to the regime, was seen as providing export earnings to help finance
industiral growth and as growing inexpensive food to lower the costs of
reproducing industrial wage labor in the cities (Caballero and Alverez,
1978). According to the Legal Decree 20610 of 1972, all CAPs located in
the Departments of Ancash, Lima, and Ica were obligated to dedicate 40
percent of their cultivable lands to basic foodstuff production. These
basic foodstuffs were subject to price controls that favored the urban
consumer. By 1976, more than 50 percent of the CAPs were conforming to
this decree (see Peru, 1977, pp. 32-35). Thus the formation, organization,

and operation of the cooperatives was largely directed from above and outside the control of the peasants who were instrumentalized to serve ends which, over time, they began to find alient to their interests.

Consequences of Cooperativization

The centralized redistributive politics of the regime had far reaching effects on many levels within the reformed sector. The centralized policy making structures of the cooperatives came into conflict with the participatory ideology promoted by the regime's mobilization agencies. The new structures were viewed by the peasants as replays of the old -- merely a change of _patrones_. Decisions were taken at the top, and the peasants were mobilized to carry out the policies commanded by the new bureaucratic-technocratic elite. For example, in the case of the CAPs, the law established four groups of workers: (1) manual workers on the land, (2) manual workers in agroindustrial plants, (3) service workers, and (4) high-level managerial officials.

Although these groups vary greatly in size, the law provided that each group be given 25 percent of the membership of the governing and managing bodies (Pasara, 1971b, p. 49). Thus, the workers were coopted into participating in a system of entreprenuerial organizations dominated by technocratic leaders oriented toward productionist goals. Politically, military reformism wanted their support in its struggle against emerging urban worker struggles. Criticism and debate from below was dubbed "politicization," "counter-revolutionary," or "subsersive." Little initiative and direction was vested in the hands of the supposed beneficiaries of the land reform. In most instances only one worker was included in the Production Committee with the rest of the twelve members

being technocrats (see Caballero, 1978b). Conflicts were largely resolved
through the traditional means of government (police) intervention or
threats of work stoppage. Increasingly, "mobilized participation" came
to be experienced by the peasants as manipulation. The persistence of
suspicion and its pervasiveness among peasants eroded the trust between
government technicians and peasants, essential for the successful operation
of the cooperative. Centralized policy making undercut the positive
responses initially elicited through the redistributive measures and
recreated an alienated peasantry. Given the role of the peasant as "object"
of cooperativization rather than as the subject actively restructuring
their social role in production, it is not surprising that the peasants
came to view cooperative organization as a new form of manipulation and
subjection.

The authority of the centralized policy-making structure was further
eroded by its very inadequate administrative performance and by the substantive policies that it pursued. One could imagine circumstances in
which the coops efficiently managed and in which substantive policies
provided tangible benefits to the peasants could have at least elicited
the passive approval or acquiescence of the peasants. In fact (as was
suggested above), the bureaucratic-centralist administration was linked
to a development strategy which subordinated agricultural development to
capital accumulation in the industrial and mining sector (Havens and coauthors, 1979). Rather than being a recipient of massive government
investments, the rural sector was viewed as a means of pumping out surplus
to finance development in the urban-industrial areas. Inadequate financing of infrastructure, resource development research, and agricultural

machinery led to a pattern of "redistribution without development." Insufficient credits and poor administration and investment decisions by coop managers led to debts without expanding the productive base to repay them. Data for the IV Agricultural Zone (Huacho, Lima, and Canete) indicates that credit for the CAPs declined 52 percent in real terms from 1970 to 1975 (Peru 1977). Increases in the cost of agro-inputs and high profit taking in processing defined the unequal exchanges which reduced peasant incomes.

To defend threatened incomes, cooperative members increasingly engaged in political and social protest against the local representative of the central government in the leadership of the coops. While the costs of agricultural implements and food at retail prices shot up, the government attempted to hold back agricultural prices paid to the co-ops, putting the co-op in a cost-price scissors. This situation was further exacerbated by austerity programs dictated by the International Monetary Fund (IMF) which led to further cutbacks in public spending (especially in the financing of debt-ridden public enterprises) at a time when agricultural debts had increased, thus limiting possibilities of new lines of government credit (see Petras and Havens, 1979; and Stallings, 1978). The centralized policy-making structure sought to extract the surplus from the co-ops thus creating multiple points of conflict and opposition -- at the level of specific policies (prices, income, credits, marketing, and so forth) and at the level of structure (the overall organization of the firm). (For details see Latin American Economic Report, 1979; Caballero, 1978b; and Montoya, 1979).

Peasant Responses --
Stages in the Anticooperative Movement

The peasant co-op members' response to the government's efforts at agrarian reform and cooperativization went through three phases, each more radical than the previous: (1) policy criticism and a "reformist approach," (2) institutional attack; and (3) dismantling of the co-op and demands for individual subdivision of land. This sequence suggests that the ongoing day-to-day experience and rational calculations of the peasantry rather than any preconceived notions of "communalism" or "individualism" shaped peasant response. As a matter of fact, peasants made various efforts to correct perceived wrongs and inadequacies within the cooperatives experience before turning away from it (Guillet, 1978). Thus in each phase peasants sought to utilize the existing institutional arrangements to maximize gains, and it was only the continued and deepening losses that deepened their alienation to the point of institutional break. Tables 8-4 and 8-5 indicate how productivity was declining in the face of declining farm prices that lowered income levels, and how wages paid to members declined at the end of the period. These constituted the essence of the deepening losses the cooperative members were experiencing. The choice of the peasants to work out of the existing institutional arrangements initially was largely based on their positive assessment of the government's action in expropriating the traditional estates and plantations. Thus the initial "goodwill" of the peasants expressed in taking the "insider" approach was conditioned by the common cause which united peasants and government against big property owners. The opportunity for collaborative efforts and successful organization thus were present. The cooperative idea did not fail because of any notions of inherent distrust

Table 8-4. Agricultural Output Per Capita for Selected Crops from
1961-1977.

Selected crop	Output per year in kilogram per person		
	1961-65	1966-70	1971-77
Wheat	13.5	10.2	9.6
Rice	28.5	33.3	32.6
Potatoes	122.9	131.8	109.8
Corn	45.2	45.9	38.1
Cassava	52.9	47.4	40.8
Barley	16.4	12.5	9.7
Cotton	34.5	21.1	13.7
Sugar	73.5	60.8	60.8
Beef	6.5	5.9	5.0

Source: Jose Maria Caballero and Elena Alvarez, "Agriculture Under Import-
Substitution Industrialization: the Peruvian Case," paper presented
at Conference on Agriculture and Industrialization in Africa and Latin
America, Dakar, December 1978.

Table 8-5. Index of Real Wages on Coastal Agro-Industrial CAPs Compared
with Metropolitan Lima from 1970-1978.

Year	Wages in Coastal CAPs	Wages in Lima
1970	100	100
1971	102	110
1972	104	117
1973	106	124
1974	113	120
1975	128	119
1976	138	123
1977	111	104
1978	84	95

Source: "La Industria Azucarera al Ritmo de la Crises," Actualidad
Economica, March 13-15, 1979.

or individualism but as a result of regime policies, which in turn reflected its overall orientation toward the class structure and the organization of political power. A classic example of this process is found in the eventual dissolution by decree of the National Agricultural Confederation (CNA) (see Havens and coauthors, 1979).

State I. During the initial period, peasant opposition essentially focused on criticizing particular aspects of the cooperatives. Attacks were directed at particular government directors, advisers, and policies. Conflicts emerged over the way the administrators functioned, the way the profits were divided, the way in which advisers intervened in decisions on crop selection, planting, and so forth. (See Amat y Lean, 1979.) This criticism was directed basically at reforming the cooperative -- to make it more responsive to its members' needs (Horton, 1974). Pressure was exercised through government-sponsored mobilization organizations, the CNA, which mediated the disputes, reviewed the sources of criticism (to isolate the radicals), and kept them within the overall confines of government-sponsored programs. As the criticism mounted, and as the central government responses were found wanting, there was a tendency to withdraw from the officially sponsored activities: disillusionment preceded mass defection and active opposition. Long-term passivity was precluded by the sharp deterioration of standard of living which reactivated peasant cooperative members, but now in nonofficial roles. The channels for this reactivation were largely found in the persistence of rural union organizations which succeeded in sustaining their existence parallel to, and in many cases within, the cooperatives. Nourished by the government's heavy-handedness in managing peasant affairs within the co-op, the peasant unions began to reemerge as the defenders of peasant rights within the co-op, adapting the class struggle perspective to the change from private owners to state managers. Thus, the class-oriented peasant organization -- Confederacion de Campesinos Peruanos (CCP) -- began to grow in size and in some areas recruit members from the government controlled CNA. The CCP defended peasants' work rights, resisted payments of the agrarian debt, and demanded higher farm prices (Rainbird and Taylor, 1977).

State II. The conflicts within the co-ops between the bureaucratic leadership and the peasants deepened and extended. Debts accumulated, prices declined, strikes and protests were repressed, substantial income differences between managers and producers persisted and became transparent to all. Increasingly, the cooperatives as an institution began to be attacked and peasants began to question whether the cooperative was the most rational choice to channel their energies. While permanent workers realized income gains until 1975, their wages have steadily declined since then (Actualidad Economica, 1979). Moreover, most CAPs employed pastoral workers who did not participate in salary gains and improved work conditions. In the critical stage they would frequently protest their own wages by cultivating private plots, abandoning co-op labor responsibilities, and assigning stoop work and hand labor to seasonal workers. However, as economic conditions continued to deteriorate, seasonal workers and permanent workers began to define common interests and struggle together against cooperative managers.

Increasingly, peasant activities shifted from requests that officials be replaced to the physical ousting of unresponsive managers. Price and income policy disputes were carried over into the capital city, became

Table 8-6. Wage Differentials on Seventy-Three Production Cooperatives
in Peru Between Permanent and Seasonal Workers, 1975

Wage Rates in soles/day	Permanent workers		seasonal workers	
	number	percent	number	percent
Less than 100	2,194	19%	2,159	49%
105-150	6,711	57	2,080	47
More than 150	2,802	24	180	4
TOTAL	11,707	100%	4,419	100%

Source: Ministry of Food, Boletin Analitico no. 1 (April) 1977.

politicized and subject to national political controversy. Parties of the
Left and Center began to respond with new and more vehement attacks on
government policy. Their organizing efforts began to be well received
within the co-ops. This was clearly the transitional period for the co-
ops, meaning either a profound rectification would have to be launched
or the whole enterprise would be called into question. For just as the
peasants were turning to political and social opposition from the Left,
to serve their interests within the co-ops, they also began parallel
activity, cultivating private land and engaging in private exchanges. The
choice to move toward "privatization" and "radicalization" were both conditioned by the adverse experience with the cooperative experience.

The decision of the peasants between individual holdings and market
relations, and collective ownership depended on the capacity of the left
wing unions to demonstrate that the latter could effectively increase
their income. Given the lack of influence which the leftist peasant
unions had over the economic transactions between agriculture and the rest
of the economy, they were hardly in a position to improve the terms of

exchange. Hence, the tendency was for peasants, who already had developed ties to the market, to seek to extend these ties and to pursue a strategy of co-op subdivision and individual ownership.

State III. The institutional crises found in the cooperatives was merely a reflection of the larger institutional crises of the military regime. After eight years the nationalist-reformist Velasco regime was overthrown and replaced by a leadership oriented toward greater freedom for private enterprise and less interested in cooperative or public ownership. Further cutbacks in public spending and government efforts to destatify the economy heightened conflicts between the regime and its mobilization agencies, leading to a break. The regime sponsored peasant unions (CNA) moved closer to the Left sponsored peasant organization, the Peruvian Peasant Confederation. More fundamental changes, however, were in store, as peasant discontent could no longer be contained within the cooperative framework: widespread peasant takeovers of cooperatives were accompanied by demands for subdivision and individual holdings. Paradoxically, Left forces were drawn into this movement against cooperatives and for private holdings. The Left could not resist the peasant choice of privatization against forced and unprofitable cooperativization. The dismantling of the co-ops was thus the culmination of a series of choices that preceded from everyday experiences in which peasants measured the costs and benefits of membership and found it wanting. The left opposition was strong enough to sustain a presence in the co-op, but not strong enough to create an alternative that could resist market pressures.

While the subdivision is perceived by the peasants as a way of escaping from the confines of the co-op, it is hardly likely to provide

any durable or substantial rewards. The individual small holder faces
many of the same problems that confronted the cooperative: lack of credit,
inflationary prices for inputs, price controls on some marketable food
items, lack of access to technical assistance and farm machinery and the
extraction of surplus by commercial middlemen, transport haulers, money
lenders, and so forth. In the short-run the individual small holder may be
able to market his produce and secure a better price, avoiding the overhead
cost of sustaining an inefficient administration. If prices are too low,
they may decide to increase their personal consumption. Moreover, by
subdividing the farm they may in effect repudiate the collective debt accumulated during the co-op's operation. In the absence of formal lines of
credit, they may secure loans on crops from the informal money market.
Finally, having control over the land, they may have at their discretion
the decisions as to what and when to plant and harvest -- thus perhaps
maximizing gains according to market fluctuations. In the middle and long
run, however, the process of subdivision will lead to excessive fragmentation beyond the yield possibilities that could support an extended household. Competition among the small holders, the natural and political
advantages that accrue to some peasants will lead to the displacement
and dispossession of others. The wide dispersion of small holders will
undermine most efforts to provide credit and technical assistance. The
predominance of urban industrial, commerical, and financial elites will
ensure that agriculture will continue to "subsidize" industrial imports
and to sustain a higher standard of living. The market exchanges will
not favor the small holders -- given the asymmetrical relations between
an oligopolistic industrial-commercial and a competitive agrarian sector.

The end result will be the general deterioration of living standards accompanied by the reemergence and accentuation of rural stratification: a few peasants may become commercial farmers, the bulk will enter the large labor pool, and probably increase the indebtedness of the small holders, leading to loss of property, a return to some form of debt-peonage, or both. In the end, the possible short-term advantages accruing to the peasants from the shift from co-ops to individual holdings will evaporate.

Peasants Against Co-ops: Irrational Traditionalism or Rational Calculation?

Peasant negative responses to the co-ops were not a reflection of a "traditional way of life," blind responses to custom and prejudice. On the contrary, the Peruvian experience suggests that no such "irrationality" guided peasant behavior. Rather we have argued that the experiential base of a series of decisions ranging from positive, to critical but supportive, preceded the outright rejection of cooperatives. At each point collective choices were made that reflected the collective interests of the peasantry and which, by and large, were based on very real concrete interests -- namely, organizational autonomy, local initiative, and income. The regime's vision of a community of shared obligations and rights was not shared by the peasants. Their view of the co-op division of labor was one in which they shared all the obligations and the officials commanded all the rights. This asymmetrical relationship reproduced within peasant consciousness the them/us dichotomy, the idea of the exchange of patrones (see Guillet, 1978). This adversary relation was heightened by the gap between the rhetoric of "local autonomy" and the reality of state tutelage. Peasants "tested" government policy commitments to the co-ops in any number of issue areas: the promise of credits and the lack of them; the accumulation of debts and the lack of growth; the exhortation to produce more and the declining terms of exchange; the vision of cooperative prosperity and the reality of deteriorating living standards.

Indeed, the terms of trade became progressively more unfavorable in three manners. First, the state set the internal price of sugar and cotton based on costs of production rather than on international market prices. This had the affect of reducing end-of-year surplus that was theoretically available for distribution to the cooperative members to supplement their wages. Since 1972, end-of-year profits were almost totally exhausted after paying the interest on the agrarian debt and management costs. Thus, cooperative members were essentially dependent on wages for their sole source of income (Vega-Centeno, 1978). The second manner of affecting the terms of trade was to force the CAPs to produce basic foodstuffs on 40 percent of their lands. These were the same basic foodstuffs that were subject to internal price controls aimed at "protecting urban consumers" (Caballero and Alvarez, 1978; p. 13).

Finally, the cost of inputs for agricultural production increased dramatically in real terms. For example, from 1974 to 1979 the price of a tractor increased 590 percent; insecticides, 530 percent; and fertilizer, 180 percent. But the farm gate prices to agricultural producers held constant in real terms. Under these circumstances the collective enterprise was rejected and the peasants turned to private subdivision as the only means of grasping a piece of immediate security. During 1978, twenty-eight highland cooperatives were taken over and parceled by peasants (Havens and coauthors, 1979). In addition, military occupation was necessary to prevent seven coastal cooperatives from ousting government administrators and replacing them with peasant-controlled administrators (Latin America Economic Report, 1979).

Concluding Remarks

We have found the notions of the abstract rationality of cooperatives wanting: the primary assumption underlying this notion was that the state and the rest of the economy were geared to the logic of the operations of the agricultural cooperatives. Furthermore, the "abstract rationality" view of the cooperatives assumes rather than demonstrates the basic harmony of interests between cooperative decision makers and members, an assumption that we found was not warranted. Clearly the success or failure of co-operative production is dependent on how well its operations fit with the larger social system; the congruity between the socioeconomic nature and policy of the state and the cooperatives is one fundamental determinant of the success and failure of cooperative activities; likewise the social relations of production between producers and decision makers defines the level of conflict and compatability within the co-op. These two levels, one located at the social formation, the other at the level of the enter-prise, and the links between them shaped the commitments and choices of the rank and file. The peasants linked central bureaucratic control with local exploitation and perceived both as irrational mechanisms for maxi-mizing production and minimizing local collective and individual benefits. The evaluation of the Peruvian agrarian reform by the Institute of Peruvian Studies indicates that more than 70 percent of cooperative members felt that lack of participation in decisions about production and distribution of surplus was the biggest single failing of the cooperative reform efforts.

Indeed, this failure was given greater importance by the members interviewed than was low wages (Mejia and Matos, 1979). Initial and subsequent peasant response to cooperative organization was rooted in an instrumental view of social reality; it was not a reflection of residual precapitalist allegiances. The changes in choice and attempts to modify the institutional setting reflected the accumulation of experiences in the contemporary setting and a recognition of the constraints imposed by market exchanges, state policies, and local structures of power. The shift from cooperatives to private parcels does not reflect any primordial attachment to markets or a private property mystique. Rather it reflects the rational response of peasants seeking to discontinue the immediate constraints of an unresponsive, exploitative state whose policies fail to meet their most essential needs (that is, increased family income in the face of rampant inflation, improved schools for children, potable water, and rural electrification). The new constraints and exploitative relations confronting the individual entreprenuer may generate a new set of responses toward a system which combines decentralized collective production and the flow of substantive payoffs to co-op members.

What are the alternatives to atomized individual holdings and centralized cooperatives? The immediate answer that comes to mind is decentralized cooperatives. But the general problems remains of locating the co-op within the overall economic strategy of the government. No matter how democratic and decentralized a co-op, if state policy allocates resources, credits and investment and sets prices to the disadvantage of the co-ops, they will be in trouble. Given the interdependent nature of the economy -- between sectors -- the success of a co-op responsive to its members depends on its centrality in the overall development plans of the state. Agricultural expansion as a major component of a growth strategy presupposes direct representatives of the democratically controlled co-ops in the seats of power. The formulation of a successful co-op policy is premised on the restructuring of the centers of decision making and a shift in development priorities -- from heavy industry to industrial expansion linked to the production of inputs in agriculture and the processing of agrarian products. The economic linkage between industry and agriculture may also facilitate social alliances between wage workers and co-op members, reinforcing the reorientation of policy. The organization of industrial production linked to agriculture could allow for the physical decentralization of production: agroindustrial complexes regionally anchored would make good sense economically as well as socially and politically. Lower transport costs is one advantage and increased interaction and communication could lead to organization of agrarian and industrial producers. The increased availability of goods generated by a shift in development priorities and the autonomy of organization resulting from decentralization could begin to meet some of the criteria upon which peasants base their choices, and facilitate the acceptance of collective forms of production.

COMMENTS

Donald N. McCloskey

Petras and Havens tell us in general that Peruvian peasants do what
is good for them, not what ideology would demand. They tell us in particular that the cooperatives imposed during the 1970s by the government in
order to shortcut a political revolution and finance an industrial revolution were bad for the peasants, and therefore disintegrated into private,
capitalist firms. Rural socialism failed not because peasants were at
heart capitalists (no more than they were at heart socialists) but because
the particular form of the socialism violated the peasants' self-interest.
It was not a matter of the heart, or even the head. It was a matter of
the stomach.

The tone in which this lesson in the limits of social engineering is
couched is admirably restrained. In a departure from the usual practice,
Petras and Havens do not club us with their ideology while declaring
ideology irrelevant. They even restrain themselves in Latinate word-
making. The sober distance they maintain, however, puzzles the reader
after it charms him. He does not know exactly where Petras and Havens
stand, in what rocky port (so to speak) they anchor. He does not know,
for example, whether they agree or disagree with the various species of

reactionary socialism that comprised the cooperative movement in Peru.
Nor does he know in the end whether they affirm or deny the dominance
of private interest over ideology and other social facts. After much
hard-nosed talk of how the individual rationalty of Jose, Andres, and
Manuel determined the fate of cooperatives, the paper suddenly in its last
paragraph shifts to macrosociology and the "congruity" of one "level" of
society with another and the "nexus" between them.

I am uncertain, therefore, which of the following thoughts suggested
by the paper are novelties and which mere restatements of the paper's
themes. Arranged in what I reckon is diminishing probability that Petras
and Havens will agree with them, they are:

1. The usual arguments for cooperatives (reported by Petras and
Havens on pages 203 and 204 are not decisive. One hears similar arguments
daily for cooperative apartments, worker control of factories, buying
food directly from farmers, and so forth.

They all assume that bigger is always better, that "eliminating the
middleman" is always a good idea. To put it the other way, they all
assume that political or bureaucratic methods of making decisions -- who
shall vacuum the hallway, who shall work overtime in the factor this week,
or, in the present context, who shall get the fertilizer -- are always
superior to the market. Sometimes they are; but, as Petras and Havens
argue later in detail, sometimes they are not. The clumsiness of a large
scale can offset its economies. The co-op idea sounds obviously true.
The very old way was (brutal) coercion; the recent way was (cut throat)
competition; and the new way is (harmonious) cooperation. By the precepts
of Sesame Street economics cooperation is always and obviously better.
Well it ain't.

2. More generally, the superiority of one form of tenure over another
is not obvious. It is usually assumed (for example, page 204) that the
sequence serfdom-wage work-sharecropping-renting-owner occupation-communi-
tarian paradise is a ladder reaching from hell to heaven. But the distance
between the rungs cannot be measured by the exercise of pure reason un-
assisted by facts. Contrary to the usual thinking, there is no theorem
in logic that says that an owner-occupier is in a better condition than
a wage worker. What _can_ be asserted confidently from the easychair is that
the condition of the working class depends on its power, not on its position. If workers have the power to move between wage work and a co-op,
and if workers are rational maximizers, then it follows logically that
their condition under the two tenures (if both exist) will be the same.
Consequently, it is not the relation of workers to the means of production
(here, the tenurial form) that fixes their condition but their competitive
relationship with other workers. The logic is thus anti-Marxist; or, to
lay my cards on the table, pro-neoclassical. A lowly serf and a holder
of many other serfs; a grand and free owner-occupier of a fishing boat
competing with thousands of similar ones in an open market can starve.
But the logic, to repeat, is mere logic, not fact. Neoclassical economics
is no more a shortcut around factual difficulties than is Marxist economics.
The abstracting power of words ("wage labor" sounds bad; "cooperative"
sounds good) fools some people, though not I believe Petras and Havens,
into thinking that a study of the particular facts of the goodness or
badness of the workers' condition is unnecessary. "The materialist conception of history," wrote Engels in 1890, "has a lot of dangerous friends,
to whom it serves as an excuse for _not_ studying history." We must all

try harder to be virtuous in this, and not presume to settle great social
issues at the blackboard.

3. A minor point on the abstracting power of words brought out in
the paper is the commodity fetishism, as one might say, of planning for
development. The commodity is the thing, and the industrial commodity
the real thing. The result is that services -- that largest sector of
even a poor economy -- are ignored and agriculture is raped (page 222) for
the good of industry. The plan seems to be based in part on a misunder-
standing of economic history, that is, that in olden days the service
sector was small and that agriculture financed industry. Neither was true.

4. The main point of the paper, alas, also illustrates the problem
of word play that stops short of proof. Petras and Havens assert (page 214)
that "the ongoing day-to-day experience and rational calcuations of the
peasantry rather than any preconceived notions of 'communalism' or 'individualism' shaped peasant response" to the cooperatives. The problem
is that the paper does not in fact offer much proof for the assertion.
This is especially disappointing to me because (like all upright and
sensible people) I am predisposed to agree with it. The proofs required
are two. First, it needs to be proven that cooperatives did in fact
worsen the lot of the participating peasantry. Were the coops in fact
forced to "grow inexpensive food" for industry (page 210)? Were the losses
in fact "deepening" (page 214)? What in fact were the "market pressures"
(page 219)? What "most essential needs" (page 224) did co-ops in fact fail
to meet? And so forth. There is a high ratio of assertion to fact in
the paper, especially statistical fact, which most of these assertions
purport to be. The precise assertion that needs to be proved is that

the co-ops hurt the peasants relative to what would have taken their place, no easy task of discernment in the confusion of other events buffeting the Peruvian countryside.

Second, it needs to be proved that peasants were not guided by ideology in rejecting the co-op, but measured the "costs and benefits of membership and found it wanting" (page 219). The task is to find evidence. Most directly, did the peasants describe themselves as making such a calculation? The only evidence on this score "indicates that more than 70 percent of cooperative members felt that lack of participation in decisions ... was the biggest single failing, ... [which was] given [even] greater importance ... than was low wages" (page 224), a statement that would delight a Hegelian, as evidence of the force of ideas and feelings over material circumstances (love of participation over wages). The paper offers no indirect evidence to offset this inadvertently damaging admission. The problem of collecting the evidence is identical to that in studies of power elites in sociology, or of class interest in political science, or of the profit motive in economics. The trick in all of these is to find an instance in which ideology and rationality diverge yet rationality is chosen. Since the Peruvian peasants chose to escape from the co-ops, the evidence will only be useful as undermining a conclusion opposite to that of the paper, namely, that the peasants were ideologues. Yet undermining one's enemies is useful work; some would say the only scientific work. In any case, it requires an exhibition of the earnings inside and outside the co-ops, and a full accounting of any side benefits (such as the greater security of co-ops). This the paper does not give.

5. So far my small disagreements with Petras and Havens have been on matters of how peasants actually do behave and how one can find out.

I end by mentioning a big disagreement on a matter of how governments ought in morality to behave towards them. The disagreement slices our field in half, and in the name of candor, therefore, is worth making explicit. I gather that Petras and Havens approve of bringing or allowing politics into questions of allocation. It will not surprise them, I am sure, to find that I would like to limit the domain of politics, preferably to night watchman and lighthouse repairman. The reason for making the declaration here is obvious: the Peruvian experiment with rural cooperatives shows with spectacular clarity, to reverse the opening sentence of the paper, how irrationally, inefficiently, and inequitably politics makes economic decisions.

COMMENTS

T.N. Srinivasan

At the outset let me say that I am not a student of Peruvian economy and society. My comments, therefore, are limited to the analytical structure of the paper. I am not qualified to comment on the facts themselves, whether they are generally accepted and even if so accepted, whether they are comprehensive or selective. I will say a few words about the experience with cooperatives in India, since the Petras paper reminds me of the discussion thirty years ago in India on cooperative farming.

The main thesis of the paper is that the peasants' response to any institutional structure, such as cooperatives, depends on how well the structure serves their interests. This thesis is illustrated by the Peruvian peasants' changing attitudes toward cooperatives from criticism of <u>participar aspects</u> and <u>personalities</u> of cooperatives at the initial

stage, to questioning of cooperatives as <u>an institution</u>, and finally to
a successful agitation of dismantling of the cooperative.

At one level it is hard to dispute the thesis: it is true almost by
definition, if the interests of the peasants, or for that matter any other
member of a society, are broadly defined and the scope for action by them
is sufficiently wide. At this level there is nothing to prove, disprove,
or illustrate. At a different level, one could view cooperatives as one
among many alternative forms of organization of production and change.
Again, at this level, as Jacques Dreze, James Meade, Jaroslav Vanek, and
others have shown, under the same assumptions under which a competitive
market equilibrium would exist (meaning thereby, the absence of economies
of scale in production, externalities, and so forth) an economy in which
production is organized in labor-managed enterprises (that is, cooperatives)
that maximize value added per member-worker has the same set of equilibria
as a private enterprise competitive economy. As such, cooperatives do not
add or subtract any institutional advantage. Of course, this result is
similar to the Lange-Lerner socialist-planned economy, reaching its ends
through mimicking markets. But this literature assumes away any problems
of incentive compatibility as well as monitoring of individual effort.
While I cannot delve deeply into these issues here, it is clear that the
success or failure of any social institution will depend to a significant
extent on how well structured are the incentives for an individual to
conform to its rules, and whether it is feasible to monitor and punish
violations and if so, how expensive it would be to do so. Of course,
it will be ideal if the institution is such that its rules are self-
enforcing, in the sense that conforming to them is in the best interests

of every member, even if others to not conform. Indeed, such a feature
is claimed for atomistic competition in perfect markets.

In analyzing peasant cooperatives one would proceed in a number of
ways: starting from a philosophical point of departure, such as the
Lockean state of nature or the Rawlsian original position, one could
ask whether a cooperative would be an institution that is likely to find
favor. The answer is likely to be in the negative. Alternatively, one
could take a historical-cum-evolutionary point of view and ask whether
cooperative organization is a stage in the evolutionary process: crudely
speaking, does it fit in the scheme of those who like to speak of progress
in historical time from the horror stage of feudalism to the Nirvana of
communism through capitalism and socialism? Here again, the answer is
likely to be in the negative though I cannot be sure, not being well versed
in this theology. A third approach would be to study cooperatives that
have functioned briefly or for extended periods of time; this boils down
essentially to a question of their stability. Thus, if a cooperative came
into being, not as a voluntary association of found members, but imposed
from the top, will it nevertheless survive without generating forces
that will undermine its functioning efficiently, if not destroy it altogether? Even if the cooperative was founded as a voluntary association of
members the question of stability still arises: the rules of procedure,
decision making, sharing of costs and benefits, and the rights as well
as duties of members may (singly or collectively) not be sufficiently
conflict-free to ensure stability.

The technology of production may have significant effects on the
prospects for success or failure of a cooperative. If the technology is
such that there is not much room for varying intensities of effort by

individual workers, and if there is a fairly well defined and rigid relationship between effort and output, and if there is not much risk or
uncertainty associated with production, a cooperative organization of
production is feasible without loss of efficiency and will probably be
stable, if other conditions on decision making and sharing are appropriate.[*]
However, it is likely that in such situations the rationale for cooperatives
as a production organization may not be there. Be that as it may, agricultural technology is perhaps the least suited for cooperative production:
there is a lot of room for varying intensity of effort in almost every
agricultural operation, such as ploughing and land preparation, weeding
and manuring, and irrigating, as well as harvesting and threshing. The
influence of weather and its uncertainty on output is such that not only
are there risks of production, but also the relationship between inputs,
particularly labor input and output is not quite simple and rigid. Thus,
the free rider problem becomes very serious in an agricultural cooperative.
Equally, the rewards for individual effort and risk taking become that
much greater if the holdings are cultivated individually.

The Peruvian case appears to fit in well with the above discussion.
The cooperatives were apparently imposed; their structure of decision
making and sharing of authority were more attuned to a hierarchical
organization than a cooperative; apparently, the actual functioning of
the cooperative was inefficient so that debts were run up, eventually
leading to the collapse of the cooperative altogether. It could not
have been otherwise; even if the state policies had not been "exploitative"
as alleged by the authors that "the shift from cooperatives to private

---

[*] Editor's Note: On the importance of monitoring, see Chapter 3 by
Popkin in this volume.

parcels does not reflect any primordial attachment to markets of a private property mystique" is beside the point; neither peasants nor any other rational individual need attach any _inherent_ value to the institution of markets and private property beyond their _instrumental_ value in achieving their goals; just as the peasants agitated against cooperatives that did not deliver the goods, they would have agitated against markets and property rights, if indeed they did not serve their purpose. This is not to suggest that those who wish to endow competitive markets and private property rights with some philosophical virtues are wrong; only that, even in the absence of these virtues, the instrumental function of markets and property rights may still exist.

Let me say a few words about India. Soon after independence in 1947 there was extensive discussion about cooperative farming in the context of land reforms. But the fervor for land reforms and cooperative farming cooled down. The Indian experience with other cooperatives in extending agricultural credit, marketing, distribution of fertilizers, and so forth has not been very happy. The cooperatives were often exploited by the more powerful large landholders for their own ends. Perhaps the successful cooperatives and communes in agriculture such as the Israeli kibbutzim or moshavim owe their success more to their ideology than to any other economic factor. Indeed, the newspaper reports emanating from China of the peasants' dissatisfaction with communes confirm that once the ideological fervor begins to wear off, the reality of private cost and benefit calculations take over.

Petras refers to "debt peonage," a phenomenon that is called "bonded labor" in the Indian literature. A bonded labor contract between a laborer and his landlord is a way of linking credit and labor transactions that serves the interests of both parties, in the absence of a smoothly function- ing credit market and a pawnable collateral other than labor on the part of the worker. It is too facile to attribute some vague notions of exploita- tion to such arrangements without a deeper study of the alternative forms of contracts available to the parties.

References

Actualidad Economica. 1979. "La Industria Azucarera al Ritmo de la Crises," Actualidad Economica (March 13-15).

Amat y Leon, Carlos. 1979. Estructura y Niveles de Ingresos Familiares en el Peru (Gobierno del Peru, Ministerio de Economia y Finanzas).

Caballero, Jose Maria. 1978a. "Los eventuales en las cooperatives costenas peruanas un modelo analitico," Economia (Lima) no. 2 (Agosto).

_____. 1978b. "La Reforma Agraria y Mas Alla: del fracaso del modelo agrarlo y del regimen militar," Critica Andina (Cuzco) no. 2, pp. 23-53.

Caballero, Jose Maria and Elena Alvarez. 1978. "Agriculture Under Import-Substitution Industrialization: The Peruvian Case," paper presented at Conference on Agriculture and Industrialization in Africa and Latin America, Dakar, December.

Erasmus, Charles. 1961. Man Takes Control (Detroit, Bobbs-Merrill).

Guillet, D. 1978. "Peasant Participation in a Peruvian Agrarian Reform Cooperative," Journal of Rural Cooperation vol. 6, no. 1, pp. 21-35.

Havens, A. Eugene and coauthors. 1979. Class Relations and Peru's Agrarian Reform (Madison, Wis., Center for Research on Politics and Society, mimeo).

Horton, Douglas. 1974. "Land Reform and Reform Enterprises in Peru" (Madison, Wis., Land Tenure Center, University of Wisconsin).

Latin America Economic Report. 1979. (July 29) p. 196.

Mejia, Jose and Rosa Diaz. 1975. Sindicalismo y Reforma Agraria (Lima, Instituto de Estudios Peruanos).

_____ and Jose Matos Mar. 1979. El Fracaso de la Reforma Agraria (Lima, Caretas).

Montoya, Rodrigo. 1979. "Changes in Rural Class Structure Under the Peruvian Agrarian Reform," Latin American Perspectives vol. 5, no. 4, pp. 113-127.

Pasara, Luis. 1971a. "Un ano de vigencia de la ley de Reforma Agraria," Derecho (Poutificia Universidad Catolica del Peru) no. 24, pp. 104-131.

_____. 1971b. "The Vicissitudes of a Labor Reform," CERES: FAO Review vol. 4, no. 5 (Sep.-Oct.) pp. 47-51.

Peru. 1977. Ministerio de Alimentacion, Boletin Analitoco no. 1.

Petras, James and A. Eugene Havens. 1979. "Peru: Economic Crises and Class Confrontation," Monthly Review vol. 30, no. 9 (February) pp. 25-42.

Rainbird, Helen and Lewis Taylor. 1977. "Relations of Production or Relations of Exploitation: A Re-Analysis of Andean Haciendas," Bulletin of the Society for Latin American Studies (U.K.) no. 27 (November) pp. 50-67.

Stallings, Barbara. 1978. "Peru and the Banks," NACLA Report on Public Debt (August).

Villaneuva, Victor. 1973. Ejercita Peruano (Lima, Editorial Juan Mejia Baca).

Vega-Centeno, Cecilia. 1978. "Comparacion de los Precios Agropecuarios del Peru con los del Area Andina 1970-1976." Pontificia Universidad Catolica del Peru: Departamento de Economica.

Wolf, Eric. 1978. "Aspects of Group Relations in a Complex Society: Mexico," American Anthropologist no. 58, pp. 1065-1078.

Chapter 9

THREE CASES OF INDUCED INSTITUTIONAL INNOVATION

Vernon W. Ruttan

The interpretation of technical and institutional change as endogenous rather than exogenous to the economic system is a relatively new development in economic thought. In a book published in the early 1970s, Yujiro Hayami and I extended and tested the theory of induced technical change against the history of agricultural development in the United States and Japan (Hayami and Ruttan, 1971). We demonstrated that in both countries technical change in agriculture had been induced along an efficient path consistent with resource endowments and relative factor prices.

The fact that much of technical change in agriculture in the two countries was produced by public sector institutions -- state (or prefect- oral) and federal (or national) agricultural experiment stations -- which obtain their resources in the political marketplace and allocate their resources through bureaucratic mechanisms, turned our attention to the problem of institutional innovation. In a more recent book, Hans Binswanger and I, along with several other colleagues, have further refined and tested

Author's Note: I am indebted to David Feeny, Richard Grabowski, James Roumasset, Clifford Russell, Theodore W. Schultz, G. Edward Schuh, and Vasant Sukhatme for comments and suggestions on an earlier draft of this paper.

the theory of induced institutional innovation that had been suggested in the Hayami-Ruttan book.

One purpose of this chapter is to present a relatively concise introduction to the theory of induced institutional innovation. A second purpose is to use the theory to interpret the process of institutional change. This second objective is accomplished in three case studies.

Institutional Innovation

A distinction is often made between institutions and organizations. Institutions are usually defined as the behavioral rules that govern patterns of action and relationships. Organizations are the decision-making units -- families, firms, bureaus -- that exercise control of resources. This appears to be a distinction without a difference. What an organization, a household, or a firm, for example, accepts as an externally given behavioral rule, is the product of tradition or decision by another organization -- a nation's court system, or the practices of organized labor relations for example.[1] In my work on institutional innovation, I have found it useful to define the concept of institution broadly to include that or organization. The term _institutional innovation_ is used to refer to change in the actual or potential performance of existing or new organizations; in the relationship between an organization and its

---

[1] According to Knight (1952, p. 51) the term 'institution' has two meanings ... One type ... may be said to be created by the 'invisible hand.' The extreme example is language, in the growth and changes of which deliberate action hardly figures; ... law is in varving ... degree of the same kind. The other type is of course, the deliberately made, of which our Federal Reserve System and this (American Economics) Association are examples. With age, the second type tends to approximate the first."

environment; or in the behavioral rules that govern the patterns of action and relationships in the organization's environment.[2]

This definition is intended to be sufficiently comprehensive, with reference to institutional innovation in agricultural development for example, to include changes in the market and nonmarket institutions which govern product and factor market relationships, ranging from the organized commodity market institutions to the patron-client relationships which often characterized exchange in traditional societies. It is also intended to include changes in public and private sector organizations designed to discover and disseminate new knowledge to farmers; to supply inputs such as water, fertilizer, and credit; or to modify market behavior through price support, procurement, or regulation. It would encompass changes which occur as a result of the cumulative effect of the private decisions of individuals, with respect to fertility behavior or migration for example, as well as those which occur as a result of group action designed to modify public decision-making processes.

Sources of Demand for Institutional Innovation

The demand for institutional innovation may arise out of the changes in relative factor endowments and relative factor prices associated with development. North and Thomas (1970, 1973) have attempted to explain the economic growth of Western Europe between 900 and 1700 primarily in terms of changes in the institutions which govern property rights. These institutional changes were, in their view, induced by the pressure of

---

[2]This definition is broader than that employed by Veblen but is consistent with that employed by Commons (1950, p.61). The definition used here encompasses the classification system employed by David and North (1971, p.9).

population against increasingly scarce resource endowments. Schultz (1968),
focusing on more recent economic history, has identified the rising economic
value of man during the process of economic development as the primary
source of institutional change. The suggestion that changing resource en-
downments mediated through changing factor price ratios act to induce
institutional innovation is, as we will show later in this chapter, consistent with considerable experience in contemporary developing countries.

The partitioning of the new income streams that result from the efficiency gains associated with technical change or improvements in institutional performance, represent a second major source of institutional
innovation. In a classical or neoclassical world, unencumbered by the use
of political resources to achieve economic objectives, the new income
streams generated by technical change would be distributed to factors
according to the Ricardian model of distribution. The gains would flow
to owners of the factors that are characterized by relatively inelastic
supply functions. It is readily perceived that the primary function served
by the institutions which direct the new income streams to the suppliers
of inelastic factors -- the factors that act as a constraint on growth
rather than as a source of growth -- is to assure their claim on the
social product.

As a result, advances in technology can be expected to set in motion
attempts by factory owners, social classes, and economic sectors to organize and initiate collective action for the purpose of redefining property
rights or to change the behavior of market institutions so as to modify
the partitioning of the new income streams (Krueger, 1974). Much of the
history of farm price support legislation in the United States, from the

mid-1920s to the present, can be interpreted as a struggle between agricultural producers and the rest of society to determine the partitioning of the new income streams that have resulted from technical progress in agriculture.

In the perspective outlined above, the changes in the factor endowments and factor prices arising out of economic growth and the new income streams arising out of technical change represent important sources of demand for institutional change. The demand for institutional change may also shift as a result of changes in cultural endowments. Even under conditions of unchanging demand, however, institutional change may arise out of improvements in the capacity of a society to supply institutional innovations, that is, as a result of factors which reduce the cost of institutional change.

Sources of Supply of Institutional Change

The issue of the supply of institutional innovation has not been adequately addressed by either the institutionalist or analytical schools in economics. The older institutional tradition treated institutional change as primarily dependent on technical change.[3] Within modern analytical economics, there is a tendency to either abstract from institutional change,[4] or to treat institutional change as if it were exogenous

---

[3]In the work of Veblen and Ayres: "It was the ... dialectical struggle and conflict between dynamic technology and static institutionalism which caused economic and political institutions slowly to be displaced and replaced, and systems of economic organization to undergo historical change and adjustment," (Zingler, 1974, p. 331). See also Seckler (1975, p. 61).

[4]According to Samuelson (1948, pp. 221-222): "The auxiliary constraints imposed upon the variables are not themselves the proper subject of welfare economics, but must be taken as given." For a critique of the failure of general equilibrium theory to incorporate institutional change, see Shubik (1976).

to the economic system.[5] Neither North and Thomas (1970, 1973) or Schultz (1968) on whom we drew for insight on the demand for institutional change, attempted to suggest a theory of the supply of institutional change.

It seems reasonable to hypothesize a close analogy between the supply of institutional change and the supply of technical change. Just as the supply curve for technical change shifts to the right as a result of advances in knowledge in science and technology, the supply curve for institutional change shifts to the right as a result of advances in knowledge in the social sciences and related professions (law, administration, social service, and planning). In the real world, property rights are costly to enforce, market exchange consumes resources, and information is scarce. Advances in knowledge in the social sciences and professions should result in a reduction in the cost of institutional change just as advances in knowledge in the natural sciences and engineering have reduced the cost of technical change.

For example, research leading to quantification of commodity supply and demand relationships can be expected to contribute toward more efficient functioning of supply management, food procurement, and food distribution programs. Research on the social and psychological factors affecting the diffusion of new technology is expected to lead to more effective performance by agricultural credit and extension services, or to more effective

---

[5]The approach to institutional innovation that is characteristic of much of the reform or planning tradition in economics is illustrated by Lerner (19744, p. 6): "In this study ... we shall assume a government that wishes to run society in the general social interest and is strong enough to override the opposition afforded by any sectional interest." This point has been made even more succinctly by Horowitz (1972, p. 49): "In the planning ideology, all planning is done by a dedicated development-oriented elite supported by loyal, self-sacrificing masses."

organization and implementation of commodity production campaigns. Research on the effects of alternative land tenure institutions or on the organization and management of group activities in agricultural production is expected to lead to institutional innovations and, in turn, to greater equity in access to political and economic resources and to greater productivity in the generation and utilization of resources in rural areas.

This is not to argue that institutional change is entirely, or even primarily, dependent on formal research leading to new knowledge in the social sciences and professions. Technical change was not delayed until research in the natural sciences and technology became institutionalized. Similarly, institutional change may occur as a result of the exercise of innovative effort by politicians, bureaucrats, entrepreneurs, and others, as they conduct their normal daily activities. The timing or pace of institutional innovation may be influenced by external contact or internal stress. If we were satisfied with the slow pace of technical and institutional change which characterizes most of trial and error, there would be no need to institutionalize research capacity in either the natural or the social sciences.

Toward a Theory of Induced Institutional Change

The relationship between technical and institutional change has represented a continuous source of concern to economists and other social scientists interested in the historic and institutional dimensions of development. There has been a persistent dualism in much of this work -- with institutional change regarded as being primarily dependent on technological change or technological regarded as being primarily dependent on institutional change (Binswanger and Ruttan, 1978, pp. 328-333). Argument

about the priority between technical and institutional change is unproductive. Technical change and institutional change are highly interdependent
and must be analyzed within the context of interdependence.

The sources of demand for technical and institutional change are
essentially similar. A rise in the price (or scarcity) of labor relative
to other factors induces technical changes designed to permit the substitution of capital for labor and, at the same time, induces institutional
changes designed to enhance the productive capacity of the human agent
and the control by the worker of the conditions of his employment. A rise
in the price (or scarcity) of land (or natural resources) induces technical
changes designed to release the constraints on production resulting from
the inelastic supply of land and, at the same time, induces institutional
changes leading to greater precision in the definition and in the allocation
of property rights in land.

The new income streams generated by technical change and by gains in
institutional efficiency induce changes in the relative demand for products
and open up new and more profitable opportunities for product innovations,
leading to greater diversity in consumption patterns. And the new income
streams generated by either technical or institutional change induce further
institutional changes desigend to modify the manner in which the new income
streams are partitioned among factor owners and to alter the distribution
of income among individuals and classes.

Shifts in the supply of superior techniques and institutions are also
generated by similar forces. The cost of the new income streams generated
by technical change are reduced by advances in knowledge in science and
technology. The cost of the new income streams generated by gains in

institutional efficiency, including gains in efficiency in conflict resolution, are reduced by advances in knowledge in the social sciences and
related professions.

The significance of the proposed theory of institutional change is
that it suggests an economic theory of induced institutional change that
is capable of generating testable hypotheses regarding (1) alternative
paths of institutional change over time for a particular society, and (2)
divergent patterns of institutional change among countries at a particular
time. It is possible to build on this model to develop a theory of induced institutional change that is not only explanatory, in the sense
that the present is explained in terms of the past, but is capable of
generating testable hypotheses regarding the future direction of institutional change, applicable in social science research to achieve more
effective institutional performance and more rapid institutional innovation.

The induced institutional innovation hypothesis implies a strong
demand for clarification of the conceptual relationships among resource
endowments, cultural endowments, technological change and institutional
change as they bear on the processes of development (Figure 9-1). It also
calls for the careful testing of those relationships against both historic and contemporary experience. In the induced innovation literature,
only the relationships among resource endowments, technical change and
institutional change have received significant attention.

The methodology that will be appropriate in testing the induced
institutional change hypothesis is not yet as rigorous as the rather
straightforward econometric tests that have confined the robustness of
the induced technical change hypothesis (Hayami and Ruttan, 1971;

Binswanger and Ruttan, 1978). Case studies will represent an important
methodological approach.

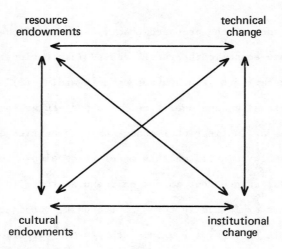

Figure 9-1. Interrelationship between resource endowments, technical
change, and institutional change.

The Impact of Higher Yields and Population Pressure on Land
Tenure and Labor Relationships: A Case from the Philippines

In this first case, I draw on the work of Kikuchi and Hayami (forthcoming) to examine the effects of increases in rice yields and population
pressure on land tenure and labor relationships in a Philippine village.
The study is unique in that it is based on a rigorous analysis of microeconomic data over a period of about twenty years.

Between 1956 and 1976, rice production per hectare in the study
village rose dramatically, from 2,529 to 6,714 kilograms (kg) per hectare
(ha) per year. This was due to two technical innovations. In 1958, the
national irrigation system was extended to the village. This permitted
double-cropping to replace single-cropping, thereby doubling the annual
production per hectare of rice land. The second major technical change

was the introduction in the late 1960s of the modern, high-yielding Green
Revolution rice varieties. The diffusion of modern varieties has been
accompanied by increased use of fertilizer and pesticides and by the
adoption of improved cultural practices such as straight-row planting
and intensive weeding.

Population growth in the village has also been rapid. Between
1966 and 1976, the number of households rose from 66 to 109, and the
population rose from 383 to 464. The number of landless households increased from 20 to 54. In 1976 half of the households in the village
owned no lnad of any kind, even houseplots. The average farm size declined
from 2.3 to 2.0 ha.

The land is farmed primarily by tenants. In 1976 only 1.7 ha of the
108 ha of cropland in the village were owned by village residents. Traditionally, share tenancy was the most common form of tenure. In both 1956
and 1966, 70 percent of the land was farmed under share tenure arrangements.
In 1963, a new agricultural land reform code, designed to break the political power of the traditional landed elite to provide greater incentives
to peasant producers of basic food crops, was passed.[6] A major feature of
the new legislation was an arrangement that permitted tenants to initiate

------

[6] Kikuchi and Hayami treat the passage and implementation of the Land
Reform Code of 1963 as exogenous to the economy of the village which they
have studied. I have interpreted the land reform of the 1960s as the
result of efforts by an emerging industrial elite to simultaneously break
the political power of the more conservative land-owning elite and to provide incentives to peasant producers to respond to the rapid growth in
demand for marketable surpluses of wage goods, primarily rice and maize,
needed to sustain rapid urban industrial development. Thus, the Land
Reform Code can be viewed as an institutional innovation designed to
facilitate realization of the opportunities for economic growth that could
be realized through rapid urban industrial development (Ruttan, 1969,
1974).

a shift from share tenure to leasehold, with rent under the leasehold set
at 25 percent of the average yield for the previous three years. Implementation of the code between the mid 1960s and the mid 1970s resulted in
a decline in the percentage farmed under share tenure to 30 percent.

The Emergence of Subleasing

The shift from share tenure to lease tenure was not, however, the only
change in tenure relationships that occurred between 1966 and 1976. There
was a sharp increase in the number of plots farmed under subtenancy arrangements. The number increased from one in 1956, to five in 1966, and
sixteen 1976. Subtenancy is illegal under the land reform code, and the
subtenancy arrangements are usually made without the formal consent of the
landowner. All cases of subtenancy was on land farmed under a leasehold
arrangement. The most common subtenancy arrangement was fifty-fifty sharing
of costs and output.

Kikuchi and Hayami (forthcoming) argue that a necessary condition for
the emergency of such a subtenancy system is that the rent paid to landlords
under the leasehold arrangement is below the equilibrium rent -- the level
which would reflect both the higher yields of rice obtained with the new
technology and the lower wage rates implied by the increase in population
pressure against the land. They note that it has been difficult for landlords to increase rental rates under the leasehold legislation. The
result, they hypothesize, is that the leasehold tenants are able to sub-
lease the land at something near the equilibrium rental rate and thus share
the economic rent with the landowners. The difference between the rent
they receive from their subtenants and the rent they pay their landlord
is the rental value of the leasehold.

To test this hypothesis, the authors used market prices to compute market values to the unpaid factor inputs (labor and land) for different tenure arrangements during the 1976 wet season. The results indicate that the share-to-land was lowest and the operators' surplus was the highest for the land under leasehold tenancy. In contrast, the share-to-land was the highest and no surplus was left for the operator who cultivated the land under subtenancy arrangement (Table 9-1). Indeed, the share-to-land when the land was farmed under subtenancy was very close to the sum of the share-to-land plus the operators' surplus under the other tenure arrangement. The results are consistent with the hypothesis. A substantial portion of the economic rent was captured by the leasehold tenants in the form of operators' surplus. On the land farmed under a subtenancy arrangement, the rent was shared between the leaseholder and the landlord. It is interesting to note that a number of leaseholders have taken advantage of the situation to capitalize the rental value of their leaseholds by selling their tenancy titles to other leases.

Emergence of the "Gama" System of Labor Contract

A second institutional change, induced by higher yields and the increase in population pressure, has been the emergence of a new pattern of labor-employer relationship between farm operators and landless workers.

Traditionally, laborers who participated in the harvesting and threshing activity received a one-sixth share of the paddy (rough rice) harvest (hunusan). By 1976, most of the farmers (83 percent) had adopted a system in which participation in the harvesting operation was limited to workers who performed the weeding operation without receiving wages (gama).

Table 9-1. Factor Shares of Rice Output Per Hectare, 1976 Wet Season
(kilograms per hectare)

	Number of plots	Area (ha)	Rice output	Current inputs	Factor Shares[a]					
					Land			Labor	Capital[b]	Operators' surplus
					Landowner	Subtenancy	Total			
Leasehold land	23	45.8	2,889 (100.0)	657 (22.7)	567 (19.6)	0 (0)	567 (19.6)	918 (31.8)	337 (11.7)	410 (14.2)
Share tenancy land	15	22.2	2,749 (100.0)	697 (25.3)	698 (25.4)	0 (0)	698 (25.4)	850 (30.9)	288 (10.5)	216 (7.9)
Subtenancy land	8	6.1	3,447 (100.0)	801 (23.2)	504 (14.6)	801[c] (23.2)	1,305 (37.8)	1,008 (29.3)	346 (10.1)	-13 (-0.4)

[a]Percentage shares are shown in parentheses

[b]Sum of irrigation fee and paid and imputed rentals or both, of carabao, tractor, and other machines.

[c]Rents to subleasors in the case of pledged plots are imputed by applying the interest rate of 40 percent per crop season (a mode in the interest rate distribution in the village).

Kikuchi and Hayami (forthcoming) interpret the emergence of the gama system as an institutional innovation designed to reduce the wage rate for harvesting to a level equal to the marginal productivity of labor. In the 1950s, when the rice yield per hectare was low and labor was less abundant, the one-sixth share may have approximated an equilibrium wage level. They hypothesized that with the higher yields and the more abundant supply of labor, a one-sixth share would undoubtedly be larger than the marginal product of labor in the harvesting operation. And they suggest that the gama innovation was introduced with less social friction than a direct reduction in the harvest share.

To test the hypothesis that the gama system was adopted rapidly primarily because it represented an institutional innovation that permitted farm operators to equate the harvesters' share of output to the marginal productivity of labor, imputed wage costs were compared with the actual harvesters' shares (Table 9-2). The results indicate a close agreement between the imputed wages and the actual harvesters' shares and are consistent with the hypothesis.

The authors conclude that in the case of changes in rental and labor relationships, the changes in insitutional arrangements governing the use of production factors were induced when disequilibria between the marginal returns and the marginal costs of factor inputs occurred as a result of changes in factor endowments and technical change. The direction of institutional change was, therefore, toward resolution of a new equilibria in factor markets.

The Kikuchi and Hayami study is particularly significant in view of the controversy that has surrounded the changes in harvesting institutions,

Table 9-2. Comparison Between the Imputed Value of Harvesters' Share and the Imputed Cost of Gama Labor

	Based on employers' data	Based on employees' data
No. of working days of Gama labor (days/ha)[a]		
Weeding	20.9	18.3
Harvesting/threshing	33.6	33.6
Imputed cost of Gama labor (P/ha)[b]		
Weeding	167.2	146.4
Harvesting/threshing	369.6	369.6
(1) Total	536.8	516.0
Actual Share of Harvesters:		
in kind (kg/ha)[c]	504.0	549.0
(2) Imputed value (P/ha)[d]	504.0	549.0
(2) – (1)	–32.8	33.0

[a] includes labor of family members who worked as Gama laborers.

[b] Imputation using market wage rates (daily wage – P8.0 for weeding, P11.0 for harvesting.

[c] One-sixth of output per hectare.

[d] Imputation using market prices (1 kg – P1).

not only in the Philippines, but in other areas in Asia in recent years. The explanations that have been offered in much of the literature rest on a political interpretation of power relationships among social classes at the village level (Collier, Wiradi, and Soentoro, 1973; Collier, Soentoro, Wiradi, and Makali, 1974). The Kikuchi and Hayami study, in the Philippines and a related study by Hayami and Hafid (1979) in Indonesia suggest an economic interpretation of institutional change consistent with the induced innovation hypothesis.

The Impact of Changing Factor Prices on Property Rights in Man and Land: The Case of Thailand

In this second case, I draw on the work of Feeny (1976, 1979) to illustrate the effect of changing factor prices on the evolution of property rights in man and land.

Before Thailand was opened up to extensive international trade in the 1850s, the Thai economy was characterized by a high land/man ratio. Real wages were relatively high. Control of manpower formed the basis of economic political and social power. Commoners were classified according to their labor obligations to the king and nobility (nai):

- slaves: primarily debt slaves or war capits

- phrai luang: required to provide three months of corvee labor or an annual fee to the king

- phrai som: required to provide corvee labor to a patron, usually nobility or an official of the king

- phrai suai: required to make payments to the king in kind, in lieu of labor services.

In the 1850s, slaves accounted for approximately 25 percent of the population. The law recognized a wide gradation in the degree of property rights and the control that a patron or owner could exercise over the

the labor of the slaves, depending primarily on whether they had been sold at the legally regulated price. Slaves acquired at less than the full price could redeem themselves, or be redeemed by their families or former owners, by paying off the debt. On balance, slavery probably served more as a form of collateral on loans, as a way of "mortgaging" future earning capacity, than as a means of defining full control over labor services.

Property rights in land in the mid-nineteenth century were not well defined. Payment of taxes on a piece of land as well as the act of clearing and developing land gave the cultivator the right to retain the land, sell it, or pass it on to heirs. But rights to an area of land were lost if the land was not cultivated for three consecutive years. Acceptance of land as valid collateral on a loan was uncommon.

Between the 1850s and World War I, Thailand experienced rapid growth in commodity exports (Table 9-3) including rice, tin, teak, and rubber. Imports of petroleum products, textiles, gunny sacks, capital goods, and other manufactured products also grew quickly. Real wages, calculated in terms of the number of kilograms of rice that could be bought with a day's labor, declined as the price of rice rose under the stimulus of export demand. Nonagricultural employment in the villages declined as a result of competition between traditional village industry and the imports of textiles and other manufactured items. Land prices rose relative to the price of labor. Land rent, calculated in terms of rice per unit of land, also rose. The interest of many of Bangkok nobility and officials turned to land investment and the development of irrigation and drainage systems designed to improve rice production.

These changes in factor price ratios were accompanied by institutional changes that led to the establishment of more comprehensive and more precise

Table 9-3. Average Annual Percentage Rates of Change in Various Indicators of Thai Economic Performance, 1850 to 1950

Period	Rice exports		Terms of trade		Population	Real wage in rice	Real land price in wage
	Quantity	Value	Rice/white shirting	Rice/gray shirting			
1864-1940	2.84	3.41			1.32		
1864-1910	4.43	5.64			0.87		
1910-1940	0.46	0.09			2.00		
1865-67 to 1939			0.465	0.85			
1865-67 to 1900			1.70	3.09			
1900-1925			-1.49	-2.20			
1925-1939			1.03	1.18			
1864-1950						-0.35	
1864-1930						-0.42	
1930-1938						3.15	
1864-1938						-0.04	
1864-1925						-0.76	
1925-1938						3.45	
1915-1940							1.41
1915-1925							-0.31
1925-1940							2.58
1911-1941					2.11		
1920-21 to 1941					2.30		

Source: Feeny, David, "Paddy, Princes and Productivity: Irrigation and Thai Agricultural Development, 1900-1940," Explorations in Economic History vol. 16 (1979) pp. 132-150.

definition of property rights in land. Between the 1860s and the 1880s titles to rice lands around Bangkok and throughout the central plain were made more specific and served as a basis for tax collection. In 1892, the government passes a comprehensive land classification law. Transferable titles which provided for exclusive use of the land and which could serve as collateral for loans were issued. Provision was made for conversion of older forms of land entitlement to the new form. In 1901 the government adopted the Torrons system of land titling which provided for cadestral surveys and central land record offices. At present, the process of titling land remains incomplete. It has been most fully applied in the intensively cultivated areas of the central plain. But the creation of secure property rights in land in Thailand is still an evolving process.

While the government of Thailand was creating a more elaborate and secure system of property rights in land during the latter half of the nineteenth century, it was also gradually dismantling its elaborate system of property rights in man. Slavery was gradually abolished in a series of steps between 1868 and 1915. Corvee labor was abolished and replaced by a head tax in 1899.

Feeny (1977, p. 15) summarizes his argument as follows:

> The appreciation of land prices led to demands for a more secure property rights system and teh ... system was forthcoming because the elite shared in the gains ... The decline of property rights in man is explained by the decline in real wages which made such ownership less attractive and wage labor more attractive. Thus, declining real wages lessened the opposition to the abolition of slavery and corvee. These actions were in the interest of the monarch who had a clear political incentive to abolish the control of manpower by his potential opposition. In sum, the changes in property rights in man and land contributed to labor mobility and security of land rights, both of which facilitated the expansion of paddy cultivation and rice exports. The (induced innovation) model successfully explains the changes in Thai property rights.

The Impact of Institutional Bias on the Direction
of Technical Change: The Case of Argentina

In the mid 1920s, agricultural development in Argentina appeared to
be proceeding along a path roughly comparable to that of the United States.
Mechanization of crop production lagged slightly behind that in the United
States. Grain yields per hectare averaged slightly higher than in the
United States. In contrast to the United States output, however, output
and yields in Argentina remained relatively stagnant between the mid 1920s
and the mid 1970s. Part of this lag in Argentine agricultural development
was due to the disruption of export markets in the 1930s and 1940s. Students of Argentine development have pointed to the political dominance of
the landed aristrocacy (de Janvry, 1973), to the rising tensions between
urban and rural interests (Smith, 1969 and 1974); and to inappropriate
domestic policies toward agriculture (Diaz, 1965).

In this third case, I examine the failure of the Argentine economy
to undertake the institutional innovations necessary to realize the
relatively inexpensive sources of growth that were potentially available
from technical change in agricultural production.

It has been argued by de Janvry (1973) that in Argentina, lack of
economic incentive for the larger farmers to adopt yield-increasing technology has been a major factor in the lag in the development of agricultural research institutions capable of generating yield-increasing
biological and chemical technologies suited to the factor endowments of
the majority of small and medium farms. He also argues that choice of
technology was biased more strongly in a labor-saving direction than it
was consistent with factor endowments.

The de Janvry model is presented in Figure 9-2. He assumes, in the case of Argentina, that inputs can be grouped into two categories: land and other forms of capital that substitute for land (landesque capital). Initially, (at t-1), it is assumed that the prices of land and other inputs are represented by unit cost, line AB; that the technology employed by the agricultural sector is represented by the isoquant I_1; and that the state of technical knowledge can be described by the innovation possibility curve, IPC_{t-1}. The initial equilibrium is at 1.

Assume now, that due to expansion of export demand, for example, the price of land rises relative to the other inputs (or that the price of the other inputs falls relative to the price of land). This new price relationship is illustrated by the unit line cost, line CD. The initial response by farm managers is to adjust their factor mix in a manner to bring about a new sector equilibrium at 2. Since costs have risen (though less than if producers had not adjusted factor proportions), there is a demand for innovations leading to some new unit isoquant I_2 on some new innovation possibility curve, IPC_t. If the new technology represented by I_2 becomes available, and if final demand is inelastic, prices will decline and eliminate the profits represented by the difference between CD and the isocost line which is tangent to I_1 at 2. As the new price ratio continues to induce further innovation, the adjustment process would be expected to continue until a new equilibrium is established at 4.

If, however, final demand is elastic -- in the case of Argentina, because of large external markets for Argentine agricultural exports -- and if the supply of land (and land substitutes) is inelastic, product prices will remain high. Land prices will continue to rise until they

internalize the higher returns from the new technology. This new adjustment is described in Figure 9-3. Step-by-step, actual demand for technical
innovation will converge toward latent demand for technology, I_6.

The significance of the de Janvry extension of the induced innovation
model is that the gains from technical change can be captured by the
owners of agricultural land in the form of rising land values rather than
by consumers in the form of lower commodity prices. He refers to this as
a land market treadmill, in contrast to the product market treadmill
described by Cochrane (1958). The land market treadmill operates with
much longer lags than the product market treadmill in translating latent
demand for technical change to effective demand. It initially affects
only the asset position and opportunity costs of landowners rather than
current costs or returns. The lag in translating the latent demand for
a shift from, for example, the technology represented by I_1 to effective
demand for I_2 technology is viewed by de Janvry as an important factor
in explaining the low level of demand for yield-increasing agricultural
technology by the landowning agricultural elite in Argentina.

A second major factor which, in de Janvry's view, contributes to the
lag in translating latent into effective demand for land-substituting
technology, is a combination of (1) elastic agricultural commodity demand
and (2) duality in Argentine agrarian structure. He argues that the
larger landowners have been able to capture a "discriminatory institutional rent" in the form of low fiscal burden, monopolization of institutional credit, and privileged access to public services. Thus large
and small landowners face different relative factor costs. The lower
costs of the large landowners become institutionalized in the price of

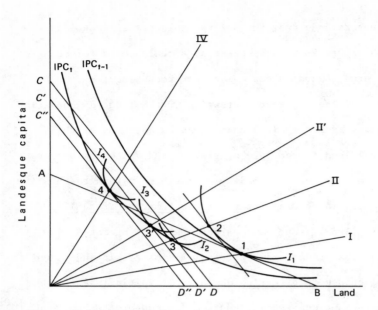

Figure 9-2. Actual demand for land-saving technical innovations.

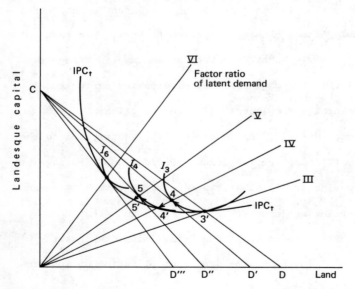

Figure 9.3. Dynamic adjustment path between actual and latent demands.

Source: Hans P. Binswanger and Vernon W. Ruttan, _Induced Innovation: Technology, Institutions, and Development_ (Baltimore, Md., The Johns Hopkins University Press, 1978), pp. 315 and 316.

urban political leadership? Part of the answer can be found in the economic interpretation of the implications of the disruption of world export markets during the 1930s and World War II. But this explanation is not adequate for most of the postwar period. Another partial answer is, in my judgment, to be found in the implications of increasingly elastic demand for Argentine agricultural commodities on world markets for domestic commodity prices. De Janvry points out that the elastic demand for Argentine agricultural exports meant that market forces woudl translate the effects of productivity gains into higher land prices rather than lower food prices. Lower food prices for urban workers could be brought about, however, through a combination of overvalued exchange rates and export taxes and quotas. The effect of these policies, designed to achieve lower food prices, was also to reduce the demand for yield-increasing technical change in agriculture on the part of both agricultural producers and urban consumers.

But the problem that de Janvry posed is not fully resolved. The land market treadmill model of induced innovation implies that the optimum path of technical change in Argentine agriculture between 1925 and 1975 should have been even more land-saving than the path followed by the United States. But the economic demand for land-saving technology induced by rising land prices remained latent. Why was it not possible for the Argentine political system to resolve the class conflicts within the agricultural sector and between the urban and rural sector in order to take advantage of the inexpensive sources of growth that could have been opened up by more rapid technical change?

land and drive down the return on land to the smaller and medium farmers. He then draws on farm management analysis to argue that intensive use of land-substituting biological and chemical technology is more profitable on small, rather than large, farms. Thus, if I_6 technology had become available, it would have created a demand for structural changes in Argentine agriculture leading to smaller farm size. On the other hand, the introduction of labor-saving mechanical technology reinforced the existing structure.

Thus, de Janvry concludes that in spite of a latent demand for yield-increasing seed-fertilizer technology in Argentine agriculture, institutional bias directed the limited research resources available for public sector research primarily in the direction of labor-saving rather than yield-increasing technical change. He argues that this explains the long delay in the evolution of a set of public sector institutions capable of inventing land-saving biological and chemical technologies and a strong set of private sector institutions capable of embodying land-saving technologies in low cost inputs.

The de Janvry rationale is only partially convincing. My own limited reading of Argentine economic and political history suggests that the answer, at least for the period following World War II, must not be found more in class-oriented urban-rural conflict than in interclass conflict within the rural sector. The large landowners have exercised much less control over the agricultural policy agenda, particularly since the revolution of 1943, than is suggested by de Janvry.

But why was there so little demand for yield-increasing advances in biological and chemical technology on the part of urban consumers and

A Perspective

The three cases examined in this paper exhibit striking differences in the efficiency with which institutional innovations were induced in response to changes in relative factor endowments and prices. In the Philippine village studied by Kikuchi and Hayami (forthcoming) "efficient" crop-sharing institutions evolved rapidly in spite of land reform legislation designed to achieve greater equity between landlords and tenants. In Thailand, the system of property rights in land and man evolved gradually in association with changes in land-labor endowments. In Argentina, the development of agricultural research institutions capable of responding to the latent demand for yield-increasing agricultural technology suited to the needs of small and medium farmers was delayed by the rural elite.

The induced innovation process as it evolved in the Philippine case would seem to approximate the results postied in the competitive theory of contracts: "If property rights are well established, contracts are easily enforced, information costs are negligible, and numbers are sufficient to make attempts to monopolize unstable, then factors of production will be allocated efficiently and receive their competitive factor payments whether markets exist or not" (Roumasset, 1978, p. 333). In the Philippine case, new land tenure and harvest-sharing institutions evolved rapidly at the village level in response to changing resource endowments and technology with little external intervention.[7]

---

[7] The suggestion that private contracting may act as a substitute for the market derives for Coase (1960). For other empirical tests, see Cheung (1969) and Roumasset (1979).

The situation in the Thai case is somewhat different. In 1850 property rights in land were largely underdeveloped. It was necessary to mobilize political and economic resources to modify the nation's legal system and to implement the changes in order to establish property rights in land in a form that provided incentives for land development. The process, as reported by Feeny (1976, 1977, 1979), was consistent with the induced innovation perspective that "institutional innovations occur because it appears profitable for individuals or groups in society to undertake the cost. Changes in market prices and technological opportunities introduce disequilibrium in existing institutional arrangements and create new opportunities for institutional innovations" (Hayami and Ruttan, 1971, pp. 60-61). This longer time period required to realize the institutional changes described in the Thai case reflect the fact that in complex societies, the allocation of substantial economic and political resources are required to bring about institutional change (Binswanger and Ruttan, 1978, pp. 327-357). It is unlikely that these institutional innovations occurred rapidly enough to bring the "contract solutions" to resource allocation in as close conformity with the implicit market solution as in the Philippine case.[8]

The Argentine case would seem to represent a case where imperfections in political markets were so severe, as a result of bias in the distribu-

---

[8]The Thai case is similar in many respects to the examples used by Demsetz (1967) in his discussion of the evolution of property rights. Roumasset (1978) uses the term "second best" (institutional) efficiency to identify contractual solutions where transaction costs are significant. In the second-best case, institutions evolve to minimize rather than to eliminate the costs of enforcement, information and exchange. In the induced institutional innovation literature, the analysis is extended to include the costs of changing property rights.

ion of political and economic resources, that they imposed ever more costly delays in the institutional innovations needed to take advantage of the relatively inexpensive sources of growth that technical change in agriculture could have made available. Interpretation of the Argentine case will have to draw on the as yet underdeveloped theory of "impure" induced institutional innovation in contrast to the pure theory of induced institutional innovation outlined in the first part of this chapter and illustrated in the Philippine case.

The public choice literature, on which most of the chapters in this volume draw, has been concerned primarily with improving institutional performance through the design of more efficient institutions. The theory of institutional innovation complements this body of literature in that it is concerned with the forces which influence the direction of institutional innovation. It identifies changing resource endowments, interpreted through changing relative factor prices, as an important source directing both technical and institutional change.

References

Binswanger, Hans P. and Vernon W. Ruttan. 1978. Induced Innovation: Technology, Institutions and Development (Baltimore, Johns Hopkins University Press).

Cheung, Stephen. 1969. The Theory of Share Tenancy (Chicago, Ill., University of Chicago Press).

Coase, R.H. 1960. "The Problem of Social Cost," The Journal of Law and Economics vol. 3 (October) pp. 1-43.

Cochrane, Willard W. 1958. Farm Prices: Myth and Reality, section III (Minneapolis, University of Minnesota Press).

Collier, William, Gunawan Wiradi, and Soentoro. 1973. "Recent Changes in Rice Harvesting Methods," Bulletin of Indonesian Economic Studies vol. 9 (July) pp. 36-42.

_____, _____, _____, and Makali. 1974. "Agricultural Technology and Institutional Change in Java," Food Research Institute Studies vol. 13 pp. 169-194.

Commons, John R. 1950. The Economics of Collective Action (New York, Macmillan).

Davis, Lance E. and Douglas C. North. 1971. Institutional Change and American Economic Growth (New York, Cambridge University Press).

de Janvry, Alain. 1973. "A Socioeconomic Model of Induced Innovation for Argentine Agricultural Development," Quarterly Journal of Economics vol. 87 (August) pp. 410-435.

Demsetz, Harold. 1967. "Toward a Theory of Property Rights," American Economic Review vol. 42 (May) pp. 347-359.

Diaz Alejandro, Carlos F. 1965. Exchange Rate Devaluation in a Semi-Industrialized Country: The Experience of Argentina, 1955-1961 (Cambridge, Mass., MIT Press).

Feeny, David Harold. 1976. "Technical and Institutional Change in Thai Agriculture, 1880-1940" Ph.D. dissertation, University of Wisconsin, Madison, Department of Economics.

_____. 1977. "From Property Rights in Man to Property Rights in Land: Institutional Change in Thai Agriculture, 1850 to 1940" working paper 77-12 (Hamilton, Ontario, Department of Economics, McMaster University).

_____. 1979. "Paddy, Princes and Productivity: Irrigation and Thai Agricultural Development, 1900-1940" Explorations in Economic History vol. 16, pp. 132-150.

Hayami, Yujiro and Vernon W. Ruttan. 1971. Agricultural Development: An International Perspective (Baltimore, Md., Johns Hopkins University Press).

_____ and Anwar Hafid. 1979. "Rice Harvesting and Welfare in Rural Java," Bulletin of Indonesian Economic Studies vol. 15 (July) pp. 94-112.

Horowitz, Irving Louis. 1972. Three Worlds of Development 2nd ed. (New York, Oxford University Press).

Kikuchi, Masao and Yujiro Hayami. forthcoming. "Inducements to Institutional Innovations in an Agrarian Community," Economic Development and Cultural Change.

Knight, Frank H. 1952. "Institutionalism and Empiricism in Economics," American Economic Review vol. 42 (May) pp. 45-55.

Krueger, Anne O. 1974. "The Political Economy of the Rent-seeking Society," American Economic Review vol. 64 (June) pp. 291-303.

Lerner, Abba P. 1944. The Economics of Control (New York, Macmillan).

North, Douglass C. and Robert P. Thomas. 1970. "An Economic Theory of the Growth of the Western World," Economic History Review 2nd series vol. 23, pp. 1-17.

_____. 1973. The Rise of the Western World (London, Cambridge University Press).

Roumasset, James A. 1978. "The New Institutional Economics and Agricultural Organization," The Philippine Economic Journal vol. 17, pp. 331-348.

_____. 1979. "Sharecropping, Production Externalities and the Theory of Contracts," American Journal of Agricultural Economics vol. 61 (November) pp. 640-647.

_____ and William James. forthcoming. "Explaining Variations in Share Contracts: Land Quality, Population Pressure and Technological Change," Australian Journal of Agricultural Economics.

Ruttan, Vernon W. 1969. "Equity and Productivity Issues in Modern Agrarian Reform Legislation," in Ugo Papi and Charles Nunn, eds., Economic Problems of Agriculture in Industrial Societies (New York, St. Martin's Press).

_____. 1974. "Equity and Productivity Objectives in Agrarian Reform Legislation: Perspectives on the New Philippine Land Reform Code," Indian Journal of Agricultural Economics vol. 19 (July-December) pp. 114-130.

Samuelson, Paul A. 1948. _Foundations of Economic Analysis_ (Cambridge, Mass., Harvard University Press).

Schultz, Theodore W. 1968. "Institutions and the Rising Economic Value of Man," _American Journal of Agricultural Economics_ vol. 50 (December) pp. 1113-1122.

Seckler, David. 1975. _Thorstein Veblen and the Institutionalists_ (London, Macmillan).

Shubik, Martin. 1976. "Beyond General Equilibrium," Discussion Paper 417, January 14 (New Haven, Cowles Foundation for Research in Economics at Yale University).

Smith, Peter H. 1969. _Politics and Beef in Argentina: Patterns of Conflict and Change_ (New York, Columbia University Press).

_____. 1974. _Argentina and the Failure of Democracy: Conflict among Political Elites, 1904-1955_ (Madison, University of Wisconsin Press).

Zingler, E.K. 1974. "Veblen vs. Commons: A Comparative Evaluation," _Kyklos_ vol. 27, pp. 322-344.

Chapter 10

DOES THE ROUTE TO DEVELOPMENT PASS THROUGH PUBLIC CHOICE?

Joe Oppenheimer

When one buys a machine such as a router or a food processor, one has come to expect not only instructions but also a set of applications. The router will come with a booklet which details many interesting projects. These are given so that the custormer can consider the applications of his or her new tool. One can also find these manuals of applications in bookstores. Indeed, before buying a food processor, I spent some time perusing a specialized recipe book, to see what I could expect a processor to do.

The idea of "considering" the applications of public choice theory to the planning of rural development projects is analogous to the functions of a chapter in one such manual. Are you interested in the analysis of rural development projects? Let us tell you about an essential new tool. Have you already invested in publich choice theory? Then do you want to try your hand in some analysis of rural development projects? But are we as enticing as Creative Food Processing Cooking (Graham, 1977)?

Author's Note: Special thanks are due to Professor Robert Bates, Jennifer Rochschield, Todd Sandler, Gordon Tullock, Eric Uslaner, and Clifford S. Russell, for their insightful comments.

Are our applications as useful as the contents of How to Do More with
Your Power Router (1975)? Can we even aspire to such heights?

   Can public choice be used to analyze plans for rural economic development? Are there applications of the theory which will allow us to make
this intellectual trip? Public choice theorists, armed with sophisticated
formalized arguments regarding the consequences of maximizing behavior
outside of markets, have things to say about how institutions work and
how individuals behave. More specifically, these theories sensitize us
to three sorts of problems: (1) the difficulties associated with the
supply of collective goods (Olson, 1965; Frohlich and Oppenheimer, 1978,
chapters 2 and 3); (2) the effect of self-interested motivations of public
leaders and officials (Niskanen, 1971; Tullock, 1965; Downs, 1957;
Frohlich and Oppenheimer, 1978, chapter 4); and (3) the inherently non-
unique identification of community choice via political aggregation
procedures and coalitional politics (Arrow, 1979; Frohlich and Oppenheimer,
1978, chapters 1 and 6). But how readily can these constructs be applied
to problems of rural development? To answer these questions I will consider the substantive characteristics of rural development plans and
public choice theory with an eye toward trying to assess the realistic
scope and limits of these applications. First, consider the limitations.

   In assessing the limitations of the public choice tools for the
analysis of rural development plans, I begin by identifying those limitations which are generic to the theory and its epistemological approach.
These difficulties, which stem from both empirical and logical characteristics of the theory, will be assessed to show how the theory's applicability may be limited. Although I am presenting the list of

damnations first, it is to raise a degree of scepticism (rather than a spirit of out and out rejectionism) in the mind of the reader.

Characteristics of Public Choice Which Limit Its

Applicability to the Analysis of Rural Development

Generic Limitations

Known replicable falsifying cases. The theory suffers from empirical difficulties. At times it makes quite precise predictions which are replicably, predictably, and measurably inaccurate.[1] None of these falsifying cases are directly in areas which are of concern to the problems of development, yet they cast a pall on the possibility of justifying the application of public choice theories. Problems in the use of theories which are false may only directly concern philosophers. But the implications of the philosophical arguments raise questions as to what prompts us to advocate the use of public choice theory for any application.

One rather severe argument has been made by Miller (1975). He points out that there are probably no epistemologically useful criteria by which to choose from among "falsified" theories. That is, once a theory is known to be false, one can show that it is impossible to talk about it being "more accurate" or "closer to the truth" than another theory.

_____

[1]Thus, under specific circumstances, one can engender intransitive preferences for individuals (May, 1953; Orether and Plott, 1979). Less surprisingly, one can construct experimental situations where strongly predicted coalitional and aggregate patterns are not obtained. For example, Plott (1979) has concocted experimental situations where the core, although existing, is not reached. But since the core is not necessarily an individual (Nash) equilibrium, this is not quite as damaging. Finally, Plott (1976a) also found with small groups ($N \leq 4$), individuals at times agree to an egalitarian outcome rather than one which would have everyone better off but unequally so.

Rather, one must choose the theory strictly on the basis of its instrumental value. And thus, once we know the theory of public choice to be
false, we must ask what claim does it have to be advocated as an instru-
ment of analysis of problems of development?

Development as a function of nondomestic factors. Public choice,
regardless of which branch of it we consider, applies the economists'
maximization model of individual choice to nonmarket situations (Frohlich
and Oppenheimer, 1978). This starting point immediately confronts us
with limitations in applying public choice models to questions of
development.

Public choice is particularly useful in analyzing the relationship
between individual choices and an aggregate choice, or set of choices.
For example, public choice may help us understand how political processes
will respond to changes in demand for a particular sort of service.[*] If
development is something which a group of citizens fight for, work for,
and politic for, and which can be delivered politically as part of the
government's policy output, then perhaps public choice will give us
considerable leverage over the relevant variables. But public choice
theory would lead us to believe that the potential demand for economic
development per se is too weak for it to motivate a government. For
development is overall growth of the nation's economy. As such, development (rather than the distribution of its dividends) may be seen as a
public good. Well known is the result that individuals will (via free
riding) understate their desire for public goods. Thus, development
proves not to be a function of explicit social choice but rather a by-

---

[*]Editor's Note: See, for example, Chapter 7 by Guttman in this volume.

product of other political decisions or a product of environment. In the latter case, public choice models may have little to say.

Quite consistently, a respectable literature argues that development in modern times is not primarily a function of internal state politics (and hence the individual choices of citizens) but rather a function of the state's position in the international system (Wallerstein, 1974; and Rubonson, 1976). The data supporting this reasoning are supplemented by our common sense. International politics sets a crucial environment for the sources of investment, loans, and the like. The demand for changing the growth rate of a less developed country may never be articulated directly. This could mean that the role of public choice theory needs to be indirect and needs to be supplemented by models of international trade, conflict, and finance.

Obviously, however, this theme can be overemphasized. If international credit, strategic importance, and the like can play a role, so do the incentives engendered by development projects. One need only consider the differences in political systems of Mexico, Cuba, and Haiti to realize that there is a great deal of variance in the political possibilities for policies about matters of development.[2] The international environment needs to be considered, but as parameters of choice rather than as replacements for the domestic political process.

Development as changes in education, information, and values. Public choice models of behavior are not well designed to deal with information acquisition. The models all begin with a supposition of values which are assumed not to change during the process of choice. But some analysts

---

[2] Of course a nation's international position is also a function of domestic choice, as the Cuban case reminds us.

of development have characterized the process of development in terms of changing values and information (Coleman, 1965). If what is to be chosen involves a change in values and information, rationality models as currently formulated can not adequately explain individuals' choices.[3]

On the other hand, quite elaborate models of information acquisition have been developed (and may be quite useful) by analysts of voting (Downs, 1957). But the less the information is directly applicable to the making of a particular choice, the less analyzable (via rationality models) is the resulting choice as whether to consume the information or not. Thus, a choice to change one's basic education may not be properly analyzable using a rationality model.

On the other hand, we can expect rationality theory to give us leverage over information acquisition about narrow, technical matters, such as supplied by agricultural extension services.

For example, a rationality model of information acquisition would tell us that individuals will purchase information only if the cost of the information is less than the probability of the information changing their behavior times the value of such changed behavior to them. Such a model immediately lends itself to the development of a publicity strategy for agricultural education services. Consumption of their services will increase as a function of the extent to which they can lead farmers to believe that such services would change their production patterns in valued fashions.

---

[3]This does not mean, however, that rationality models tell us nothing about choices involving alternative values or information levels. Extensions of the basic choice models deal with choices of values and learning (Roberts and Holdren, 1970). But these are not yet sufficiently integrated into public choice theories to be of use to planners of projects.

Development as a coercively imposed policy. Often the development
policies of a government are not democratically chosen by its citizens
but rather are forced upon them. One need not consider the Soviet cases
to realize that. In Taiwan, South Korea, Brazil, and other countries,
authoritarian elites have forcibly imposed economic development policies
on their citizens. Public choice theories are poorly equipped to deal
with coerced choices or coercive processes (but see Hanson, 1978; Frohlich
and Oppenheimer, 1971a, chapters 7 to 9; 1973 and 1974; as well as Tullock,
1969 and 1971). Rather, the theoretical insights have been strongest with
regard to particular voluntary institutionalized processes such as elections (Downs, 1957; Romer and Rosenthal, 1978; Oppenheimer, 1979; Kramer,
1977), voting processes in general (Plott, 1967; Kramer, 1973; Arrow,
1963; and Shepsle, 1978), interest group, revolutionary, and other mass
mobilization organizational problems (Olson, 1965; Coleman, 1979; Tullock,
1971), bureaucratic behaviors (Tullock, 1965; Niskanan, 1971; Miller,
1977) and citizen roles (Hirschman, 1970; Downs, 1957; Frohlich and
coauthors, 1978).

Yet the models of public choice are often premised on the self-
interest of political leaders, and this can be generalized to coercive
situations. Leaders freed of regular democratic processes and maximizing
their private benefits will not find force alone a rational strategy
(Frohlich and Oppenheimer, 1974). Rather they will find their tenure
in office longer and easier if they also supply collective goods to the
society. Their interest in the supportive attitude of the populace and
coalitional support leads to their strategic use of such programs as
development plans. Leaders who rule by guns and butter would, obviously,

seek complementarities between the two. But there have been few theorems produced about these coercive political systems.

Limitations Stemming from Theorems

It is not only these generic difficulties of the rationality models which make for difficulties. Many of the findings of the theory lead us to know, ex ante, that any prescriptions and applications of the public choice theory (and probably any other individual choice model) to problems of institutional planning must be relatively limited.

General instabilities and applying public choice to development. Are we looking for a tool with which to predict outcomes from institutional processes? If so, then probably the most debilitating roadblock for any micro or behavioral theory is the mass of general instability findings which public choice theories have generated. These results cluster around two great theorems: Kenneth Arrow's famous impossibility theorem and the proof of the nonexistence of the core in many n-person games (Gillies, 1953). These results have at least three implications for the problems of planning for development.

First, these results show that there is often no simple (predictable, unique, or stable) translation of individual values or choices into a collective decision via a democratic process or set of procedures. In other words, the same individual choices from among alternatives are likely to aggregate into different results as a function of such things as the ordering of the agenda and the process of coalition formation (Gilliges, 1953). This makes it impossible to develop a unique or determinate, or stable prediction of an outcome from most mechanical (for example, vote counting) political processes even when we can specify

all the choices (such as votes) of the actors involved. The consequences
of these findings run deep.

Second, it follows that no simple model of democratic institutional
behavior can be built using only the assumptions of individual behavior.
Such models, developed by economists to deal with markets, will not be
possible in politics without utilizing ad hoc assumptions (such as that
no coalitions will form). What to do? Other social considerations need
to be incorporated in the models: considerations regarding the nature
of bargaining, coalition formation, and so forth, before the bridges
to a macrotheory can be outlined (Oppenheimer, 1980). The theory thus
sensitizes us to the effect of the detailed political arrangements on
the strategic use of policies by the political leaders. Public choice
theorists have been interested in precisely defining under what institutional arrangements power is given to whom (Shepsle, 1978). But this
line of inquiry has problems. First, the formal rules are only a minor
aspect of many political processes. Informal rules and behavior patterns
are of considerable importance and far more difficult for an analyst to
discover. Second, the range of variation of these rules is enormous.
Given that power to affect the agendas of institutions is infinitely
variable, any general theory which is developed will be difficult to
apply to real institutions so as to predict precise outcomes.

Third, since the theories predict that the outcome is a function
of the ordering of the agenda (via cycles) one wants to consider who
has the power to order the agenda and what are their motives. Much
of public choice has been developed around conjectures as to what the
generic motivations of political actors might be. But consider then the

analysis of motivations of actors. The difficulty is that here, unlike in market contexts, there is no single, measurable item such as profits which can be cited as a generic motivator. Even in democratic systems, the simple maximization of votes (Downs, 1957; Kramer, 1973) would, at times, seem to make little sense. After all, if victory is at stake, then one need not maximize, one need only win (for example, get a simple majority). Certainly, once one has a commanding majority (for example, 75 percent) one's interest in still more votes would decrease. In more complex systems, the problem becomes even tougher. Political scientists traditionally utilize such concepts as power, and public or national interest to denote a rather diffuse interest of politicians. Public choice theorists have been more concrete and specific referring to such things as the budget of the head of a bureau (Niskanen, 1971) or the probability of reelection for a legislator (Mayhew, 1974). But these narrower theories all have their detractors and their known difficulties.

How serious are problems of instabilities to the tasks of development planning? Consider the sources of instability. Black (1958) has shown that under a certain set of conditions, no cycles or instabilities need be anticipated. These conditions (generalized in Sen, 1970) require that the individuals perceive only one dimension along which to evaluate the issue. Is this condition likely to be met when the issue is development?

If development issues are considered to be simple questions about how much current consumption to forego and to invest in economic growth, the issue is formulated in terms which could well meet Black's criteria. That issue might be perceived as having only one dimension (how much to save or invest). Individuals each could have their "most preferred

savings rate" and would find themselves ever more disappointed the further
they found themselves from that rate. Ah, if life were that simple.

Usually development is not just a simple issue. Indeed, in part
to create support for what would otherwise be considered a pure public
good it is politically wise to disaggregate the issue to engender active
support. In any case, development involves discrete tasks and projects
(irrigation, roads, schools, and so forth) and investments. Savings must
come from some person's income stream. These investments and changes
confer benefits on some individuals and costs on others. A graphic example
of the imposition of costs from economic development came to the fore recently. The fervor of the Moslem community of Iran against the "western-
ization" of the country indicated the deeply felt costs imposed on the
more traditional elements of the society. As such, the issue is distributional, multidimensional, and complex. Not only should we build
a road but where, and across whose pasture becomes an issue.

As situations become more competitive, as isssues are more multidimensional, the chance for stability in outcome through any coalitional
process decreases. At the extreme, in a purely redistributive (zero-sum)
situation, one can expect no stability unless it is imposed by such
ad hoc, or extraneous elements as tradition, the order of the agenda,
the rules governing how bargaining between coalition members takes place,
and so forth. The issues of development, there is both the complex
distributional question and the simpler collective good growth question.
Political actors will focus on different aspects of the development
question. Peasant revolutions usually begin by focusing on redistribution.
Sitting governments tend to focus on the aggregate gains from development.

But the ability to form destabilizing coaltions on the distrubtional
issues belies government's approach just as certainly as the ability to
identify the public good aspects of the problem can introduce a degree
of stabilizing cooperation in a situation of class strife. Public choice
theory can neither tell us which aspect will receive emphasis nor the
outcome which will result. Rather it holds open virtually all possibilities because of the redistributional characteristics of the issues.

The preceding paragraphs have indicated that there are a number of
reasons to suggest that the theory may not be ideally suited for application to some of the problems of development. Of course, the attractiveness
of a theory depends, at least in part, on the relative strengths of its
competitors and hence, the public choice theorists may have a useful role
to play in the analysis of rural development projects. But one would hope
that the above critiques would lead readers to scepticism. They should
be on the lookout both for more useful instruments of analysis in this
area, and for the additional elements of theory which might make our
theories applicable to a wider range of questions of interest to the
analysts of development.

The Scope of Public Choice's Positive Application
To Rural Development Planning

Even if the above pages lead one to lowered expectations from any
manual on how to design rural development projects using public choice,
such a manual may still have useful content. Indeed, some implications
of the theory are quite profound and useful for those interested in
development. But, unfortunately, they are also relatively diffuse and
general, thereby serving roles best described as "advisory" or "heuristic."

Let us consider some of the major implications of the theory for rural planning.

Implications of Leadership Motivations for Rural Development Plans.

The political interests of leaders and those of the citizenry are rarely the same. Rather, political leadership usually has interests which derive, via complex procedural and other ties, from those of the citizenry. The relationship may, or may not preserve the essential interests of the citizens when the politician takes a stand. The likelihood of the citizens' interests being properly expressed by the leadership of a group, an area, or a jurisdiction is certainly, in part, a function of the existence of democratic procedures.

What is the "typical" political structure in LDCs? Certainly we can safely assume (1) nondemocratic rules where the establishment and continuance of governmental authority is by considerable coercion supplemented by support purchased through bribes and payoffs; (2) an information sector (often with media ownership or control by the government) emanating from a capital city; and (3) market forces permitted to induce private capital flows between economic sectors, at least to some extent.

But of course, rural economic development can stem from a few factors only. These are changing the investment pattern; changing the production patterns (without the use of investment); and changing the relative price levels for agricultural products. If development is seen in terms of real growth of production, and not growth of consumption, then only if the changes in the relative prices affect investment and production can they relate to development. Thus, rural economic development plans must have to do with investment and production, and how decisions regarding these variables are to be made. Typical policies which have manipulated these factors to foster rural economic development have been (1) the extension of agricultural (and other) educational services to the rural producer; (2) the use of tax policies to change the patterns of production and ownership in the rural sector; (3) national or local investment in social overhead capital (roads, irrigation projects, and so forth) to subsidize and encourage agricultural investments; (4) the development of financial services to help the agricultural producers change their investment patterns; and (5) the changing of land tenure rules, so as to increase productivity and equity.

But plans are not only economic policies. For governments which adopt them, plans become political strategies to engender political support for the government. Thus, just as these rural development plans change the payoffs from economic activities, so do they change the political base for the government. And just as the plan will have differing effects in different economic systems, so will its political environment change its consequences. The planner must expect the government to use plans strategically for their own ends. Hence another factor which determines the effect of any governmental plan will necessarily be the political context of its adoption.

For example, consider a tyrannical government's plan to build roads. Is the government helped by the roads because the roads foster the development of markets or rather because they enable the government to transport troops and hence deliver coercion? Roads, after all, can connect the military to the rural countryside just as easily as they can connect the rural production centers with markets and distribution points.

Road systems desigend for these different purposes would obviously not need to be the same. How likely is the road plan to be subverted for the strategic bolstering of the government and what effects would such changes have on the economic productivity of the plan? Can the plan be so designed so that the strategic input by the government does not permit the government to subvert the plans?

The particular strategic distortion which political forces will bring to bear on the implementation of any of the above mentioned development strategies will, in part, be determined by these political characteristics. The design of institutional and procedural frameworks will determine, in part, how all encompassing these strategic distortions can become. Decentralization, for example, leads to a certain degree of geographical containment of these effects. On the other hand, there are historical cases (such as China, between the two world wars) where the decentralization of control led to an increase in the overall strategic use of politics for the aggrandizement of leaders.

Implications of Collective Good Theory for the Design of Programs

One of the main concerns of public choice has been the behavior of individuals, in situations where all share the same thing and no one can be excluded if anyone gets it. The resulting theory (of collective or public goods) has been used to analyze the design of those political institutions responsible for the collective delivery of goods and services. Such a good could be a roadway, an irrigation system, or an educational facility. True, none of these items are necessarily purely collectively supplied: Service facilities are geographically located so as to make access a function of placement. Entry requirements for the use of irrigation and educational facilities may easily be imposed. Thus,

not everyone is a user of the service. (For the analysis of such situa-

tions, see Buchanan, 1965). But the existence and quality of the facili-

ties themselves constitute an environmental change which is shared by all

in the region. Further, and more important, the individuals who are direct

clients or beneficiaries of a project share the project's deisgn, infra-

structure, and so forth. In this sense, they share the properties of

the program which are collectively supplied to all those directly served

by the program. Thus, at least in these fashions, the project design

may usefully be seen to be a collective good for consumers (Frohlich and

Oppenheimer, 1971a and 1972).

When a collective good is supplied to a group of individuals they

each have incentives to be free riders.[4] But usually, if the good is

supplied by a government, the tax structure dictates how they all are

going to share the cost of the good. When this occurs, how is free rider

behavior still relevant? What other problems exist in supplying a col-

lective good under such circumstances?

First consider free rider behavior. If your share of the cost of

a collectively supplied program is fixed, your behavior cannot be one

of a free rider. Yet what happens when you object to or support an

aspect of the program? Imagine, for example, your children are attending

a school with an insufficiently nutritious lunch program. Now, any change

with respect to the lunch program will come about becaue of some pressure.

---

[4]Imagine a group of families who could all secure a benefit if any
subset of them got it. If the benefit could only be obtained if some
in the group bore a cost, all will hope others will bear the costs rather
than them (Olson, 1965; Frohlich and Oppenheimer, 1971b; Hardin, 1971).

It will take both time and effort. Perhaps another parent will complain. In general, the collective nature of the project will prevent some of the individuals from taking the effort needed to relieve minor irritations or get improvements made in the program. This difficulty will be greater the higher the clients perceive the costs of effective action. When high costs are expected, individuals will not even bother to find out what they could do to change things. They will rationally remain ignorant (Downs, 1957). Thus, the program is likely to become ever more divorced from the needs of the target group if there are costs to political action.

But this difficulty would also occur when collective action is needed to support a program. Thus, in calculating which plans to adopt, and how best to administer them, governments will pay attention to the relative difficulty of gaining support from the supply of public goods. Nothing that supports is more easily garnered from streams of private goods, development plans are likely to be used to insure a maximization of the flow of private benefits. Guttman's analysis in Chapter 7 of the distribution of agricultural services in India (pp. 183-202) is a case in point. Similarly, as Petras and Havens report in Chapter 8 (pp. 203-237), the land reform programs in Peru were administered so as to maximize the support of the government. What needs to be done to minimize or negate this tendency?

To improve the long-term quality of collective projects one needs to encourage feedback from the program's clients. High costs of information and action, as well as low feelings of efficacy, are likely to prevent participation and information acquisition. One needs to design projects so as to minimize these three characteristics in the administration of programs. The clients need information as to how to effect the

details of the projects: who is responsible, how does one contact this
group, and so forth. Further, the participation or complaint process
should be easily begun and relatively costless to engage in. Indeed, it
probably needs to be subsidized. But most important, since we know how
inefficacious single individuals are likely to be vis-a-vis an administrative institution, one must ensure the civil rights to organize around
complaints regarding the structure of the program. One must encourage
collective action.

Of course, in less developed countries, this leads to considerable
difficulties for there the political process is usually nonparticipatory.
Hence, our first findings are prescriptions for the political processes
surrounding the development projects. And these prescriptions may well
be hard to satisfy.

But supplying collective goods within a fixed tax system leads to
other problems. Most democratic procedures (and also nondemocratic ones),
when coupled with a system of fixed tax shares, lead to inefficient (that
is, non-Paretian) outcomes (Mueller, 19791, chapter 3). These non-Pareto
outcomes are generally coupled with another feature: the political
processes and institutions in use can not help but make some feel that
the program is not satisfactory. For by fixing tax shares and yet supplying programs collectively, some will want more, while others want less.
This, after all, was the finding of Lindahl (1919), and no realized
political process gets around this problem.[5] To illustrate, imagine a
village of voters considering the possibility of an irrigation ditch and

---

[5]The theory of clubs would allow for a possible remedy for some of
these programs. But the remedy requires (1) a "market-like" mobility of
individuals between clubs or jurisdictions (Buchanan, 1965); and (2) no
necessary distributional problem underlying such arrangements (Miller, 1976).

its maintenance. The cost would be shared on an equal basis. Now each individual will find a ditch worthwile only if his or her cost share is less than the benefits that individual is to reap from the project. But with majority rule the village will allow for a project large enough so that just fewer than half find themselves with tax shares so large that they would wish, at that price, there would be no ditch. Any (nonunanimous) rule with fixed tax shares generates this sort of alienation.

Thus, opening a political process to complaints and organizing with low costs of participation is _sure_ to lead to protests. The difficulty which ensues from the inevitability of protest is how to ensure that the response to protest improves the program for the society rather than merely serving to reward a particular interest group. This is especially true given the motives of politicians.

Theorists have attempted to construct models which show how to avoid free riding and other demand distorting acts to ensure optimal social choice when individual choice is self-interested. But what these models show is how peculiar would be any process in which self-interested individuals do not free ride. In making such processes result in optimal choices, sociologically prevalent phenomena must be ruled out, for example, coalitions (Mueller, 1979, chapter 4 for an overview). The conclusion seems to be inescapable: responsive political processes cannot be expected to generate optimal choices, when the individuals are all self-interested.

But how extensive is self-interested behavior? If collective action is well approximated by a prisoner's dilemma game, do people in all societies respond to such situations similarly? The answer is no.

Societal traditions vary as to how people are to relate to possible cooperation and competition. Thus, we would expect that the effect and success of similar policies will vary by these "cultural" parameters. For to the extent that the society has a long tradition of indigenous community organizing and infrastructure for cooperation it will be less likely to fall prey to the prisoner dilemma characteristics of collective action. Hence, when a strong tradition of cooperation and community sharing exists, as it did, for example, during the early years of Israeli statehood, communal arrangements for property owners (as in the kibbutzim) need not engender free riding behavior.

Various experimental probes have examined how important free riding is. The final results are not in yet, but certain conjectures look likely to be confirmed. First, absolute free riding, in general, is not the "modal" response to collective goods problems (Sweeney, 1973). Rather, a high proportion of the population can be expected to engage in limited free riding (Marwell and Ames, 1980). Furthermore, free-riding and, in general, response to prisoner dilemma situations, varies by culture (Chammah, 1972; Marwell and Ames, 1980). Third, the structure of the situation can make a great difference in the amount of free riding one ought to expect. Coordinating expectations so that individuals feel their contribution may make the difference changes the motivations of the individuals (Marwell and Ames, 1979 and 1980; Frohlich and Oppenheimer, 1971b; Frohlich and coauthors, 1978). Having a "lumpy," rather than a "continuous" good makes a difference also (Frohlich and Oppenheimer, 1971b; Marwell and Ames, 1980; Forhlich and coauthors, 1975). Finally, the repetitive nature of the interaction and the degree to which the individuals continue to

confront collective good problems without prior organizing is relevant
(Isaac, McCue and Plott, 1980; Marwell and Ames, 1980).

Implications of Social Choice Theory for the Design of Political Processes

Another branch of public choice theory is useful in considering
whether one could construct general political processes which would lead
to a stable aggregation of individual preferences.

Processes are far more likely to avoid cycles if different issues
are handled by different processes. This prevents the formation of multi-
issued coalitions, the platform of which may reflect a multitude of "small"
groups all of whom support each other's issues for purposes of increasing
their political clout (Oppenheimer, 1975). Such coalitions are inherently
unstable. Thus, any bureaucratic response to such coalitions also is a
response quite arbitrarily related to the preferences and needs of the
clients.

But even were each project to be separately administered so as to
decrease the chance for multi-issue coalitions, instabilities and cycles
are possible. For coalitions based on the distributive aspects of any
issue are also subject to the problems of cycles and instabilities. And
the political pressures for collectively supplied changes in project
design cannot readily be separated by most processes from advocacy of
distributional shifts. After all, the changes in such things as the
water loss rate in an irrigation ditch affect individuals differently
depending upon how far along the ditch their plots are. Thus, the
characteristics of programs which lead to complaints and the suggestions
would often confer changes in the distribution of benefits. To some
extent, this cannot be avoided.

One can, however, try to constrain the distributive issues. Typically, one does this by fixing the tax scheme by processes independent
of those which deal with the questions of program design. However, by
ensuring that the payment for the programs and projects is financed in a
particular and fixed fashion, and by ensuring therefore that some of the
distributional questions are excluded from the political process having to
do with program design; that is, by leaving out, or separating, the cost
side from the benefit side, one runs into the other previously mentioned
problems. Let us see how. The proposed solution can be seen to be a
"decentralized," and libertarian process. Each issue area would have its
own decision mechanism.

Institutionalized services, delivered within an environment respect-
ful of civil liberties, where the costs of action and information to the
clients are small, and where the process is not subject to multi-issue
coalition building, the costs of provision or tax shares has been decided
ex ante, may stay quite responsive to the needs of the clients. But by
dividing the services into autonomous policy areas, each with their own
interest group which lobbies for changes, we have constructed a quasi-
pluralist system. Such a system, when decentralized, allows for no
logrolling across issues. And the cost of this is that we end up with
possibly Pareto-inefficient outcomes.

By politically separating the programs, and thereby securing control
over them by differing subgroups of the population, one is inviting the
difficulties associated with Sen's liberal paradox (Sen, 1970, chapter 6).
This is the finding of Miller (1979). The paradox stems from the following sort of interaction. Let N be the group to decide about an irrigation

ditch via process P. Let M (an entirely different group) similarly decide
about extension services, via Q. It may be that both programs are approved
yet the individuals in M would have preferred not to have the ditch and
those in N would have preferred no services. If their preferences regarding the programs they did not decide were stronger than those where
they made the decisions, then the outcome will <u>unanimously</u> be found un-
desirable.

By ensuring that the clients have control, one also ensures that when
the externalities of the programs (for example, their cost as reflected
in the tax increases for the rest of the population) outweigh the direct
effects of the program, there will be no mechanism for taking into account
the interests of the nonclients. By construing the problem as a source
of instability, one creates a new difficulty. This can lead to truly
bizarre results which no one in the society desires. The conflict here
is directly between stability and efficiency. To gain efficiency one
need introduce the characteristics which support cycles and arbitrary
relationships between the preferences of the individuals and the outcomes
of the political process.[6]

Similar difficulties confront other attempts to construct political
processes to generate support for desirable programs (Plott, 1976b).
Generally, accepted processes either need to rule out sociologically
prevalent patterns (for example, coalitions) or efficiency to insure
nonarbitrary (that is, cyclic) results.

---

[6]This is also a critique of Tiebout's (1956) justification for decentralization of programs and proliferation of independent municipalities
within a metropolitan area (Miller, 1979).

Conclusions

What then does public choice tell us about planning for rural development? Such plans take a number of forms. Public choice's concern for the motives of leaders tips off that the policies designed to promote development can be expected to be adopted for other reasons: reasons of increasing political control or support for the government. How is this likely to manifest itself?

Tax and price policies designed to encourage investment are likely to be so administered as to enhance the inherent stability of the government. Roads, irrigation projects, and other social overhead capital investments are likely to be distributed with a maximum concern for the returns to supporters of the regime and to increase the government's ability to deliver coercion among potential dissidents. Such distortions often lead to wastefulness.

The naive planner may hope that by coupling a development plan with a particular political support process, manipulation can be avoided. All political processes are subject to strategic manipulation (Schwartz, 1979). To have a reasonable chance of avoiding such manipulation we need to sacrifice some of our goals.

To reiterate, if we ask for more from standard political institutions, if we demand efficiency, we often end up with cyclic or, what is more likely, manipulated outcomes. To avoid this, we usually must forego efficiency. Public choice tells us that we cannot have our cake and eat it too. We are limited in what we can obtain from a civil libertarian, democratic process. Yet the theory demonstrates that such processes are needed to maintain a reasonable degree of responsiveness of the programs

to the clients they are to serve. Public choi chus makes us aware of
the tradeoffs which we must make. It informs us regarding the reasonable
expectations we can have of the institutions. If markets do not engender
an acceptable growth pattern, political intervention may be called for.
It would mean projects and programs designed to achieve specific outcomes.
Public choice informs us as to what our expectations ought to be, given
the need to intervene in market processes.

Perhaps a router can speed the making of joints for drawers while
a food processor makes it possible for all of us to make pâté. Public
choice theory enables the analyst to obtain a bit of wisdom which otherwise might have to come only from the more experienced sage. It tells us
of inherent conflicts between our goals which we might otherwise not
perceive. It forces us to consider our choices more carefully than we
otherwise might. If this is a relatively thankless task, it is not a
trivial one. But it does not go far toward the design of programs.
Certainly, it may give us some rough and tumble objectives to consider
in institutional design. But to rural development from public choice?
I am afraid we just can't get there from here -- at least not without
some other vehicles.

References

Alinsky, Saul. 1969. *Reveille for Radicals* (New York, Random House).

Arrow, Kenneth. 1963. *Social Choice and Individual Values* 2nd ed. (New York, Wiley).

Black, Duncan. 1958. *The Theory of Committees and Elections* (Cambridge, England, Cambridge University Press).

Buchanan, James. 1965. "An Economic Theory of Clubs," *Economica* vol. 32, (February) pp. 1-14.

Chammah, Albert. 1972. "Five Strategies to Create Cooperation or Foment Competition," and "Gaming and Simulation Aspects of Conflict," both in *Proceedings of the Third Course given by the International Summer School on Disarmament and Arms Control of the Italian Pugwash Movement* (New York, Gordon and Breach) pp. 273-291 and 293-312.

Coleman, James S., ed. 1965. *Education and Political Development* (Princeton, N.J., Princeton University Press).

_____. 1979. "Future Directions for Work in Public Choice," in Clifford S. Russell, ed. *Collective Decision Making* (Baltimore, Md., Johns Hopkins University Press for Resources for the Future).

Downs, Anthony. 1957. *An Economic Theory of Democracy* (New York, Harper & Row).

Frohlich, Norman, Tom Hunt, Joe Oppenheimer, and R. Harrison Wagner. 1975. "Individual Contributions for Collective Goods: Alternative Models," *Journal of Conflict Resolution* vol. 19 (June) pp. 310-329.

_____ and Joe A. Oppenheimer. 1971a. *An Entrepreneurial Theory of Politics* (Princeton, N.J., Princeton University Press).

_____ and _____. 1971b. "I Get By with a Little Help From My Friends," *World Politics* vol. 23, no. 1 (October) pp. 104-120.

_____ and _____. 1972. "A Reformulation of the Collective Good-Private Good Distinction," paper given at the 1972 Public Choice Society Meetings, Pittsburgh, Pa.

_____ and _____. 1973. "Governmental Violence and Tax Revenue," in Herbert Hirsch and David Perry, eds., *Violence as Politics* (New York, Harper & Row) pp. 72-88.

_____ and _____. 1974. "The Carrot and the Stick: Optimal Program Mixes for Entrepreneurial Political Leaders," *Public Choice* vol. 19 (Fall) pp. 43-61.

_____ and _____. 1978. Modern Political Economy (Englewood Cliffs, N.J., Prentice-Hall).

_____, _____, Jeffrey Smith, and Oran Young. 1978. "A Test of Downsian Voter Rationality: 1964 Presidential Voting," American Political Science Review vol. 72, no. 1 (March) pp. 178-197.

Gillies, D. 1953. "Some Theorems on n-Person Games," Ph.D. Thesis, Department of Mathematics, Princeton University.

Graham, Ethel Lang. 1977. Creative Food Processor Cooking (Baltimore, Md., Ottenheimer).

Grether, David and Charles R. Plott. 1979. "Economic Theory of Choice and the Preference Reversal Phenomenon," American Economic Review vol. 69, no. 4 (September) pp. 623-638.

Hanson, Roger A. 1978. "Toward an Understanding of Politics Through Public Goods Theory," in William Loehr and Todd Sandler, eds., Public Goods and Public Policy (Beverly Hills, Sage).

Hardin, Russell. 1971. "Collective Action as an Agreeable n-Prisoners' Dilemma," Behavioral Science vol. 16 (Sept./Oct.) pp. 472-481.

Hirschman, Albert O. 1970. Exit, Voice and Loyalty (Cambridge, Mass., Harvard University Press).

Isaac, R. Mark, Kenneth McCue and Charles Plott. 1980. "Free Riding Behavior for Continuous Public Good Provision," paper presented at Public Choice meetings, San Francisco (March).

Kramer, Gerald H. 1973. "On a Class of Equilibrium Conditions for Majority Rule," Econometrica vol. 41 (March) pp. 285-297.

_____. 1977. "A Dynamical Model of Political Equilibrium," Journal of Economic Theory vol. 16, no. 2, pp. 310-334.

Lindahl, Erik. 1919. "Just Taxation -- a Positive Solution," (translated from the original German) in R.A. Musgrave and A.T. Peacocks, eds. Classics in the Theory of Public Finance (New York, St. Martins, 1967).

Marwell, Gerald and Ruth E. Ames. 1980. "Economists Free Ride. Does Anyone Else?" paper presented at Public Choice meetings, San Francisco (March).

_____ and _____. 1980. "Experiments on the Provision of Public Goods, I and II," American Journal of Sociology vol. 84, no. 6, pp. 1335-1361; ;and vol. 85, no. 4, pp. 926-137.

May, Kenneth. 1953. "Intransitivity, Utility and the Aggregation of Preference Patterns," Econometrica vol. 22, pp. 1-13.

Mayhew, David. R. 1974. Congress: The Electoral Connection (New Haven, Conn., Yale University Press).

Miller, David. 1975. "The Accuracy of Predictions," Synthese vol. 30, pp. 151-191.

Miller, Gary A. 1976. Fragmentation and Inequality: The Politics of Metropolitan Organization. unpublished Ph.D. dissertation, Department of Government, University of Texas, Austin.

_____. 1977. "Bureaucratic Compliance as a Game on the Unit Square," Public Choice vol. 19 (Spring) pp. 37-51.

_____. 1979. Interest Groups, Parties, and Plural Policy Arenas, Social Science Working Paper No. 276 (Pasadena, California Institute of Technology).

Mueller, Dennis. 1979. Public Choice (Cambridge, Cambridge University Press).

Niskanen, William A., Jr. 1971. Bureaucracy and Representative Government (Chicago, Aldine).

Olson, Mancur, Jr. 1965. The Logic of Collective Action (Cambridge, Harvard University Press).

Oppenheiner, Joe A. 1975. "Some Political Implications of Vote Trading and the Voting Paradox," American Political Science Review vol. 69, no. 3 (September) pp. 963-966.

_____. 1979. "Outcomes of Logrolling in the Bargaining Set and Democratic Theory," Public Choice vol. 34, no. 2 (July).

_____. 1980. "Small Steps Forward for Political Economy," World Politics forthcoming.

Plott, Charles R. 1967. "A Notion of Equilibrium and Its Possibility under Majority Rule," American Economic Review vol. 57 (September) pp. 787-806.

_____. 1976a. Verbal communique with the author regarding some of Plott's unreported experimental outcomes.

_____. 1976b. "Axiomatic Social Choice Theory: An Overview and Interpretation," American Journal of Political Science vol. 20, pp. 511-596.

_____. 1979. "The Application of Laboratory Experimental Methods to Public Choice," in Clifford S. Russell, ed. Collective Decision Making (Baltimore, Md., Johns Hopkins University Press for Resources for the Future) pp. 137-160.

Rapoport, Anatol and Albert Chammah. 1971. _Prisoners' Dilemma_ (Ann Arbor, University of Michigan Press).

Roberts, Blaine and Bob Holdren. 1970. _Theory of Social Process: An Economic Analysis_ (Ames, Iowa State University Press).

Romer, Thomas and Howard Rosenthal. 1978. "Political Resource Allocation Controlled Agendas, and the Status Quo," _Public Choice_ vol. 33, no. 4 pp. 27-43.

Rubinson, Richard. 1976. "The World Economy and the Distribution of Income Within States: A Cross National Study," _American Sociological Review_ vol. 41, no. 4 (August) pp. 638-659.

Schwartz, Thomas. 1979. "The Universal Instability Theorem" (Austin, University of Texas, mimeo.)

Shepsle, Kenneth A. 1978. "Structure Induced and Preference Induced Equilibrium in Multidimensional Voting Models," (St. Louis, Mo., Washington University Press, mimeo.)

Sen, Amatra K. 1970. _Collective Choice and Social Welfare_ (San Francisco, Calif., Holden Day).

Sweeney, John W., Jr. 1973. "An Experimental Investigation of the Free Rider Problem," _Social Science Research_ vol. 2, no. 3-4, pp. 277-292.

Tiebout, C.M. 1976. "A Pure Theory of Public Expenditures," _Journal of Political Economy_ vol. 64 (October) pp. 416-424.

Tullock, Gordon. 1965. _The Politics of Bureaucracy_ (Washington, D.C., Public Affairs Press).

_____. 1969. "An Economic Approach to Crime," _Social Science Quarterly_ vol. 50, no. 1 (June) pp. 59-71.

_____. 1971. "The Paradox of Revolution," _Public Choice_ vol. 11 (Fall).

Wallerstein, Immanuel. 1974. "The Rise and Future Demise of the Capitalist World System: Concepts for Comparative Analysis," _Comparative Studies in Society and History_ vol. 16, pp. 387-415.